Heritage Signature® Auction #6058

Rare Books

September 13-14, 2011 | Beverly Hills

LIVE AUCTION Signature® Floor Session
(Floor, Telephone, HERITAGE Live!™ Internet, Fax, and Mail)

Heritage Auctions, Beverly Hills
9478 W. Olympic Blvd. • Beverly Hills, CA 90212

Session 1
Tuesday, September 13 • 2:00 PM PT • Lots 37001–37144

HERITAGE Live!™ Internet, Fax, & Mail <u>only</u> Session

Session 2
Wednesday, September 14 • 3:00 PM CT • Lots 37145–37428

LOT SETTLEMENT AND PICK-UP
Available immediately following the floor session on Tuesday, September 13 or on Wednesday, September 14 by 12:00 PM CT. After 12:00 PM CT Wednesday, September 14, all lots will be transported back to our Dallas Headquarters and shipped from there.

Extended Payment Terms available. Email: Credit@HA.com

Lots are sold at an approximate rate of 100 lots per hour, but it is not uncommon to sell 75 lots or 125 lots in any given hour.

This auction is subject to a 19.5% Buyer's Premium.

Heritage Numismatic Auctions, Inc.: CA Bond #RSB2004175; CA Auctioneer Bonds: Samuel Foose #RSB2004178; Robert Korver #RSB2004179; Bob Merrill #RSB2004177; Leo Frese #RSB2004176; Jeff Engelken #RSB2004180; Jacob Walker #RSB2005394; Scott Peterson #RSB2005395; Shaunda Fry #RSB2005396; Mike Sadler #RSB2005412; Andrea Voss #RSB2004676; Teia Baber #RSB2005525; Cori Mikeals #RSB2005645; Carolyn Mani #RSB2005661; Chris Dykstra #RSB2005738; Alissa Ford #RSB2005920.

LOT VIEWING
Heritage Auctions, Beverly Hills
9478 W. Olympic Blvd. • Beverly Hills, CA 90212
Saturday, September 10 – Monday, September 12
9:00 AM – 5:00 PM PT

View lots & auction results online at HA.com/6058

BIDDING METHODS:
HERITAGE Live!™ Bidding
Bid live on your computer or mobile, anywhere in the world, during the Auction using our HERITAGE Live!™ program at HA.com/Live

Live Floor Bidding
Bid in person during the floor sessions.

Live Telephone Bidding (floor sessions only)
Phone bidding must be arranged on or before Monday, September 12, by 12:00 PM CT.
Client Service: 866-835-3243.

Internet Bidding
Internet absentee bidding ends at 10:00 PM CT the evening before each session. HA.com/6058

Fax Bidding
Fax bids must be received on or before Monday, September 12, by 12:00 PM CT. Fax: 214-409-1425

Mail Bidding
Mail bids must be received on or before Monday, September 12.

Phone: 214-528-3500 • 800-872-6467
Fax: 214-409-1425
Direct Client Service Line: 866-835-3243
Email: Bid@HA-com

This Auction is Presented and cataloged by Heritage Auctions
© 2011 Heritage Auctioneers & Galleries, Inc.

HERITAGE HA.com
A U C T I O N S

Steve Ivy
CEO
Co-Chairman of the Board

Jim Halperin
Co-Chairman of the Board

Greg Rohan
President

Paul Minshull
Chief Operating Officer

Todd Imhof
Executive Vice President

Rare Books Specialists

James Gannon
Director, Rare Books

Joe Fay
Manager, Rare Books

3500 Maple Avenue • Dallas, Texas 75219
Phone 214-528-3500 • 800-872-6467
HA.com/Books

Consignment Directors: James Gannon and Joe Fay

Cataloged by: Erik Bosse, Paula Bosse, Joe Fay, Dave Golemon, Brandon Kennedy, Harlan Kidd, and Nancy Ruppert

MAIL/FAX BID SHEET

Heritage Auctions • HA.com
Direct Client Service Line—Toll Free:
866-835-3243
3500 Maple Avenue
Dallas, Texas 75219-3941

ALL INFORMATION MUST BE COMPLETED AND FORM SIGNED

NAME _____

ADDRESS _____

CITY/STATE/ZIP _____

DAYTIME PHONE (_____)_____

CLIENT # (if known)_____ BIDDER #_____

E-MAIL ADDRESS _____

CELL PHONE _____

EVENING PHONE (_____)_____

Would you like a FAX or e-mail confirming receipt of your bids? If so,

please print your FAX # _____

or e-mail address here: _____

I would like to limit my bidding to a total of $ _____

at the hammer amount for all lots listed on this bid sheet. I am aware
that by utilizing the Budget Bidding feature all bids on this sheet will be
affected. If I intend to have regular bidding on other lots I will need to
use a separate bid sheet.

Payment by check may result in your property not being released until
purchase funds clear our bank. Checks must be drawn on a U.S. bank.
(Bid in whole dollar amounts only.)

A Buyer's Premium of 15% will be added to the successful hammer price bid on lots in
Coin and Currency auctions or 19.5% on lots in all other auctions.

Non-Internet bids (including but not limited to, podium, fax, phone and mail
bids) may be submitted at any time and are treated similar to floor bids. These
types of bids must be on-increment or at a half increment (called a cut bid). Any
podium, fax, phone or mail bids that do not conform to a full or half increment
will be rounded up or down to the nearest full or half increment and will be
considered your high bid.

Current Bid	Bid Increment
< - $10	$1
$10 - $29	$2
$30 - $49	$3
$50 - $99	$5
$100 - $199	$10
$200 - $299	$20
$300 - $499	$25
$500 - $999	$50
$1,000 - $1,999	$100
$2,000 - $2,999	$200
$3,000 - $4,999	$250
$5,000 - $9,999	$500

$10,000 - $19,999	$1,000
$20,000 - $29,999	$2,000
$30,000 - $49,999	$2,500
$50,000 - $99,999	$5,000
$100,000 - $199,999	$10,000
$200,000 - $299,999	$20,000
$300,000 - $499,999	$25,000
$500,000 - $999,999	$50,000
$1,000,000 - $1,999,999	$100,000
$2,000,000- $2,999,999	$200,000
$3,000,000- $4,999,999	$250,000
$5,000,000 - $9,999,999	$500,000
>$10,000,000	$1,000,000

These bids are for Auction: #_____ Auction Description _____ (ex. See catalog spine for auction # and description)

LOT NO.	AMOUNT	LOT NO.	AMOUNT	LOT NO.	AMOUNT	LOT NO.	AMOUNT

PLEASE COMPLETE THIS INFORMATION:

1. IF NECESSARY, PLEASE INCREASE MY BIDS BY:
   ☐ 10%   ☐ 20%   ☐ 30%
   Lots will be purchased as much below top bids as possible.

2. ☐ I HAVE PREVIOUSLY BOUGHT FROM HERITAGE

3. ☐ I HAVE A RESALE PERMIT
   (please contact 1-800-872-6467)

I have read and agree to all of the Terms and Conditions of Auction: inclusive of
paying interest at the lesser of 1.5% per month (18% per annum) or the maximum
contract interest rate under applicable state law from the date of auction.

REFERENCES: New bidders who are unknown to us must furnish satisfactory industry references or a valid credit card in advance of the auction date.

REV. 4-14-11

SUBTOTAL	
TOTAL from other side	
TOTAL BID	

_____
(Signature required) *Please make a copy of your bid sheet for your records.*

FAX HOTLINE: 214-409-1425

1

LOT NO.	AMOUNT	LOT NO.	AMOUNT	LOT NO.	AMOUNT	LOT NO.	AMOUNT
							TOTAL this side

Please make a copy of your bid sheet for your records.

Auction Highlights

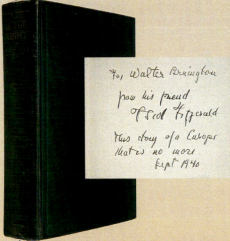

F. Scott Fitzgerald. *Tender is the Night. A Romance.* New York: Charles Scribner's Sons, 1934. First edition, third printing. **Inscribed by Fitzgerald on the front free endpaper, "For Walter Bruington / from his friend / F Scott Fitzgerald / This story of a Europe / that is no more. / Sept 1940."**
Estimate: $6,000 and up
HA.com/6058-26001

H. A. Rey. *Curious George.* Boston: Houghton Mifflin Company, 1941. First edition in a wonderful example of the rare dust jacket.
Estimate: $15,000 and up
HA.com/6058-28001

[Aitken Bible]. *The Holy Bible, Containing the Old and New Testaments: Newly Translated out of the Original Tongues...* Philadelphia: Printed and Sold by R. Aitken, 1782. First edition of the first complete Bible in English to be published in America, and the only Bible ever authorized by Congress.
Estimate: $40,000 and up
HA.com/6058-65001

Jean Toomer. *Cane.* Woodcuts by Martin Puryear. San Francisco: Arion Press, 2000. First edition, number 30 of 400 copies **signed and numbered by Puryear.** One of a limited number of copies housed in the special wooden box created by Puryear, and **with the extra suite of seven woodblock prints, also numbered 30 of 50, each signed by Puryear.**
Estimate: $10,000 and up
HA.com/6058-37003

Aesop. *Vita et Fabellae Aesopi...Gabriae Fabellae... Collectio Proverbiorum Tarrhaei &c.* [Venice]: Aldus Manutius, [1505]. Very rare Greek-only edition of Aesop, which Dibdin described as "among the rarer and more beautiful productions of the Aldine Press."
Estimate: $7,500 and up
HA.com/6058-69002

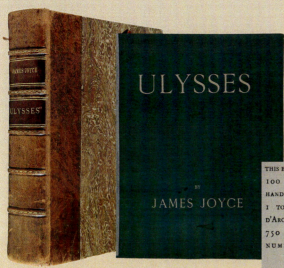

James Joyce. *Ulysses*. Paris: Shakespeare and Company, 1922. First edition. One of 750 numbered copies on handmade paper (this copy being No. 540), out of a total edition of 1,000 copies. Bound in modern antique-style half marbled sheep, with original front and rear covers bound in.
Estimate: $10,000 and up
HA.com/6058-88001

John James Audubon (1785-1851). White-headed Eagle-Plate CXXVI (Havell Edition). A striking hand-colored aquatint engraving by R. Havell from the first edition of The Birds of America (London: 1827-1838).
Estimate: $5,000 and up
HA.com/6058-25001

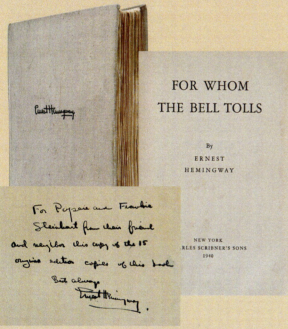

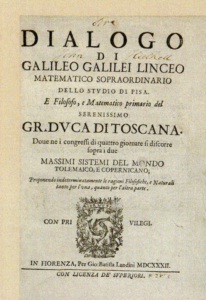

Galileo Galilei. *Dialogo... Doue ne I congressi di Quattro giornate si discorre sopra I due Massimi Sistemi del Mondo Tolemaico, e Copernicano...* Florence: Giovanni Batista Landini, 1632. First edition of Galileo's statement and defense of the Copernican system of heliocentrism, a work which resulted in Galileo's 1633 trial for heresy in Rome.
Estimate: $30,000 and up
HA.com/6058-70001

Ernest Hemingway. *For Whom the Bell Tolls*. New York: Charles Scribner's Sons, 1940. First edition, **one of fifteen author's copies with uncut edges inscribed and signed by Hemingway to his Havana neighbors, Popsie and Frankie Steinhart.**
Estimate: $20,000 and up
HA.com/6058-53001

J. K. Rowling. *Harry Potter and the Philosopher's Stone*. [London]: Bloomsbury, [1997]. The exceedingly rare first printing of Rowling's first Harry Potter book, **with a Rowling Signed Photo and transmittal Autograph Note Signed on her own stationery.**
Estimate: $20,000 and up
HA.com/6058-22001

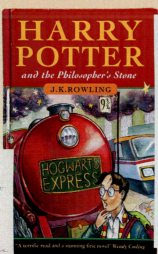

Table of Contents

SESSION ONE

Floor, Telephone, Heritage Live!™, Internet, Fax, and Mail Signature® Auction #6058
Tuesday, September 13, 2011 | 2:00PM PT | Lots 37001 – 37144
Beverly Hills

A 19.5% Buyer's Premium ($14 minimum) Will Be Added To All Lots
To view full descriptions, enlargeable images and bid online, visit HA.com/6058

"The Bible of the Revolution"

 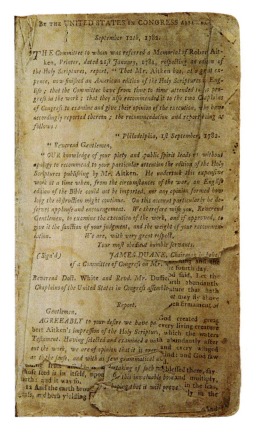

37001 [The Aitken Bible]. *The Holy Bible, Containing the Old and New Testaments: Newly translated out of the Original Tongues...* Philadelphia: Printed and Sold by R. Aitken, 1782. First edition, and the first printing in America of the complete Bible in English. Two twelvemo volumes in one. A-2Z^12 3A^6 (-3A6); ^2A-U^6 W^6 X-2D^6; lacking the general title page (often missing, as it was bound in as a cancel, and is often missing in many of the surviving copies), a partial leaf and whole leaf (with very little remnants in the gutter) in Isaiah (2O6 and 2O7), a bit less than half of the lower portion of the New Testament title page, and the last five leaves of Revelations (2D2-2D6). Note: the blank between the Old and New Testaments, 3A6, often noted as missing, is reckoned in the ESTC copy as the title leaf, printed as 3A6, removed, and then bound in as a cancel before A1. Original full leather binding with seven raised spine bands. Binding worn and abraded, with corners exposed, but holding strong. Contemporary ink inscriptions to pastedowns. Small printed note regarding Congressional involvement in printing scripture affixed to front pastedown. Text unevenly toned, with moderate staining and foxing throughout. A number of leaves creased, bumped or with a creased bottom corner. A few leaves with minor marginal chipping. A handful of leaves unevenly inked. The Congressional endorsement (A1) with two significant areas of loss and some chipping to page edges. Two-inch curved, closed tear to 2M1, extending into fourteen lines of text. Approximately one quarter of 2Q12 torn away but sewn back in with contemporary or nineteenth-century thread. One-and-a-quarter-inch horizontal closed tear to 2N1, affecting most of a few lines in the right column of text. A well-thumbed, but sound example of the rarest of American Bibles, and the only Bible ever authorized by the American Congress.

No English-language Bible had been published in America during the colonial period, as the English Crown held the copyright to the King James version, and printed all Bibles in London. Wright's census of the Aitken Bible could turn up only thirty-two copies, and less than fifty are known. Evans refers to this Bible as, "[t]he first edition of the Bible printed in the English language in America; and among the rarest issues of the press in America."

"The first Bible printed in English in this country with an American imprint" (Sabin p.132).

This copy originally comes from a Pittsburgh-area family who later moved to Ohio. Contemporary ink inscription on rear pastedown from a member of this family.

Evans 17473. Hills 11. Sabin 5165.

Estimate: $40,000-up
Starting Bid: $20,000

Once-Classified Lecture Series on Nuclear Physics from Los Alamos

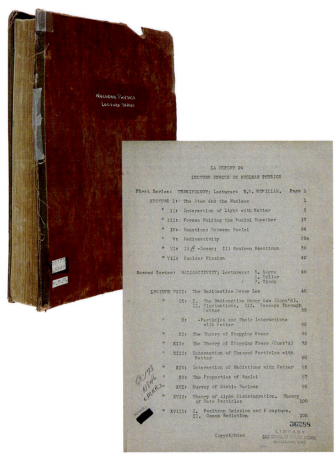

37002 **[The Atomic Bomb]. [Edward Teller, Edwin M. McMillan, Robert F. Christy, and others].** *LA Report 24. Lecture Series on Nuclear Physics.* [Los Alamos Scientific Laboratories, 1943-1944]. Octavo. [vi], 329 pages. Mimeographed text on loose-leaf sheets (rectos only) with binder holes in the left margin. Fastened between brown side-bound Acco report covers, with a handwritten title on the front cover in white ink, reading, "NUCLEAR PHYSICS LECTURE SERIES." Some wear and tape repair to the covers. Ex-library, formerly part of Case Western University's Case School of Applied Science, Department of Physics. Call number pasted to front cover. Library bookplate to inside front cover. Library call number in pencil and stamps, one of which is marked through in black, on the first page. Library stamp to verso of last page. Library checkout card and pocket still affixed to inside back cover. Text is clean. Very good condition.

A rare, pre-publication edition of forty-one lectures delivered between September 14, 1943 and March 2, 1944 by various scientists developing the atomic bomb. The lectures were delivered in six series: Terminology, Radioactivity, Neutron Physics, Two-Body Problem, The Statistical Theory of Nuclear Reactions, and Diffusion Theory. Among the lecturers were numerous future Nobel Prize winners, such as Edwin M. McMillan, Emilio Segre, Felix Bloch, Robert F. Christy, a student of Robert Oppenheimer's, and Edward Teller, "the father of the hydrogen bomb."

Estimate: $1,500-up
Starting Bid: $750

Important Biography of Frederick Douglass, Signed by Author Charles W. Chesnutt

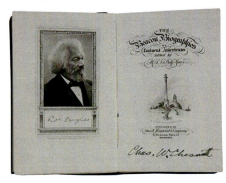

37003 **Charles W. Chesnutt.** *Frederick Douglass.* Boston: Small, Maynard, 1899. First edition. **Signed by Chesnutt.** Twelvemo. 144 pages. Publisher's limp black leather with gilt titles and decoration to spine. Top edge gilt with others untrimmed. Engraved frontisportrait of Douglass. Minor rubbing and scuffing to binding with boards heavily abraded along top edge. Front hinge cracked and joint tender. Textblock clean. Overall good condition.

Estimate: $1,500-up
Starting Bid: $750

Limited Editions, Both Signed by Eisenhower

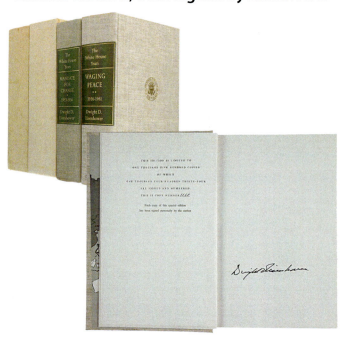

37004 **Dwight D. Eisenhower.** *The White House Years: Mandate for Change 1953-1956.* [and:] *The White House Years: Waging Peace 1956-1961.* New York: Doubleday & Company, Inc., 1963-1965. Numbers 228 and 1,166, respectively of 1,500 limited edition copies each **signed by Eisenhower on a tipped-in leaf facing the limitation page.** Two octavo volumes. Volume I: xviii, [1, List of Maps], [1]-650 pages. Volume II: xxiii, [1]-741 pages. Each volume illustrated with photographs. Publisher's tan cloth with gilt-lettered spine title labels and the Presidential seal in gilt on the front cover. Pictorial cartographic endpapers. Fore-edge and bottom edge uncut. Some signatures unopened. Each housed in the publisher's paper slipcase with the title label on one side, and the original clear plastic dust jackets. Minimal edge wear to boards. Spine of *Mandate for Change* a bit bowed. Mild wear to slipcases, with one spine bump. A handsome pair in near fine condition.

Estimate: $1,500-up
Starting Bid: $750

Probably the Finest Production from Ben Franklin's Press

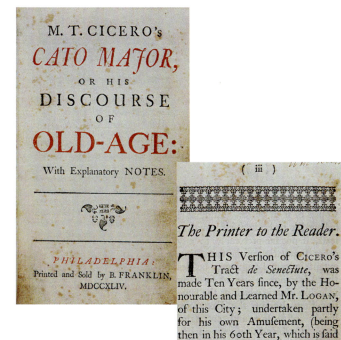

37005 **[Benjamin Franklin, printer]. M[arcus] T[ulius] Cicero.** *M. T. Cicero's Cato Major, or His Discourse of Old-Age: With Explanatory Notes.* Philadelphia: Printed and Sold by B. Franklin, 1744. First edition, first state, with "ony" on page 27. Small quarto (7.75 x 4.75 inches). viii, 159 pages. Translated and with notes by James Logan [1674-1751]. Title page in red and black with printer's device. Full calf period binding professionally rebacked to style. Raised bands. Gilt borders to boards. Front free endpaper with inked name of previous owner Samuel Witt, dated 1759. Edges somewhat worn. Foxing throughout. In custom half morocco slipcase and cloth chemise. Overall, a very good, tight copy.

"Probably the finest production of Franklin's press, and really a splendid specimen of the art" (Sabin). Franklin states in his preliminary printer's statement: "I have, *Gentle Reader*, as thou seest, printed this Piece of *Cicero's* in a large and fair Character, that those who begin to think on the Subject of OLD AGE, (which seldom happens till their Sight is somewhat impair'd by its Approaches) may not, in Reading, by the *Pain* small letters give the Eyes, feel the *Pleasure* of the Mind in the least allayed...I shall add to these few Lines my hearty Wish, that this first Translation of a *Classic* in this Western World, may be followed with many others, performed with equal Judgment and Success; and be a happy Omen, that *Philadelphia* shall become the Seat of the *American* Muses."

ESTC W20709. Evans 5261. Sabin 11379.

Estimate: $4,500-up
Starting Bid: $2,250

One of the Great American State Papers, Establishing the Honor and Credit of the United States

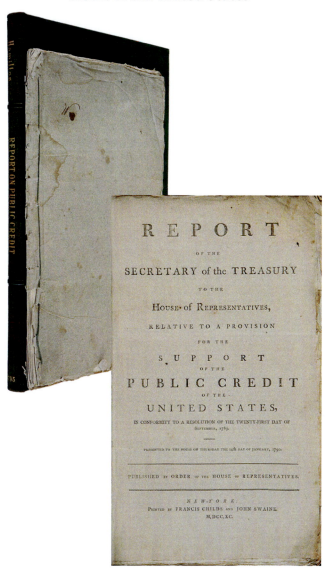

37006 **Alexander Hamilton.** *Report of the Secretary of the Treasury to the House of Representatives Relative to a Provision for the Support of the Public Credit of the United States...Presented to the House on Thursday, the 14th Day of January 1790.* New York: Francis Childs and John Swaine, 1790. Folio. 51 pages. Untrimmed, in original side-sewn blue-gray wrappers, which show moderate chipping. Inked name with date on rear wrapper: "William Imlay December 1, 1800." In custom half morocco box. Very good.

"One of the great American state papers, being the first report on public credit. In it Hamilton recommends that the U.S. pay all its war debts, at par value, as well as assume all war debts of the states, thereby establishing both in domestic and foreign circles the honor and credit of the United States. He also presents here for the first time his ideas and plans for a strong central government. By this document the federalist philosophy of American government began, and on or against its principles every statesman for a hundred years based his political career" (Jenkins).

Church 1253. Evans 22998. Jenkins, *Early American Imprints* I - 186.

Estimate: $10,000-up
Starting Bid: $5,000

Hamilton's Works in Three Volumes, with the Sixth Edition of *The Federalist*

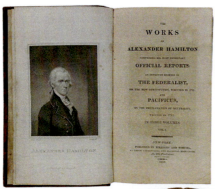

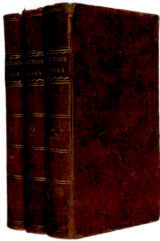

37007   **Alexander Hamilton.** ***The Works of Alexander Hamilton***: *Comprising His Most Important Official Reports; an Improved Edition of the Federalist, on the New Constitution, Written in 1788; and Pacifus, on the Proclamation of Neutrality, Written in 1793. In Three Volumes.* New York: Published by Williams and Whiting, 1810. First edition of Hamilton's works, and sixth edition of the Federalist. Three octavo volumes. vii, [1, blank], [1, contents], [1, blank], 325, [1, blank]; [2, general title], [i-ii, Federalist title], [iii]-iv [contents], 368; [2, general title], [i-ii, Federalist Volume II title], [iii]-iv [contents], 368 pages. Complete with three engraved frontispiece portraits of Alexander Hamilton, John Jay, and James Madison, respectively. Contemporary full calf. Smooth spines numbered and ruled in gilt in compartments with red morocco labels with gilt titles. Covers showing wear with a few minor abrasions, particularly at the corners and spine. Edges sprinkled blue. Endpapers have some spotting. Light foxing to preliminaries and terminals. Some even toning throughout. A few leaves standing proud in Volume I. Light offsetting of frontispieces. Ownership signature of John P. Binns in each volume. A newspaper clipping noting *Federalist* articles' authorship on front pastedown. All very good.

"In these documents are constelled more than the learning and the wisdom of other days. The native, the original conceptions of this creative genius, give life and light to every subject. Every page bears its own peculiar testimony to the vastness of his mind — the soundness of his judgment — the clearness of his views — and the integrity of his heart. The humblest peasant, who loves his country and participates in her weal and wo, as well as the statesman and politician whose feelings and interests are more particularly identified with the subject, will read these Reports with mingled wonder and delight" (from the Preface)."The sixth edition [of the Federalist] was published in 1810 by Williams and Whiting of New York, and formed the second and third volumes of the 'Writings of Hamilton' [*sic.*]."

Estimate: $2,500-up
Starting Bid: $1,250

With a Handsome Fold-Out Map of the Island of Barbados, Circa 1750

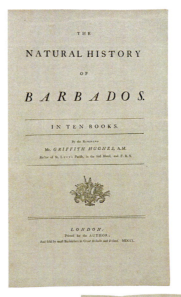

37008   **Griffith Hughes.** ***The Natural History of Barbados.*** In Ten Books. London: Printed for the Author, 1750. First edition. Folio. [xxiv], 250,*251-*254, 251-314, [20] pages. With a fold-out map of the island of Barbados and thirty inserted woodcut plates (numbered and bound in this order: 1-9, X*, 11-23, 25, 27, 24, 24, 28-29). Woodcut chapter headings, initials, and endpieces. Contemporary full leather with gilt spine titles and five raised bands. All edges sprinkled red. Binding worn and abraded. Corners exposed. Unfortunately, a former owner or librarian has strengthened both joints with strips of black cloth tape running the length of the spine, covering most of the spine gilt and raised bands. Minor foxing to text. Small portion of the top corner of L1 torn away. Some offsetting from the plates to facing pages. Overall, a very good copy, which formerly belonged to the Donald Angus Collection at the Pineapple Research Institute of Hawaii.

"The book is handsomely printed, and the plates are finely executed from drawings by Ehret..." (Sabin 33582).

Estimate: $2,500-up
Starting Bid: $1,250

First Edition in English of Jefferson's Classic

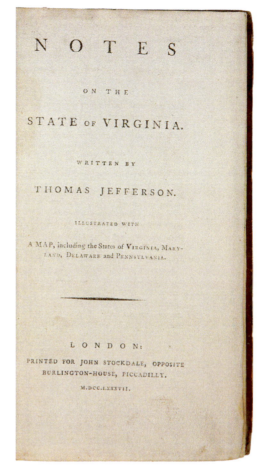

37009   **Thomas Jefferson.** *Notes on the State of Virginia.* Illustrated with a Map, including the States of Virginia, Maryland, Delaware and Pennsylvania. London: Printed for John Stockdale, 1787. First edition in English. Octavo. [vi], [1]-382 pages. With a large folding map, hand-colored in outline, bound just before the text, titled, "A Map of the country between Albemarle Sound, and Lake Erie, comprehending the whole of Virginia, Maryland, Delaware and Pennsylvania, with parts of several other of the United States of America." Contemporary full leather with gilt titles on a red morocco spine label (partially perished). Significant wear and abrading to boards. Corners exposed. Spine is approximately three-fifths perished. Front board re-attached along hinge. Very minor foxing, but mostly a wonderfully clean text. A few leaves with creased corners. Two-and-a-half-inch closed tear to the map, affecting the "T" in "ATLANTIC OCEAN." Light foxing to map, and some fold-line tape repairs to the verso. Overall, a wonderful, clean copy of Jefferson's classic work in very good condition.

John Stockdale, Jefferson's longtime bookseller, wrote to the author on November 20, 1786 to inquire about publishing the *Notes* in English: "Some time past two French Gentlemen call'd upon me, with a Copy of your Minutes of Virginia, with a View to have it Printed, but I inform'd them that I had some reason to believe that a New Edition was coming out with corrections by the Author, and ... a large Map was [being engraved] for the Work. I have some doubts wether it would pay the expences, at same time have a Wish to Publish it, with your Name, as I am convinced it is a Work of great Merit" (Thomas Jefferson Papers 10:545).

On February 1, 1787, Jefferson wrote Stockdale: "You have two or three times proposed to me the printing my Notes on Virginia. I never did intend to have them made public ... [b]ut as a translation of them is coming out, I have concluded to let the original appear also. I have therefore corrected a copy, and made some additions. I have moreover had a map engraved, which is worth more than the book. If you chuse to print the work I will send you the corrected copy, and when it shall be nearly printed I will send the plate of the map" (Thomas Jefferson Papers, 11:107).

Howes J78. Sabin 35896.

Estimate: $20,000-up
Starting Bid: $10,000

Inscribed by Martin Luther King, Jr. to Julia Roberts' Parents

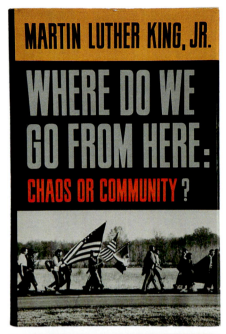

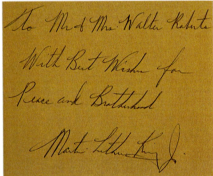

Early Work on Barbados with Engraved Plates and Charts

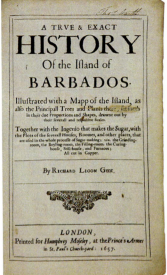

37010   Martin Luther King, Jr. *Where Do We Go from Here: Chaos or Community?* New York, Evanston, and London: Harper& Row, [1967]. First edition. **Inscribed "To Mr. and Mrs. Walter Roberts With Best Wishes for Peace and Brotherhood Martin Luther King, Jr."** on the front free endpaper. Octavo. 209 pages. Publisher's black cloth over mustard paper boards with gilt and red spine titles. Mustard endpapers. Deckled fore-edge. Original dust jacket. Minimal shelf wear to the boards. A few pencil underlines and dog-eared pages in the first part of the text. A crisp dust jacket with only minimal rubbing and one tiny fingernail bruise to the spine tail. Overall, a bright, tight copy in near fine condition.

The Robertses and Kings were well-acquainted with each other in and around Atlanta, Georgia. Martin Luther King's children attended the Roberts' acting school for children in Decatur, Georgia, and when Julia Roberts was born, Mrs. King picked up the hospital bill. A close association copy of King's fifth book with a warm personal inscription.

Estimate: $3,000-up
Starting Bid: $1,500

37011   Richard Ligon. *A True & Exact History of the Island of Barbados.* London: Humphrey Moseley, 1657. First edition. Folio. 122 pages (page 97 mis-numbered as "98"). Collated as complete minus imprimatur leaf, with a folding engraved map, nine engraved plates and charts, some folding, folding letterpress index leaf. Contemporary leather binding with a somewhat crudely repaired spine. Boards wellworn and scuffed, mainly at the extremities. Contents toned with scattered light-to-moderate foxing and some dampstaining, else a good copy of this rare work. James Edward Colleton bookplate on the verso of the title page; bookplate of the Donald Angus Collection mounted to the front pastedown.

Sabin 41057. Wing, L2075.

Estimate: $2,500-up
Starting Bid: $1,250

With 120 Hand-Colored Lithographed Plates of Native Americans

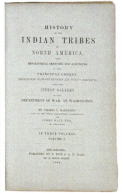

37012   **Thomas L. McKenney & James Hall:** *History of the Indian Tribes of North America* with *Biographical Sketches and Anecdotes of the Principal Chiefs Embellished with One Hundred and Twenty Portraits from the Indian Gallery in the Department of War, at Washington.* Volumes I and II: Philadelphia: D. Rice & A. N. Hart, 1854. Volume III: Philadelphia: J. T. Bowen, 1850. Mixed edition (Volumes I and II from the second octavo edition; Volume III from the first octavo edition). Quarto. iv, 333, [1, blank]; xvii, [1, blank], [9]-290; iv, [17]-392 pages. With 120 hand-colored portrait plates with tissue guards. Publisher's full blind-tooled leather with gilt titles on banded spines. All edges gilt. Bindings worn, abraded and frayed. Volume I rebacked with the remaining portions of the original spine leather laid down. Spine head of Volume II chipped. Bindings shaken, with all hinges cracked, the front hinge in Volume III reinforced with white tape. Scattered foxing. Preliminaries to Volume III a bit more foxed than the other two volumes. Text unevenly toned. Penciled ownership signatures to front free endpapers. Red Jacket plate in Volume I partially detached. Keokuk plate in Volume II detached and heavily edge-worn. Most plates with very little or no foxing or spotting. Very good. A one-page Typed Letter Signed by Frederick Goff on Library of Congress stationery is laid in, responding to the owner of this copy about market value and availability of this particular set.

From the preface: "The folio edition...has been pronounced by the learned and polished both of Europe and America, to be one of the most valuable and interesting productions of the present age...This universal appeal of the folio edition of the work, has induced the publishers of the present edition to alter the size to *royal octavo,* and thus place it within reach of the thousands, who, with taste and learning equal to the patrons of the large edition, have no less capacity to appreciate its worth and beauties."

Howes M-129 ("the most colorful portraits of Indians ever executed"). Sabin 43411 (describing the 1850 octavo edition).

Estimate: $6,000-up
Starting Bid: $3,000

First Edition of a Key Work in the Run-Up to the American Revolution

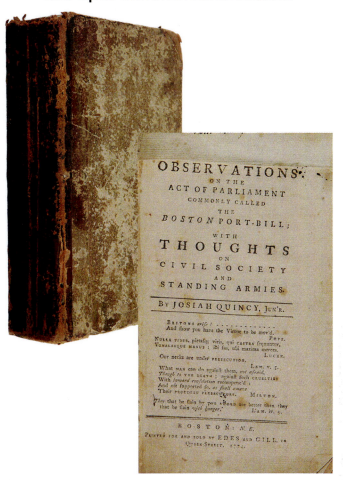

37013   **Josiah Quincy, Jun'r.** *Observations on the Act of Parliament Commonly Called the Boston Port-Bill; with Thoughts on Civil Society and Standing Armies.* Boston: Printed for and Sold by Edes and Gill, in Queen Street, 1774. First edition. Quarto (8.125 x 4.94 inches, 20.7 x 12.5 cm). [ii], [1]-82 pages. In an unsophisticated contemporary binding with old leather backstrip and corners over paper-covered boards. Leather heavily worn and flaking; three leather corners missing. Boards substantially rubbed, with some peeling and paper loss; one corner worn away. Front hinge cracked. Foxing and toning to pages throughout. Title page has had the top .875 inches cut away. In better than good condition. [Bound with:] **Excerpts from approximately a dozen publications spanning 1774 to 1788**, including pages from *Royal American Magazine* (1774) and *Columbian Magazine* (1788); the rest is comprised of excerpts from *The History of the Proceedings and Debates of the House of Commons* and the *House of Lords* from 1777 and 1778. Pages throughout toned and foxed, with a couple of instances of minor dampstaining. Sammelband of Revolutionary War-era writings in overall good or better condition in a worn period binding.

Not only was Josiah Quincy a Harvard-educated lawyer (he acted as John Adams' co-counsel in defending the soldiers involved in the Boston Massacre), he was also a patriot and a powerful orator and essayist who spoke out forcefully against British oppression in the American colonies. In this important work that helped spark the American Revolution, Quincy effectively protested the Intolerable Acts, and he urgently—and soaringly—exhorted his fellow Americans to rebel against the British and to fight for independence.

Church 1109. Evans 13561. Howes Q18. Sabin 67192.

Estimate: $3,000-up
Starting Bid: $1,500

Limited to Only 100 Copies, this a Presentation Copy, Inscribed by Roosevelt

One of Only 100 Copies, this with a Presentation Inscription from FDR to Secretary Wickard

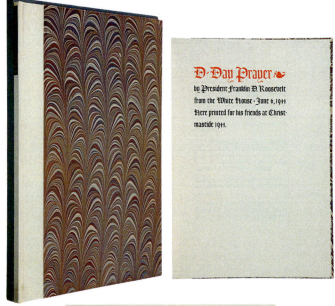

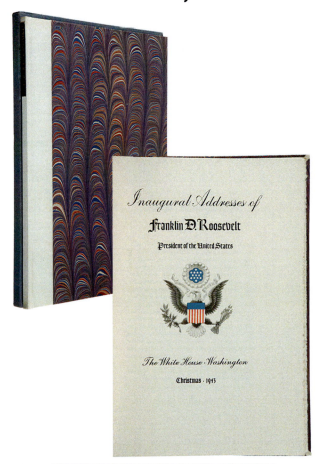

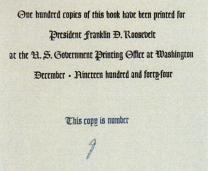

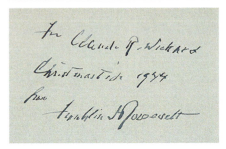

37014 [Claude R. Wickard]. Franklin D. Roosevelt. *D-Day Prayer by President Franklin D. Roosevelt from the White House, June 6, 1944, Here Printed for His Friends at Christmastide 1944.* Washington, DC: U.S. Government Printing Office, December 1944. Edition limited to 100 copies, of which this is number 9. **Presentation copy, inscribed by the President to his Secretary of Agriculture: "For Claude R. Wickard / Christmastide 1944 / from Franklin D. Roosevelt."** Small slim quarto. Unpaginated (four pages of text). Printed in black, blue, and red. Vellum-backed marble paper boards. Gilt-stamped green leather title label to spine. In original acetate wrappers. A fine copy in slipcase.

From the collection of Claude R. Wickard (1893-1967) who served as Secretary of Agriculture in Roosevelt's cabinet from 1940 to 1945. He resigned the cabinet post in 1945 to head the Rural Electrification Administration, a New Deal agency created by FDR to promote and encourage rural electrification.

Estimate: $10,000-up
Starting Bid: $5,000

37015 [Claude R. Wickard]. Franklin D. Roosevelt. *Inaugural Addresses of Franklin D. Roosevelt, President of the United States.* Washington, DC: The White House, Christmas 1943. Edition limited to 100 copies, of which this is number 10. **Presentation copy, inscribed by the President to his Secretary of Agriculture: "For Claude R. Wickard / with the affectionate regards of / Franklin D. Roosevelt / Christmas / 1943."** Small slim quarto. 24 pages. Vellum-backed marble paper boards. Gilt-stamped black leather title label to spine. Top edge gilt. A couple of very faint areas of yellowing to vellum. Laid in is original White House mailing label. In original acetate wrappers. A fine copy in slipcase.

Estimate: $6,000-up
Starting Bid: $3,000

One of Only Twenty Lettered Copies, Presented to Members of FDR's Cabinet

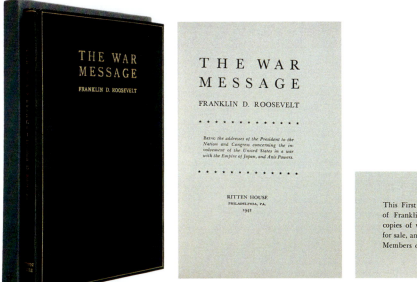

37016   [Claude R. Wickard]. **Franklin D. Roosevelt.** *The War Message. Being the addresses of the President to the nation and Congress concerning the involvement of the United States in a war with the Empire of Japan, and Axis Powers.* Philadelphia: Ritten House, 1942. First edition, one of 20 lettered copies (this being letter "J") reserved for Members of the Cabinet and for presentation. Small octavo. 64 pages. Full navy blue morocco. Lettered and bordered in gilt, all edges gilt. Red ribbon marker. In lightly sunned slipcase, with letter "J" in ink at foot of spine. A fine copy, from the collection of FDR's Secretary of Agriculture, Claude R. Wickard.

Estimate: $5,000-up
Starting Bid: $2,500

One of Only Sixty Copies, This Inscribed by President Truman

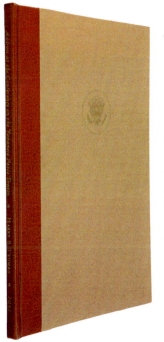 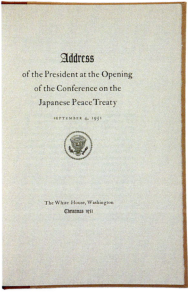

37017   [Claude R. Wickard]. **Harry S. Truman.** *Address of the President at the Opening of the Conference on the Japanese Peace Treaty, September 4, 1951.* Washington, DC: The White House, Christmas 1951. One of 60 copies printed for President Truman, of which this is number 52. **Presentation copy, inscribed by the President**: **"To Hon. Claude R. Wickard, / with best wishes for a / Merry Christmas. / Harry S. Truman / Dec. 25, 1951."** Tall, slim octavo. 12 pages. Quarter orange morocco over tan paper boards, with gilt lettering to spine and gilt-stamped presidential seal on front board. Laid in is original White House mailing label with poinsettia Christmas sticker. Fine.

Estimate: $4,000-up
Starting Bid: $2,000

Rare Burton Work on Zanzibar, in the Publisher's Original Cloth

37018 Richard F. Burton. *Zanzibar; City, Island, and Coast.* London: Tinsley Brothers, 1872. First edition. Two octavo volumes. xii [xiii-xiv, sectional title, blank], 503 [504, imprint]; vi [vii-viii, sectional title, blank], 519 [520, imprint] pages. Volume I with one folding map, four plates (including frontispiece), and four plans; Volume II with seven plates (including frontispiece). Chocolate brown cloth with gilt vignette on the front boards of each volume and titles stamped in gilt on the spine. Bindings exhibit signs of professional repair/restoration. Contents quite nice. In general a fine set.

Richard Francis Burton was undergoing financial difficulties during this period and so pressured John Tinsley, the publisher, into advancing the publication date. As a result the books were poorly bound which is the chief reason that so many copies are either found in poor condition or have been professionally restored as has this beautiful set. Though finally published in 1872, most of the information and narrative for this Burton work is from 1857 or earlier, when Burton's manuscript went missing (intentionally, according to Burton) and was discovered and returned to him in 1865, some eight years later.

Estimate: $1,500-up
Starting Bid: $750

First Edition of Cook's First Voyage

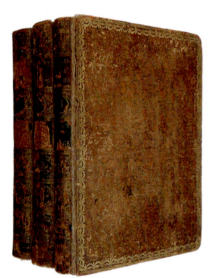 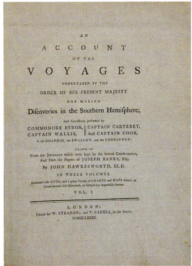 

37019 [Captain James Cook]. John Hawkesworth. *An Account of the Voyages Undertaken by the Order of His Present Majesty for Making Discoveries in the Southern Hemisphere,* And successively performed by Commodore Byron, Captain Wallis, Captain Carteret, And Captain Cook, In the *Dolphin,* the *Swallow,* and the *Endeavour:* Drawn up From the Journals which were kept by the several Commanders, And from the Papers of Joseph Banks, Esq; By John Hawkesworth, LL.D. In Three Volumes. Illustrated with Cuts, and a great Variety of Charts and Maps relative to Countries now first discovered, or hitherto but imperfectly known. London: Printed for W. Strahan; and T. Cadell, 1773. First edition. Three large quarto volumes (approximately 11.25 x 9 inches). xxxvi, [1-3], 4-139 (also numbered 360), blank , [361-363], 364-676; [xvi], 410; [vi], [411], 412-799, blank pages. 51 plates and charts, some folding. All volumes collate complete. Period calf bindings, with gilt floral borders to boards, inner dentelles, and gilt titles and decorations to spine and to red and black leather spine labels. Leather quite worn and rubbed, with loss to leather at extremities, sometimes with loss to boards. A few spine labels missing. Old repairs, but bindings still quite sturdy. Minor occasional foxing. Occasional chips or tears to leaves; tear to fold-out chart of New South Wales, measuring approximately 1.25 inches. An overall very good copy.

First edition of the classic work detailing Cook's first voyage (1768-1771) as he explored the Pacific, charting Australia, New Zealand, and Tahiti.

Holmes 5.

Estimate: $4,000-up
Starting Bid: $2,000

With Wonderful Hand-Colored Illustrations of the Orient

37020 **James Forbes. *Oriental Memoirs*:** *Selected and Abridged from a Series of Familiar Letters Written During Seventeen Years Residence in India: Including Observations on Parts of Africa and South America, and a Narrative of Occurrences in Four India Voyages.* London: White, Cochrane, and Co., 1813. First edition. Four quarto volumes. [4], [i]-xxiii, [1], [1]-481 pages, [1]; [i]-xv, [1], [1]-542 pages; [i]-xii, [1]-487 pages; [i]-xi, [1], [1]-425 pages, [1], [1] errata, [1], [4] bookbinder directions, [2]. Engraved frontispiece. Ninety-two total illustrations, including eighty-four engravings and eight lithographs, twenty-eight of these illustrations hand-colored, some heightened with gum arabic. Bound in contemporary full tan russia with lightly diced covers. Decorative triple fillet borders with gilt-stamped floral device at corners. Five raised gilt-stamped bands with six gilt-stamped compartments and titles on spine. Gilt-ruled edges and turn-ins. All edges gilt. Marbled endpapers. Joints starting, as is common. Covers and extremities rubbed with minor abrasions. Light foxing throughout. Some spotting and offsetting to plates. Pair of bookplates within each volume. A generally near fine set of a beautifully illustrated travel memoir.

Abbey, *Travel* 3876.

Estimate: $3,000-up
Starting Bid: $1,500

Early Illustrated Work on Travelling and Hunting in Tibet

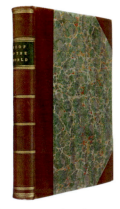 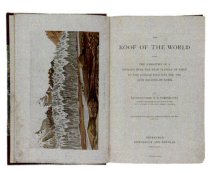 

37021 **Lieutenant-Colonel T. E. Gordon. *The Roof of the World,*** *Being the Narrative of a Journey Over the High Plateau of Tibet to the Russian Frontier and the Oxus Sources on Pamir.* Edinburgh: Edmonston and Douglas, 1876. First edition. Octavo. xiv, 172 pages. With twenty-four tinted lithograph plates (including frontispiece), forty-two other tinted illustrations in text, and a folding map. Bound in half leather over marbled boards. Titles stamped in gilt on a green morocco spine label. Minimal shelf wear to binding. The contents generally sound with some foxing and light dampstains to the plates, a small closed tear on the folding map, and an unobtrusive former owner's blind stamp on a couple of the preliminary pages. Very good condition.

Gordon broke new ground through the Tian Shan and Pamir highlands as he was one of the first Europeans to explore and hunt sheep in the area. He preceded other hunters like Demidoff and Littledale, Swayne, and others by several decades.

Cordier 2820. Neat G35. Royal Geographical Society Catalogue, p. 188. Yakushi, G88.

Estimate: $1,500-up
Starting Bid: $750

Ten Double-Page Views of the Grand Canyon

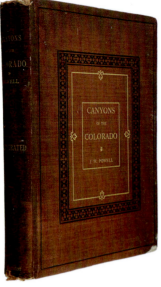
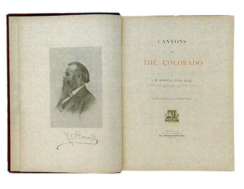
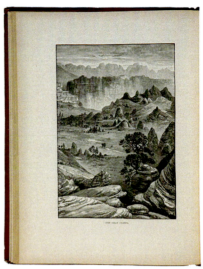

37022   J[ohn] W[esley] Powell. *Canyons of the Colorado.* Meadville: Flood & Vincent, The Chautauqua-Century Press, 1895. Quarto. xiv, 400 pages. One-page advertisement for the Santa Fé Railroad. Title printed in red and black. Frontispiece. Index. Numerous plates, including ten double-page views of the Grand Canyon, and text illustrations. Contemporary maroon cloth over beveled boards. Gilt lettering to the spine; gilt lettering, and black and gilt ruling to front board. Spine darkened and with moderate chipping to head and foot. Corners bumped; extremities scuffed. Stains to lower corner of front board and bottom edge. Hinges cracked. Five leaves with split along the gutter for about six inches. Internally clean and free of foxing; illustrations sharp and vibrant. Overall a very good, bright copy of this scarce and important narrative of the West.

"This book differs in so many respects from the report of 1875 [*Exploration of the Colorado River of the West and Its Tributaries; Explored in 1869, 1870, 1871, and 1872, under the Direction of the Secretary of the Smithsonian Institution*] that it is here given the status of a separate title. Not only has the narrative been revised and augmented, but there are several new chapters and a great many new illustrations. Included in the latter are adaptations from the superb sketches of William H. Holmes which are featured in the Dutton atlas [*Tertiary History of the Grand Cañon District, with Atlas* (Washington: 1882)]...Altogether, it is a handsome book; also a scarce one" (Farquhar).

Decker 36-333. Farquhar, *Colorado River*, p. 43. Graff 3335. Howes P527.

Estimate: $3,000-up
Starting Bid: $1,500

Volume I of Roberts' *Holy Land*

37023   David Roberts. *The Holy Land*, *Syria, Idumea, Arabia, Egypt & Nubia*. From drawings made on the spot by David Roberts, R.A. With historical descriptions, by the Revd. George Croly, L.L.D. Lithographed by Louis Haghe. Vol. I. London: F. G. Moon, 1842. Large folio (24.125 x 17.125 inches). Volume I only. Unpaginated. Portrait frontispiece. Forty-three tinted lithographed plates (twenty-two full-page, twenty-one half-page), including title vignette. Half bound in nineteenth-century maroon leather over marbled paper boards. Elaborate gilt spine, gilt rules, all edges gilt. Marbled endpapers. Leather and boards rubbed and scuffed with some surface loss to paper. Both hinges damaged; front hinge cracked at preliminary blanks. Some pages with water stains to lower margin; larger water stain to lower margin of approximately last ten leaves, with only one barely touching border of Plate 39 ("Jacob's Well"). Significant foxing throughout, affecting text and image areas of many plates. A few short tears to margins throughout, a few corners missing at front. Plate 21 ("Jerusalem from the North") with several gouges in image area. Good or better.

Abbey, *Travel* 385.

Estimate: $1,500-up
Starting Bid: $750

Deluxe Quarto Edition, One of 250 Copies Signed By Stanley

 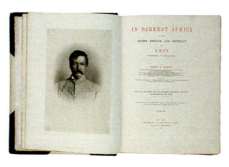 

37024   **Henry M. Stanley.** *In Darkest Africa or the Quest, Rescue, and Retreat of Emin, Governor of Equatoria.* New York: Charles Scribner's Sons, 1890. Demy Quarto Edition de Luxe. Limited to 250 numbered copies, of which this is number 69, **signed by the author on a special limitation page** bound in front. Two quarto volumes. [i]-xv, 529; [i]-xv, 472 pages. With **six etched plates signed in pencil by G. Montbard**, and 150 woodcut illustrations. Four maps, three of which are folding; two are linen-backed. Titles printed in red and black. Engraved portrait frontispiece of Stanley printed on India paper. Satin book marks. Original dark brown half morocco over vellum boards with title, flag of Emin Pasha, and Stanley's signature stamped in gilt on boards and spines. Top edges gilt, others untrimmed. Moderate edge wear to boards, spine, and corners. Minor spotting to vellum. Some slight offsetting to the preliminary pages, etchings uniformly toned, and moderate browning to the untrimmed edges. Previous owner's stamp to front free endpapers. Else, a handsome set in very good condition.

Estimate: $3,000-up
Starting Bid: $1,500

Scarce Translation of Frederick the Great's "Strategical Instructions" — Inscribed by Thomas Carlyle

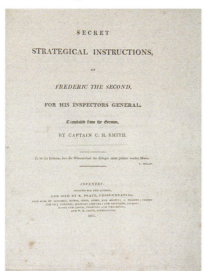 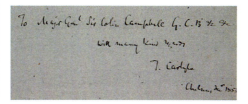

37025   **[Frederick II, King of Prussia.] C. H. Smith.** *Secret Strategical Instructions, of Frederic the Second, For His Inspectors General.* Translated from the German, by Captain C. H. Smith. Coventry: Printed for the Author, 1811. First edition in English. Small folio. x, [11-]28 pages plus 31 hand-colored engraved plates containing maps and plans, five of which are folding. Plate 21 with the tipped-in errata flap. Half-bound in red polished calf over marbled paper boards. Gilt spine and top edge. Marbled endpapers. Minor rubbing to extremities. Foxing throughout. A few pencil notations. **This copy inscribed by Thomas Carlyle to Sir Colin Campbell in 1855** (signed "T. Carlyle"). **Also inscribed by archaeologist Eric Birley to Major-General Clayton Bissell in 1948.** Fine. Quite scarce.

In the "Editor's Preface to the German and French Editions," Frederick the Great's strategic prowess as displayed in these *Instructions* is described thusly: "Here Frederic [*sic*] fully displays the art, by which he was so constantly victorious: — the manner of misleading the Enemy respecting the real point of attack — even the art of rapidly passing from the defensive to the offensive state, keeping in view all the chances of success. By these principles, peculiarly his own, he was enabled often to accomplish great actions with small comparative means."

Estimate: $3,000-up
Starting Bid: $1,500

With Contemporary Hand-colored Coats of Arms Throughout

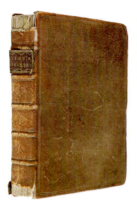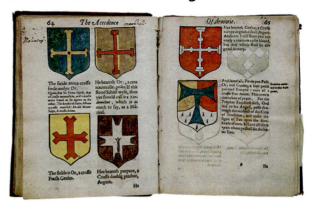

37026   **Gerard Leigh.** *The Accedence of Armorie.* London: Printed [by William Jaggard] for Iohn Iaggard, 1612. Third edition. Quarto. [iv, "Of the Oiniet" and engraved title page (remargined), missing six leaves of preliminaries], 241, [3] pages. Hand-colored folding plate of Atlas and Hercules tipped to Q3. STC 15393. [bound with:] **Edmund Bolton.** *The Elements of Armories.* London: Printed by George Eld, 1610. First edition. [xvi], 193 (2B gathering not present), [13, 2E4 (final leaf) missing] pages. STC 3220. With many dozens of hand-colored arms and illustrations throughout. Likely nineteenth-century suede with blind-stamped borders and decorations to boards and a red leather spine title label lettered in gilt. Edges sprinkled red. Spine ends partially perished. Rubbing and abrading to boards. Corners exposed. Hinges tender. Contemporary marginalia throughout the first title; on only a few leaves of the second. Scattered spotting and staining, mostly to the first title. Three bookplates to preliminaries. Long contemporary inscription on verso of preliminary leaf of *Accedence* by John England, member of a Yorkshire family mentioned in the text. Good condition.

Estimate: $2,000-up
Starting Bid: $1,000

Lord Shelburne's Copy, in Exquisite Eighteenth-Century Bindings

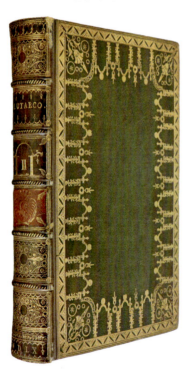

37027   **[Plutarch].** *La Prima [-Secunda] Parte della Vite di Plutarco.* *Tradotta da M. Lodovico Domenichi....* Venice: Gabriel Giolito de Ferrari, 1560. Two quarto volumes. [vii], 973; [vii], 535, 350. Woodcut titles and capitals. Beautifully bound in eighteenth-century full polished green morocco over boards. Broad gilt ornamental borders. Raised bands. Compartments decorated with gilt designs and lettering, as well as a later red morocco monogram of Lord Shelburne. Lavishly gauffered gilt edges, with red scalloped borders. Marbled endpapers. Bookplates to the front pastedowns of Henrietta Louisa Fermor, Countess of Pomfret (? - 1761). Bookplates to the rear pastedowns of William Petty, first Marquess of Landsdowne, and second Earl of Shelburne (1737-1805). Lord Shelburne presided as the Prime Minister of Great Britain from 1782 to 1783. Some minor rubbing to the extremities, and slight darkening to the spines. In chemises and a single half-morocco slipcase. A handsome set in near fine condition.

Estimate: $7,500-up
Starting Bid: $3,750

With Thirty-Eight Fine Engraved Portraits Depicting the History of the Royal Lineage of Holland

   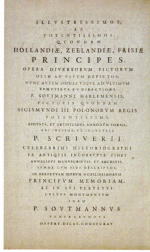

37028 **Petrus Scriverius.** *Principes Hollandiæ, Zelandiæ et Westfrisiæ.* Haarlem. Pieter Soutman, 1650. First edition. Folio (approximately 21.5 x 14 inches). [2, blank], [4], [126], [2, blank] pages. Complete with engraved title, 38 engraved portraits, and one plate of the coat-of-arms of Haarlem, with the city in the background. Contemporary full vellum, covers paneled in gilt with gilt central floral medallion and gilt floral cornerpieces. Binding soiled and worn, with spine mostly perished, text worn at edges, plates browned and somewhat worn. Shaken. Good condition.

Petrus Scriverius (Latinized form of Pieter Schrijver or Schryver, 1576-1660) was an important Dutch writer and scholar who lived in Leiden studying classical literature and the history of the Netherlands. He is best remembered for his histories of the Netherlands and of particular provinces, including the present work. "...The Batavian myth that formed the foundation for Holland's identity was above all a provincial myth, with almost ethnic features. Medieval history was also given a distinctly provincial slant in Holland. Precisely in the year 1650 the Leiden scholar Petrus Scriverius, whose earlier *Old Batavia Now Called Holland* had given a strongly pro-Holland interpretation of the story of the Batavian origin of the Dutch population, published a monumental and royally illustrated *Principes Hollandiae, et. ...*(Haarlem, 1650), a revised version of the history of the Counts of Holland from Dirk I to Philip II. For Scriverius the Holland counts and their province were the natural successors of the Batavian people." (-Willem Frijhoff, Dutch Culture in a Euriopean Perspective, 1650.) This book is a beautiful collection of engraved portraits and histories of the most important citizens of the Netherlands. Some portraits after Jan Van Eyck, Rubens, or Lucas van Leyden.

Estimate: $1,500-up
Starting Bid: $750

Perhaps the Most Comprehensive Collection of Alchemical Works in the Western World

37029 **[Lazarus Zetzner].** *Theatrum Chemicum, Praecipuosse Lectorum Auctorum Tractatus de Chemiae et Lapidis Philosophici Antiquitate, veritate, iure, praestantia & operationibus....* [Oberursel]: Ursellis, 1602. Unknown edition. Two volumes in one. Octavo. 901, [22] index; 630, [6] index pages. Several illustrations in text including one folding table. Bound in vellum. Staining and trivial tears to several pages, else very good condition.

Theatrum Chemicum was a compendium of early alchemical writings published in six volumes over the course of six decades. The first three volumes were published in 1602, while the final sixth volume was published in its entirety in 1661. *Theatrum Chemicum* is probably the most comprehensive collection of alchemical writings ever published in the Western world. Lazarus Zetzner is credited with editing and publishing the work, though he was undoubtedly the author of much of it.

Estimate: $2,500-up
Starting Bid: $1,250

Attractive English Bible from 1579

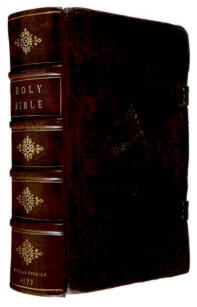

37030 **[Bible in English].** *The Bible. Translated According to the Ebrew and Greeke, and conferred with the best translations in divers languages.* London: Christopher Barker, 1579. Octavo. Double-column pages. Full calf over boards. Recently rebound with new backstrip, retaining original boards with some restoration to the corners. New leather stays to the original brass clasps and hasps. Some fading to the red edges. Scattered foxing and some occasional staining and marginalia to the pages. Overall, a bright, attractive copy in very good condition.

An early edition of the Geneva translation of the Bible.

Estimate: $1,500-up
Starting Bid: $750

The Earliest Original Collection of Lutheran Hymns in North America

37031 **[Evangelical Lutheran Ministerium of Pennsylvania and the Adjacent States].** *Erbauliche Lieder-Sammlung zum Gottesdienstlichen Gebrauch in den Vereinigten Evangelisch Lutherischen Gemeinen in Nord-America....* Erste Auflage. Germantaun [Pennsylvania]: Gedruckt bey Leibert und Billmeyer, 1786. First edition. Twelvemo. [14], 592, 8 pages. Wood-engraved frontispiece portrait of Martin Luther (defaced) by F. Reiche. [bound with:] *Anhang zu dem Gesangbuch der Vereinigten Evangelisch-Lutherischen Gemeinen in Nord-Amerika.* Germantaun: Gedruckt bey Michael Billmeyer, 1790. First edition. Twelvemo. 80 pages. [bound with:] *Kurze Andachten, einer Gottsuchenden....* Germantaun: Gedruckt bey Leibert und Billmeyer, 1786. First edition. Twelvemo. [26] pages. Early full calf over boards. Spine with five raised bands. Pair of brass and leather clasps intact. Foxing and occasional moderate staining throughout. Joints weak. Some chipping to the extremities of the binding. Overall, a very good, tight copy.

Entered into the record by Jonathan Bayard Smith, Prothonotary of the Court of common Pleas of Philadelphia County. J. B. Smith was a member of the Continental Congress and a signer of the Articles of Confederation.

This is the first appearance of a new hymnal, authorized by the Lutheran Synod. "The preface, signed by twenty-five members of the Ministerium, written by Muhlenberg, its senior member, states the reasons which guided him in the selection of hymns; and alludes to his forty-four years of 'toilsome pilgrimage' in the Western Continent" (Evans, *American Bibliography*).

Evans 19628, 22495.

Estimate: $5,000-up
Starting Bid: $2,500

First Limited Edition Of Scientology's Third Text

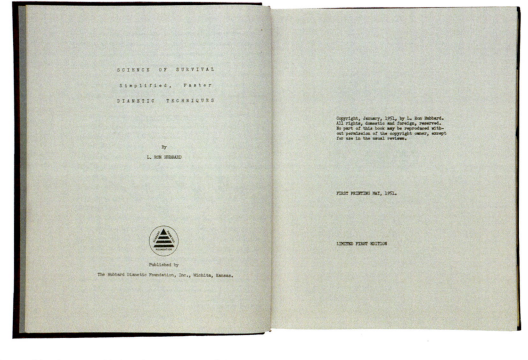

37032 **L. Ron Hubbard**. *Science of Survival: Simplified, Faster Dianetic Techniques*. Wichita, Kansas: The Hubbard Dianetic Foundation, Inc., [May, 1951]. First printing, limited first edition. Quarto. 541 pages. Large fold-out Hubbard Chart of Human Evaluation and Dianetic Processing (part 1), with sample checklist and sample coupons at rear. Publisher's limp red leatherette boards with gilt spine titles and ruling. Printed paper over board slipcase with spine titles. Very slight wear to boards, spine, and corners. Sample checklist and fold-out chart at rear somewhat toned. Slipcase has moderate wear with bumped head and minor loss. Otherwise, a near fine copy of this scarce early Dianetics title.

Text appears to have been printed from hand-corrected sheets. Facsimile handwritten dedication from Hubbard is printed below the "This Copy of the Limited Manuscript Edition was prepared especially for (blank)" and directly precedes the title page. Also included is a facsimile handwritten Acknowledgment and a "Dear Reader" letter also in Hubbard's hand. This book is dedicated to Alexis Valerie Hubbard, his daughter from his second marriage and is removed from future editions.

Hubbard states in the Preface, "This book is late. It is a whole year late. Actually, it should have been the first book." With *Science of Survival*, Hubbard introduced the thetan, the tone scale, and past lives, all key elements of Scientology in the future. A description of how theta interacts with the physical universe of matter, energy, space and time (MEST) first appears in this text as well. The Chart of Human Evaluation is the keystone of the book, demonstrating the tone scale as well as the components of emotion — the "triangle" of Affinity, Reality and Communication (ARC).

Estimate: $2,500-up
Starting Bid: $1,250

Illuminated Leaf

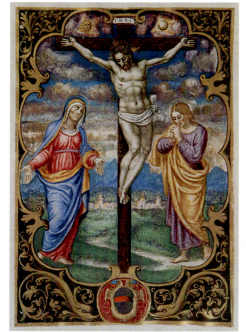

37033 **[Illuminated Manuscript Leaf]. Scene of the Crucifixion.** [N.p., n.d., circa eighteenth century]. Double-sided vellum leaf emulating an illuminated manuscript. One side with the scene of the Crucifixion, in red, blue, yellow, white, purple, green, and brown, framed in a gilt cartouche inside a gilt border. On the verso, manuscript text in Latin, in gold, blue, and black. Vellum puckered at edges of sheet; mild discoloration to text side. In generally fine condition. Leaf measures approximately 8.6875 x 6 inches; framed and glazed to an overall 23 x 19.5 inches.

Estimate: $1,800-up
Starting Bid: $900

First Edition of "The Book of Mormon," Belonging to John Wesley Brackenbury, Son of the First Mormon "Martyr" and Stepson of Joseph Smith, with Seventeen Original Photographs of Members of the Brackenbury, Smith, and Curtis Families

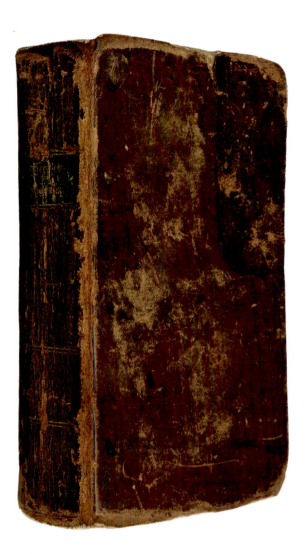

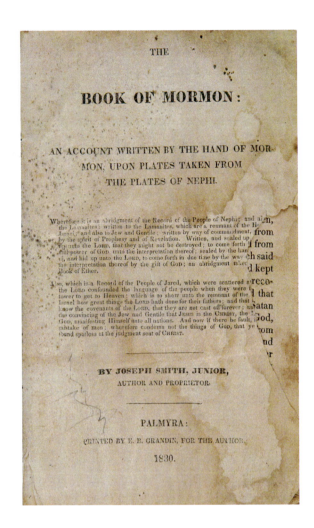

37034 **Joseph Smith, Junior.** *The Book of Mormon: An Account Written by the Hand of Mormon, Upon Plates Taken From the Plates of Nephi.* By Joseph Smith, Junior, Author and Proprietor. Palmyra, [New York]: Printed by E. B. Grandin, for the Author, 1830. First edition. **John Wesley Brackenbury's copy, with his name on front pastedown: "J. W. Brackenbury / His Book / White Cloud / Kansas" written in pencil by the owner, John Wesley Brackenbury. "John W. Brackenbury / Independence / Mo." in pencil on rear pastedown. Brackenbury's seal reading "John W. Brackenbury / Notary Public / Jackson Co., MO" on Testimony leaf at rear.** Octavo. iv, [5], 588 [2] pages.

With the two-page preface at the front and the testimonial leaf at the back, both of which appeared only in the first issue of this book. Also with the misprint "122" on page 212. Without the index, which was issued at a later date and was not included in the first edition. Lacking only the front free endpaper leaf and the final blank. Original full sheep binding. Smooth spine with black morocco label with gilt lettering and seven double gilt rules. Some rubbing to boards and along joints, with a few light scratches. Edges and extremities worn, with pasteboards exposed at corners and edges. Some loss at spine ends. Early repair to section of leather on front board and to section of leather on rear board. Mild puckering to both pastedowns. Dampstaining throughout, most apparent to first 100 pages and to last 100 pages. Toning, and foxing throughout. Large chip to fore-edge of title leaf, affecting text on recto and verso; two other leaves with minor chip to bottom edge, not affecting any text. Pencil notes throughout, in the hand of the owner, John W. Brackenbury, an "early Saint" of the Mormon Church. Despite some cosmetic imperfections, the binding is still square and quite sturdy. A very good copy.

This copy belonged to John Wesley Brackenbury (1829-1902), the son of Joseph Blanchett Brackenbury (1788-1832), a very early follower of Joseph Smith who was baptized as a Latter-Day Saint in 1831, only a year after the Mormon Church was founded. He was ordained an Elder the next day and became a High Priest six months later (ordained by Oliver Cowdery, one of the Three Witnesses of the golden plates). One of the first missionaries for the Church of Jesus Christ of Latter-Day Saints, the elder Brackenbury was sent on a mission to New York State in January of 1832, where he was poisoned with arsenic by townsfolk fervently opposed to Mormonism. Brackenbury's murder, while serving a mission, resulted in his becoming what has been described as the faith's "first martyr."

Brackenbury's widow and young children struggled after his death. They were ultimately driven out of their home in Jackson County, Missouri by an anti-Mormon mob. After spending a night hiding in a cornfield, three-year-old John and his family returned to their home the next morning. John Wesley Brackenbury recalled later: "In the morning when we came back to the house, I remember that the house was torn down to the eaves, and the rafters were all off it, and I remember going into the house and there was a large table sitting in the middle of the room, and a big large pan of honey sitting on it. Then they took us away from there, off into the woods to a school house, and there were the women, children, and an old man there, but I do not remember the old man's name. We stood there all day, women, children, and this old man, there all day, crying, and in great distress."

After spending a somewhat nomadic few years travelling the Midwest and Far West, following the LDS Saints, the family ended up in Nauvoo, where, in the early 1840s, Elizabeth Davis Goldsmith Brackenbury Durfee, the widowed mother of John Wesley Brackenbury, married Joseph Smith, founder of the Latter-Day Saint movement and author of *The Book of Mormon*, becoming the twelfth of Smith's plural wives. Years after Smith's death, the Brackenburys eventually made their way back to Independence, Missouri, the place Joseph Smith had proclaimed "the New Jerusalem" or "the City of Zion."

As the son of very early Mormon followers, and as the stepson of the founder of the movement, it is no surprise that John Wesley Brackenbury kept and studied *The Book of Mormon* all of his life. As a child he was baptized to the Church of Jesus Christ of Latter-Day Saints, and in 1866 he was baptized into the Reorganized Church of Latter-Day Saints, a splinter Mormon group led by Joseph Smith III who founded the group as Prophet-President after the death of his father, Joseph Smith, Jr. The RLDS was based in Independence, Missouri in Jackson County, John Brackenbury's family's home for most of his life. An ever-faithful follower until his death in 1902, he was serving as a member of the Quorum of Elders as late as 1900.

Along with *The Book of Mormon*, this lot also includes seventeen original photographs, mostly cabinet portraits (and one tintype), made circa 1900, of members of the Brackenbury, Smith, and Curtis families of Missouri, Kansas, and Iowa — including four portraits of John Wesley Brackenbury. Many of the photographs bear the printed stamp of the Lamoni, Iowa studios run by Brackenbury's son Charles (Lawhorn & Brackenbury, Julian &

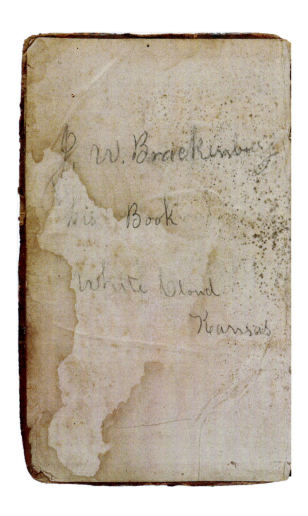

First Quorum Of
Elders.
APRIL, 1900.
1. Samuel Ackerley
2. F. L. Sawley
3. Thomas Whiting
4. T. R. White
5. N. C. Enge
6. Thomas Hougas
7. E. H. Durand
8. A. W. Moffet
9. S. V. Bailey
10. E. A. Blakeslee
11. Alfred White
12. H. N. Snively
13. Wm. Newton
14. J. W. Brackenbury
15. D. S. Holmes
16. W. R. Pickering
17. H. J. Davison
18. Geo. Smith
19. E. Hayer
20. R. N. Burwell
21. W. W. Gaylord
22. E. Short
23. J. M. Stubbart
24. P. P. Starke
25. Lehi Ellison

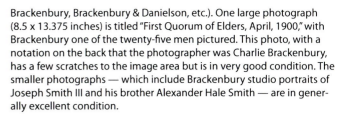

Brackenbury, Brackenbury & Danielson, etc.). One large photograph (8.5 x 13.375 inches) is titled "First Quorum of Elders, April, 1900," with Brackenbury one of the twenty-five men pictured. This photo, with a notation on the back that the photographer was Charlie Brackenbury, has a few scratches to the image area but is in very good condition. The smaller photographs — which include Brackenbury studio portraits of Joseph Smith III and his brother Alexander Hale Smith — are in generally excellent condition.

Photographs in this collection include: **John Wesley Brackenbury** (two identical photographs, one in an oval mat, one in a square mat); **"First Quorum of Elders - April 1900"**; **Joseph Smith III** (eldest surviving son of LDS church founder Joseph Smith, Jr. and his first wife Emma Hale Smith; Joseph Smith III was anointed prophet-leader when his father died and was the head of the Reorganized Latter-Day Saints; **A. H. (Alexander Hale)** Smith (third surviving son of Joseph Smith Jr. and Emma Hale Smith; **Woman seated next to a man propped up in bed (appears to be J. W. Brackenbury and, perhaps, his wife Nannie Curtis Brackenbury; Charles Brackenbury** (son of JWB, the photographer who took most of these photographs); **Alice and Charles Brackenbury** (daughter-in-law and son of JWB); **Vivian Brackenbury** (granddaughter of JWB); **Walice [sic] Brackenbury** (grandson of JWB); **Hazle [sic] Brackenbury**; **Luna Noble** (daughter of JWB); **Nell & Walter Pierson** (JWB's daughter and son-in-law); **Unidentified woman**; **"Tintype of Smith or Curtis"**; **Group of 10 women**; and **Group of 22 men and women**. (Further information on photos available at HA.com.)

This copy of *The Book of Mormon* and these photographs have been kept together and passed down through generations of Brackenbury's family. These items, never before offered for sale, are consigned from a direct descendant of John Wesley Brackenbury.

The Book of Mormon has had a profound influence, not only on John Wesley Brackenbury and his immediate family, but also on nineteenth-century religious thought. Its impact on American history is notable, too, particularly for the pivotal role it played in this country's Western expansion. *The Book of Mormon*, rare in the first edition, is not only a highly-prized sacred text but is also one of the most collectible books on religion issued in the United States.

Church 1342. Crawley 1. Crawley & Flake, *A Mormon Fifty,* 1. Flake 595. Grolier, *100 American,* 37. Howes S623. Sabin 83038. Streeter Sale 2262.

Estimate: $80,000-up
Starting Bid: $40,000

Published by the Vatican Secret Archives

37035 **[Knights Templar].** *Processus Contra Templarios. Exemplaria praetiosa III.* First edition. Two folio volumes. Limited to 799 numbered sets, this being number 398. Text volume in Latin, Italian, and English, printed on specially made cotton paper, with three engraved plates, accompanying portfolio containing facsimile manuscripts and Papal seals in elaborate leather pockets decorated in gilt, publisher's vellum over wooden boards, text volume lettered in gilt, spine of portfolio with onlaid leather strapwork and ties, preserved in single wallet-style limp goatskin portfolio, with ties, original velour bag and original packaging material.

This lavishly-designed production originated from the Vatican Secret Archives and possesses all of the pomp and extravagance one might expect from the Stato della Città del Vaticano. The work documents the papal hearings which eventually led to the suppression of the Templar order. From the prospectus: "The ancient parchments, and among them the Chinon paper which includes the papal acquittal upon the accusations against the Knights Templar, the private agenda with notes likely written by [P]ope Clemens V. The surviving acts of the pontiff inquiry, kept at the Vatican Secret Archive, show to what extent the pope himself aimed to save and preserve the existence of the Templar Order, assigning it a new role upon restoration of its habits and rules."

Estimate: $4,000-up
Starting Bid: $2,000

From the Havell Edition

37036 **John James Audubon (1785-1851). White-headed Eagle — Plate CXXVI (Havell Edition).** A striking hand-colored aquatint engraving by R. Havell from the first edition of *The Birds of America* (London: 1827-1838). Watermarked "Whatman 1834" (the "J" appears to be obscured by the image). In very good condition with a few short tears (and two between 2 and 2.5 inches in length) along edges, most professionally repaired; one tear inside image area measuring approximately one inch, professionally repaired. Some professional paper fills. Some faint areas of dampstaining, toning, and very minor foxing to image area. Two pieces of mounting tape at top edge, affixed to verso. Has been trimmed inside platemark. 36.875 x 24.75 inches. An overall bright copy of this depiction of an immature bald eagle.

Estimate: $5,000-up
Starting Bid: $2,500

Lockwood Octavo Edition of Audubon's *Birds of America*

Presentation Copy from Darwin to the Translator of His Works into French, with Three Autograph Letters Signed by Charles Darwin

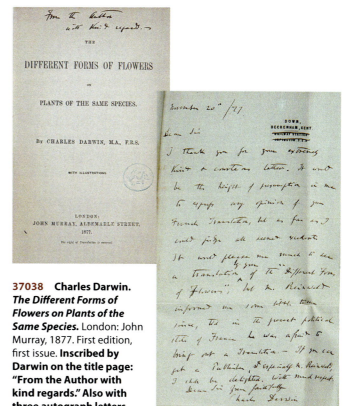

37038   Charles Darwin. ***The Different Forms of Flowers on Plants of the Same Species.*** London: John Murray, 1877. First edition, first issue. **Inscribed by Darwin on the title page: "From the Author with kind regards." Also with three autograph letters signed by Darwin** tipped in. **Edouard Heckel's copy with his ink notes on blank preliminary page, and with his monogrammed anchor stamp on title page.** Octavo. viii, 352 pages, plus 32 pages of publisher's advertisements dated March, 1877. Illustrations. Green cloth with gilt titles and gilt decorative borders and device to spine, and with blind-stamped line pattern to boards. Brown coated endpapers. Mild rubbing to binding; minor wrinkling to boards. Two small ink stains to rear board. Text block is intact but has completely (and cleanly) separated from binding. Front free endpaper chipped. Binder's stamp on rear pastedown. Book in good condition, in a custom clamshell box; letters are in very good or better condition.

Edouard Heckel was the translator of several of Darwin's works into French, including this one. Tipped in at the beginning of the book are **three autograph letters signed by Charles Darwin** (one signed "Ch. Darwin"), written to Heckel. Each letter is on notepaper measuring 8 x 5 inches and all are folded together to fit inside the dimensions of the book. All have the address "Down, Beckenham, Kent, Railway Station, Orpington, S.E. R." printed in the top right corner.

The letters cover the period November, 1877 to August 13, 1878, as Heckel was preparing the French translation of *Different Forms of Flowers*. Darwin offers praise, suggestions, and appreciation in these three letters. Heckel's translation, *Des différentes formes de fleurs dans les plantes de la même espèce* was published in Paris in July, 1878 by Reinwald.

Estimate: $3,000-up
Starting Bid: $1,500

37037   John James Audubon. ***The Birds of America,*** *Drawings Made in the United States and their Territories.* New York: George R. Lockwood, [1870]. Later Lockwood edition with the biographical essay on Audubon in Volume I. Eight octavo volumes. xv, 246; vii, 199; viii, 233; viii, 321; viii, 346; vii, 298; vii, 285; viii, 256. With 500 full-color lithograph plates after J. J. and J. W. Audubon by W. E. Hitchcock, R. Trembly, and others, printed and finished by hand by J. T. Bowen of Philadelphia. Complete. Ex-library. Half morocco over boards, except for Volume II, which has been bound in buckram. Boards detached from five volumes. Some loss to the backstrips. Internally sound. Overall, a very good set with the complete plates in clean and bright condition.

Sabin 2364.

Estimate: $15,000-up
Starting Bid: $7,500

Twelve Principal Works by Charles Darwin

37039   Charles Darwin. Works of Charles Darwin in Fifteen Volumes, including: *Journal of Researches* into Natural History and Geology of the Countries Visited During the Voyage of H. M. S. Beagle.... [and:] *The Structure and Distribution of Coral Reefs.* [and:] *Geological Observations* on the Volcanic Islands and Parks of South America.... [and:] *The Origin of Species* by Means of Natural Selection.... Two volumes. [and:] *The Variation of Animals and Plants Under Domestication.* Two volumes. [and:] *The Descent of Man* and Selection in Relation to Sex. [and:] *The Expressions of the Emotions in Man and Animals.* [and:] *Insectivorous Plants.* [and:] *The Different Forms of Flowers on Plants of the Same Species.* [and:] *The Power of Movement in Plants.* [and:] *The Formation of Vegetable Mould Through the Action of Worms.* [and:] *The Life and Letters of Charles Darwin....* Two volumes. New York: D. Appleton and Company, 1898. Uniformly bound octavo volumes in half red morocco over marbled boards. Gilt lettering to spines. Top edge gilt. Many illustrations and maps throughout. Some rubbing to the extremities. Very good.

Estimate: $1,500-up
Starting Bid: $750

Over 100 Hand-Colored Engravings of Birds

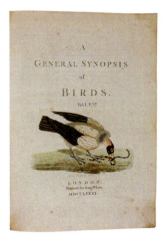

37040   John Latham. *A General Synopsis of Birds.* In three volumes. Volume I: London: Benjamin White, 1781. Volume II & III: London: Leigh & Sotheby, 1783, 1785. First edition. Three octavo volumes. vi, 788, [34]; 808, [38]; 628, [44], 298, [15]. Volume II bound with the first supplement, dated 1787. **119 hand-color plates, plus seven hand-colored frontispieces.** Modern binding of brown buckram over boards. Gilt lettering to spines. Scattered moderate foxing throughout. Shadow offset to most pages facing the prints. Slight staining to the fore-edge of Volume III. Near fine.

Freeman 2175. Sitwell, p. 114.

Estimate: $1,500-up
Starting Bid: $750

Limited to 500 Numbered Copies, with Hand-Colored Plates of Deer

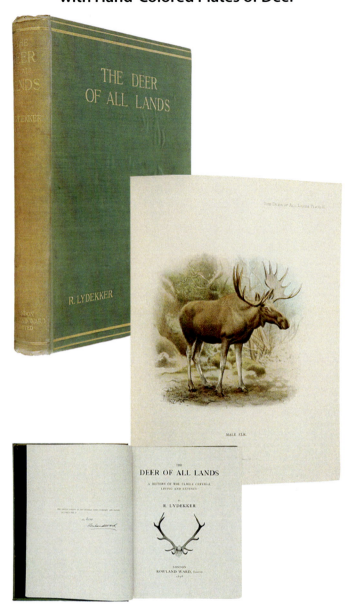

37041   R. Lydekker. *The Deer of All Lands*. A History of the Family Cervidae Living and Extinct. London: Rowland Ward, 1898. **One of five hundred numbered copies signed by the publisher, of which this is number 214.** Quarto. 329 pages. Twenty-four hand-colored plates with numerous reproductions and illustrations. Publisher's green cloth with gilt-stamped titles and ruling to front cover and spine. Shelfwear to extremities with slight bubbling to boards. Hinges starting. Spine faded. Armorial bookplate on front pastedown and blindstamp to front free endpaper. Light spotting to a few plates. Very slight toning to page edges. A very good copy of a much sought-after book with beautiful hand-colored plates.

Estimate: $1,500-up
Starting Bid: $750

One of Sixty Copies Signed By The Famed Naturalist

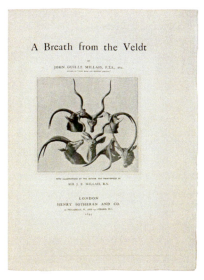

37042   John Guille Millais. *A Breath from the Veldt*. London: Henry Sotheran and Co., 1895. Special edition. One of 60 copies, of which this is number 54, **signed signed and dated by the author**. Imperial folio. 236 pages. Illustrations by the author and frontispiece by Sir J. E. Millais. Half bound in crimson morocco over cream boards with black-stamped titles and vignettes of sable and kudu antelope on front board. Gilt-stamped titles and decoration on spine. Printed on handmade deckle edge paper for this extra large format. Top edge gilt. Foxed boards show wear with some soiling. Spine lightly rubbed and bottom corners bumped. Some foxing to plates and minor offsetting throughout. Light toning to page edges. A much sought-after title in this format with wonderful illustrations. Very good.

Estimate: $2,000-up
Starting Bid: $1,000

With Twenty Wonderful Hand-Colored Plates of Parrakeets

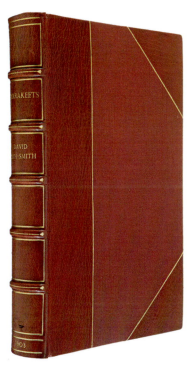

37043   David Seth-Smith. *Parrakeets. A Handbook to the Imported Species*. London: R. H. Porter, 1903. First edition. Octavo. xx, 281 pages. **Twenty hand-colored plates.** Illustrations in text. Bound by Sangorski & Sutcliffe for Bernard Quaritch. Half red morocco over red cloth boards. Raised bands. Gilt lettering to spines. Top edges gilt. A beautiful edition in fine condition.

Estimate: $1,500-up
Starting Bid: $750

With Fifteen Hand-Colored Plates

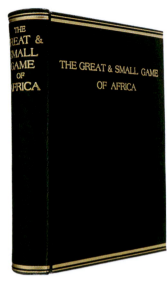 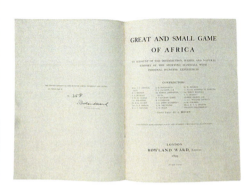 

37044   **H. A. Bryden**, General Editor. *Great and Small Game of Africa. An Account of the Distribution, Habits, and Natural History of the Sporting Mammals, with Personal Hunting Experiences.* London: Rowland Ward, 1899. **One of 500 numbered copies, of which this is number 358, signed by the publisher.** Folio. [i]-xx, [1]-612 pages. Fifteen hand-colored plates, with numerous reproductions and illustrations. Modern full leather with gilt-stamped titles and ruling to front cover and spine. Light indentation to page edges of text block. Plates and pages edges lightly toned. A few torn, toned pages repaired or restored. Ownership signature. Very good.

Estimate: $1,500-up
Starting Bid: $750

Scarce Hunting Book on Trip to Kamchatka

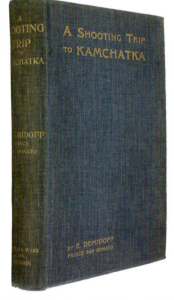  

37045   **Elim Demidoff, Prince San Donato.** *A Shooting Trip to Kamchatka.* London: Rowland Ward, 1904. First edition. Octavo. xvi, 302, [5] publisher's catalog pages. With five photogravures, numerous illustrations in text, and two colored folding maps. Original blue cloth over beveled boards with titles stamped in gilt. Top edge roughly trimmed, all others untrimmed. Browning to spine, light shelf wear elsewhere. Contents sound save for a slight dampstain at the bottom edge of the text block. Otherwise, a very good copy of this rather scarce work.

Estimate: $1,500-up
Starting Bid: $750

Lydekker's Scarce Work on Game Animals, Limited to Only 250 Copies

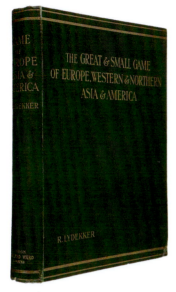 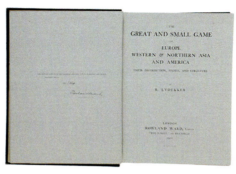 

37046 **R. Lydekker.** *The Great and Small Game of Europe, Western & Northern Asia, and America, Their Distribution, Habits, and Structure.* London: Rowland Ward, 1901. Limited edition of 250 hand-numbered copies signed by the publisher, of which this is number 164. Quarto. xx, 445 pages. Eight hand-colored plates under tissue guards and seventy-five additional illustrations in text. Original green cloth with titles stamped in gilt on the front board and spine. Former owner's bookplate mounted to the front pastedown. Boards with modest wear and bumped lower corners. Internal pages and plates clean and crisp. Most pages uncut at the top edge. Near fine. An exceptionally scarce book, especially in this condition.

Estimate: $1,500-up
Starting Bid: $750

The Handsome Limited Edition Signed by Theodore Roosevelt

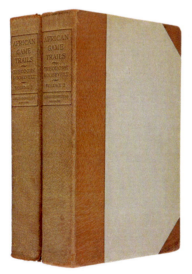 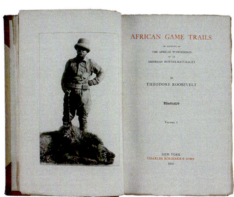 

37047 **Theodore Roosevelt.** *African Game Trails:* An Account of the African Wanderings of an American Hunter-Naturalist. New York: Charles Scribner's Sons, 1910. First edition, limited to 500 sets of which this is number 342, **signed by Roosevelt** on the limitation page in the first volume. Two octavo volumes. xvi, [2], 268, viii, [2], 269-529 pages. With fifty illustrated or photographic plates. Publisher's tan three-quarter leather over beige paper boards. Titles stamped in blind with blind-ruled borders on spines. All edges untrimmed. Some wear to the bindings, especially the joints and spine ends. Corners rubbed and/or exposed. A few small abrasions and light soiling to paper boards of each volume. Spine tail of Volume I with a tiny split. Light offsetting to endpapers from binding leather. Internally very clean. A very good copy.

Estimate: $4,000-up
Starting Bid: $2,000

Limited and Signed by Teddy Roosevelt

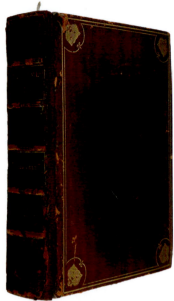

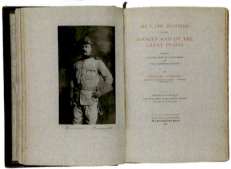

37048 **Theodore Roosevelt.** ***Big Game Hunting in the Rockies and On the Great Plains*** *Comprising "Hunting Trips of a Ranchman" and "The Wilderness Hunter."* New York: G. P. Putnam's Sons (The Knickerbocker Press), 1899. First edition, limited to 1,000 hand-numbered copies, of which this is number 88, **signed by Theodore Roosevelt** beneath the frontispiece photograph. Large quarto. [2], xxix, [1, blank], 323, [1, blank], viii, 476 pages. With fifty-five illustrations by artists such as Remington, Frost, Beard, Sanford, and Gifford. Descriptive tissue guards. Contemporarily rebound in full brown leather with decorative animal head vignettes and rules stamped in gilt on the boards. Raised bands. Titles in gilt on morocco labels. Marbled endpapers. Top edge gilt. Joints repaired but sound. Boards moderately scuffed with modest bumping to the extremities. Spine worn. Endpaper repaired. Captioned tissue cover over the frontispiece torn in half and detached, but present and complete. Small morocco bookplate affixed to the front pastedown: "Ex-Libris Frank J. Hogan." Contents bright. An overall very good copy of this scarce work.

Phillips, *American Sporting Books*, pp. 317-318. Riling 1478. Wheelock, p. 7.

Estimate: $3,000-up
Starting Bid: $1,500

One of Only 200 Copies, Signed by Theodore Roosevelt, In the Original Buckram Binding

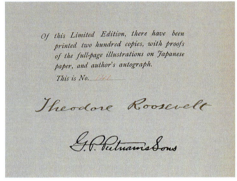

37049 **Theodore Roosevelt.** ***The Wilderness Hunter.*** *An Account of the Big Game of the United States and Its Chase With Horse, Hound, and Rifle.* New York and London: G. P. Putnam's Sons, 1893. First edition limited to 200 hand-numbered copies, of which this is number 141, **signed by Theodore Roosevelt.** Quarto. xvi, 472 pages. Proof illustrations on Japanese paper including the frontispiece and twenty-three plates after drawings by A. B. Frost, Henry Sandham, J. Carter Beard, C. Harry Eaton, and Frederick Remington under captioned tissue guards. Original tan buckram with gilt-stamped titles on the front board and spine. Top edges gilt. Light spotting to boards with some toning on the spine panel. Contents clean and crisp. Contemporary gift inscription on the front free endpaper. Small photograph of Roosevelt centrally mounted to the front pastedown. A very good copy of this rather scarce title.

Estimate: $1,500-up
Starting Bid: $750

120 Issues of the Scarce and Influential Alchemy Journal

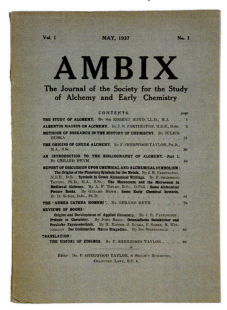

A Twentieth-Century Classic of Scientific Literature

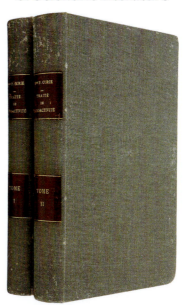

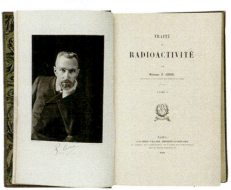

37050   AMBIX. *The Journal of the Society for the Study (History) of Alchemy and (Early) Chemistry.* Published for the Society for the History of Alchemy and Chemistry. Cambridge/London: W. Heffer and Sons/ Taylor and Francis, 1937-1997. First editions. 120 octavo issues. Bound in printed wrappers. Some toning to wrappers and page edges of early issues. Occasional spine and cover chipping, with Vol. I, No. 2 covers detached but present. A few issues have neat ownership signature on upper right of front cover. Some prospectuses laid in. Overall, copies of this widely influential and extremely scarce early scientific journal are in very good or better condition. To put a collection of this periodical together piecemeal would be virtually impossible.

"The Society (SHAC), founded in 1937, has consistently maintained the highest standards of scholarship in all aspects of the history for alchemy and chemistry from early times to present. The journals coverage is wide and varied, ranging from studies in exoteric and esoteric alchemy to recent chemistry. The presentation of scientific ideas, methods and discoveries is made as non-technical as possible, consistent with academic rigour and scientific accuracy."

Estimate: $2,000-up
Starting Bid: $1,000

37051   Marie Curie. *Traité de Radioactivité.* Paris: Gauthier-Vallars, 1910. First edition. Two octavo volumes. xiii, 426; 548 pages. Frontispiece. Seven plates. Modern gray cloth over boards. Leather title labels to spine. "Hommage" blind-stamped to both half-title pages (intended as a presentation copy). Some light spots to boards from minor insect damage. Overall, a very good, bright, tight set of this classic of scientific literature.

Estimate: $1,500-up
Starting Bid: $750

"Cogito Ergo Sum."

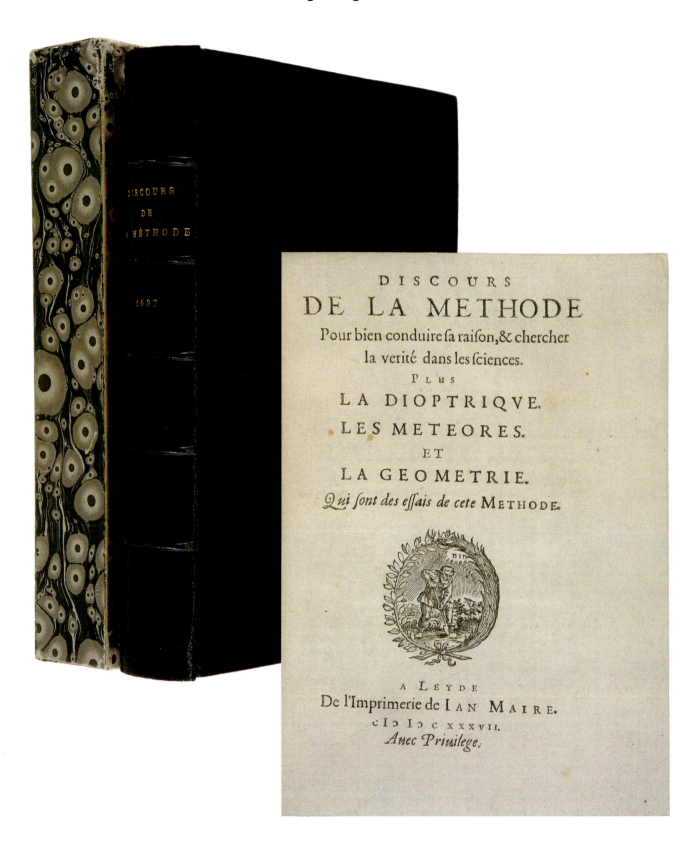

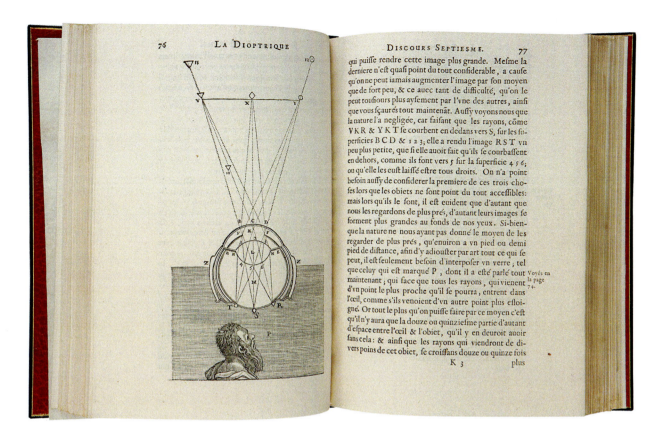

37052 René Descartes. *Discours de la Méthode pour bien conduire sa raison, & chercher la vérité dans les sciences.* *Plus la Dioptrique. Les Météores. Et la Géométrie.* Leyde [Leiden]: Jan Maire, 1637. First edition of Descartes' first published work. Quarto. 78, [2, section title], 413, [1, advertisement], [33, Table], [1, blank] pages. 3K4, the Dutch privilege leaf, in facsimile on old paper. Woodcut device on title page. Woodcut diagrams and initials. Late-nineteenth-century full black morocco by Georges Huser with gilt spine titles inside five raised bands. Red morocco pastedowns ruled in gilt. All edges gilt. Original vellum covers bound in (one partially detached). Housed in a decorative paper and leather slipcase. Text carefully washed, with only very minor occasional foxing. Minor paper flaw to D3. An excellent copy of the foundational work of modern science and philosophy.

This work contains the first appearance of one of the most famous and important phrases in the history of science and philosophy. "Cogito ergo sum" appeared for the first time in the present work in French, as "Je pense donc je suis" that translates into the English proposition "I think, therefore I am". Descartes was writing in French in order to reach a larger audience. The phrase first appeared in the better known Latin form "Cogito ergo sum" in the later published *Principles of Philosophy* (1644).

"It is no exaggeration to say that Descartes was the first of modern philosophers and one of the first modern scientists; in both branches of learning his influence has been vast... The revolution he caused can be most easily found in his reassertion of the principle (lost in the middle ages) that knowledge, if it is to have any value, must be intelligence and not erudition. His application of modern algebraic arithmetic to ancient geometry created the analytical geometry which was the basis of the post-Euclidian development of that science. His statement of the elementary laws of matter and movement in the physical universe, the theory of vertices, and many other speculations threw light on every branch of science from optics to biology... All this found its starting-point in the 'Discourse on the Method for Proper Reasoning and Investigating Truth in the Sciences'" (*Printing and the Mind of Man*, second edition, p. 77).

Dibner 81. Guibert, *Discours*, 1. Horblitt 24. Krivatsy/NLM 3114. Norman I, 621. *Printing and the Man*, second edition, 129. STCN 163704. Tchemerzine IV 286.

Estimate: $60,000-up
Starting Bid: $30,000

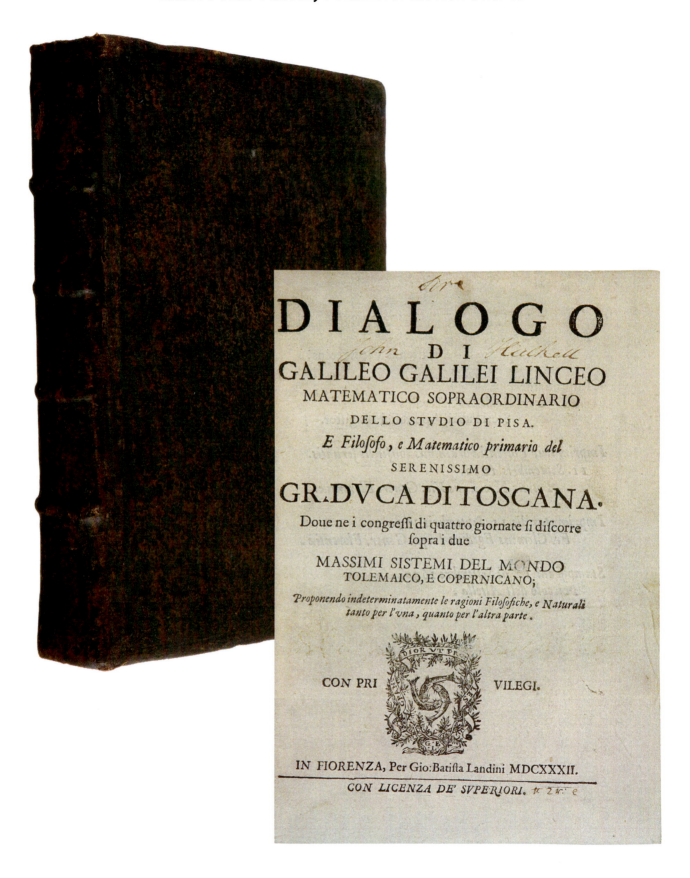

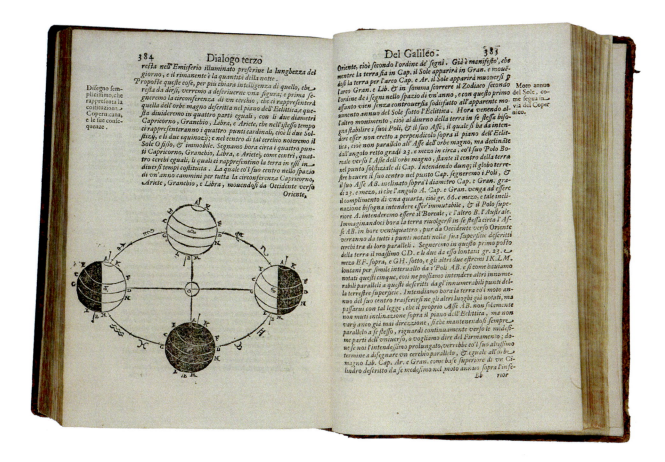

37053 **Galileo Galilei.** *Dialogo...Doue ne I congressi di Quattro giornate si discorre sopra I due Massimi Sistemi del Mondo Tolemaico, e Copernicano...* Florence: Giovanni Batista Landini, 1632. First edition. Quarto. [viii], 458, [32] pages, with Errata leaf (2F6) and final blank present. Page 92 with correction slip supplying side note pasted in the margin. Woodcut device on title page, with thirty-one woodcut diagrams and illustrations, woodcut decorations and woodcut initials. Contemporary mottled calf with double-ruled borders and floral blindstamped devices in the corners. Text edges sprinkled red. Spine head renewed. Boards somewhat worn, with corners rubbed. Front hinge a touch tender after the endpaper. Minor marginal spotting to some leaves. Engraved frontispiece supplied in facsimile. Letter "H" added by hand to diagram on M8v. A one-and-three-eights-inch horizontal marginal tear to S6. Leaves 2B3/2B4 (with 2B4 missigned as "2B2") nested incorrectly and so bound. Signature of John Halkett, seventh baronet of Pitfirrane on title page. Bookplate of Halkett family on front pastedown. A clean copy, with wide margins, of Galileo's foundational work of modern science and philosophy. Galileo's statement and defense of the Copernican system of heliocentrism, a work which resulted in the author's 1633 trial for heresy in Rome.

"The *Dialogo* was designed both as an appeal to the great public and as an escape from silence. In the form of an open discussion between three friends — intellectually speaking, a radical, a conservative, and an agnostic — it is a masterly polemic for the new science. It displays all the great discoveries in the heavens which the ancients had ignored; it inveighs against the sterility, wilfulness, and ignorance of those who defend their systems; it revels in the simplicity of Copernican thought and, above all, it teaches that the movement of the earth makes sense in philosophy, that is, in physics. Astronomy and the science of motion, rightly understood, says Galileo, are hand in glove. There is no need to fear that the earth's rotation will cause it to fly to pieces. So Galileo picked up one thread that led straight to Newton. The *Dialogo*, far more than any other work, made the heliocentric system a commonplace. Every fear of Galileo's enemies was justified; only their attempts to stifle thought were vain" (*Printing and the Mind of Man*, second edition, p. 77).

Bibliografia Galileiana 128. Carli & Favaro 28. Cinti 89. Dibner 8. Horblit 18c. Norman 858. *Printing and the Mind of Man*, second edition, 128. Riccardi I, 511. Sparrow 74.

Estimate: $30,000-up
Starting Bid: $15,000

First Edition of Pasteur

37054 **Louis Pasteur.** *Quelque Réflexions sur la Science en France.* Paris: Gauthier-Villars, 1871. First edition. Octavo. 40 pages. Printed wrappers. Moderate foxing throughout. Damp-staining to upper corner. Ink name of previous owner to front wrapper. Occasional penciled underling. Splitting down the spine two inches. In custom chemise and slipcase. One of Pasteur's principle works in very good condition.

This slender volume contains three essays. "Les Laboratoires" was first published in 1868. "Suppression du Cumul dans L'Enseignement des Sciences Physiques et Naturelles," and "Pourquoi la France n'a pas Trouvé D'Hommes Supérieurs au Moment du Péril" were published here for the first time.

Estimate: $1,500-up
Starting Bid: $750

The Earliest English Work on Medical Psychology

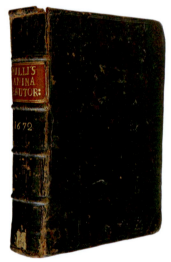 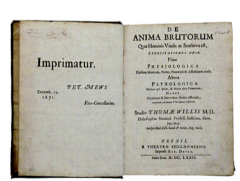 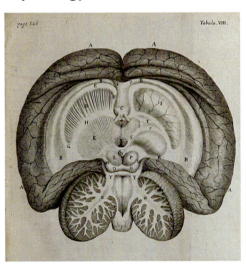

37055 **Thomas Willis.** *De Anima Brutorum Quae Hominis Vitalis ac Sensitiva est, Exercitationes Duae. Prior Physiologica...Altera Pathologica...* Oxford: Theatro Sheldoniano [Sheldonian Theatre], 1672. First edition. Quarto. [lvi], 563, [11, Index], [1, blank] pages. Includes the five-page publisher's catalog, but the errata slip was neither cancelled in nor pasted onto any leaf (therefore, likely a first issue). With eight engraved plates, five of which are folding. Contemporary full brown leather with gilt spine titles in compartments with four raised bands. Binding worn and abraded, with short splits to the joints at the spine head. Corners bumped and rubbed. Hinges starting but still strong. Minor occasional foxing or spotting within the text. Very good.

A rare and important work, regarded by Willis as his greatest work, and generally accepted as the first book on medical psychology. F. J. Cole, in his *A History of Comparative Anatomy*, wrote that the book is "a solid contribution to the armamentarium of the comparative anatomist." This is the rarer Oxford imprint, being also printed in London the same year for more general circulation. Ownership signature of antiquarian book collector Cuthbert Tunstall, later Cuthbert Constable, on the title page. The bookplate of his son, William Constable, affixed to the front pastedown.

Madan 2953. Wing W2825.

Estimate: $1,500-up
Starting Bid: $750

Texts on Astronomy

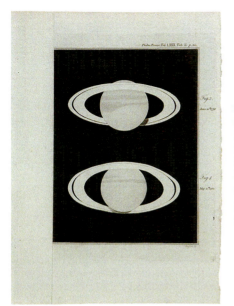

37056   Thirteen William Herschel Texts on Astronomy, from *Philosophical Transactions*. Disbound quarto sections in oversized wrappers. Some stapled, some uncut, with a few trimmed. Some with illustrative plates, a few of which are folding. Edges somewhat toned with light rippling to sections. Occasional offsetting of plates. An interesting collection of works by the German-born British astronomer, best known for his discovery of Uranus and his work regarding Saturn's rings. Herschel also discovered two moons for both aforementioned planets and coined the word "asteroid." All in very good condition. (Detailed list at HA.com)

Estimate: $1,500-up
Starting Bid: $750

One of Twenty-Five Copies Signed by George Barbier with an Original Watercolor

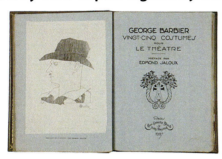 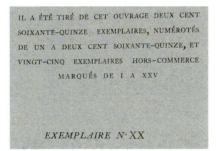

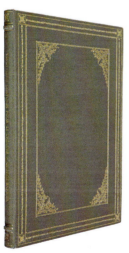  

37057   George Barbier. *Vingt-Cinq Costumes pour le Théâtre.* Préface par Edmond Jaloux. Paris: Chex Camille Bloch & Jules Meynial, 1927. First edition. One of twenty-five numbered copies "hors-commerce," out of a total edition of 300 copies. **With an original watercolor drawing by Barbier, signed "Aux amis Marty [Charles Martin?] / bien cordial souvenir de / George Barbier 1928."** Quarto. 20 pages. Mounted etched frontispiece portrait of Barbier by Charles Martin, and twenty-five mounted plates reproducing costume designs by Barbier, colored through stencils and heightened with gold and silver. Descriptive tissue guards. Bound by Sangorski & Sutcliffe in full gray crushed morocco. Covers decoratively paneled in gilt, gilt spine with two raised bands, gilt board edges and turn-ins. Top edge gilt, others uncut. Marbled endpapers. A little minor toning. Otherwise a fine copy.

Colas 218. Hiler, p. 64.

Estimate: $5,000-up
Starting Bid: $4,500

Limited to 125 Copies, Signed by Mark Beard

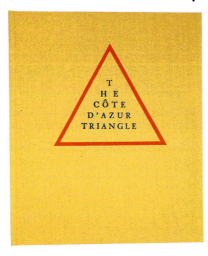

37058 **[Mark Beard, illustrator].** Harry Kondoleon. *The Côte d'Azur Triangle.* New York: Vincent FitzGerald & Co., 1985. First edition, limited to 125 numbered copies, of which this is number 38, **signed by Kondoleon and illustrator Mark Beard.** Folio. Illustrated with colored lithographs. Original yellow cloth over boards. Title in blue on front board. Clamshell case. Fine.

The seventh title printed by Vincent FitzGerald and the third to feature the artwork of Mark Beard.

Estimate: $2,000-up
Starting Bid: $1,000

Kiki Smith's Gorgeous 1997 Production

37059 **Mei-Mei Berssenbrugge. Kiki Smith.** *Endocrinology.* [N.p., Long Island, New York]: Universal Limited Art Editions, Inc., [1997]. Number 14 of 40 limited editions **signed and numbered by Berssenbrugge and Smith** on the limitation page. Large folio. Printed in Caslon Italic on Mohawk Superfine cut and mounted as irregular strips on natural fibre Nepalese paper. With twenty-one organic lithographs printed in blue by Kiki Smith with hand-written words by her in blue ink on mounted strips. Photograph of the artist mounted to each cover. Publisher's linen-backed cardboard covers with uncut edges. A gorgeously produced artist's book in fine condition.

Estimate: $2,000-up
Starting Bid: $1,000

Inscribed by Dali, with an Original Drawing

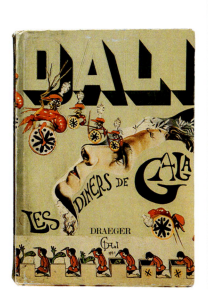

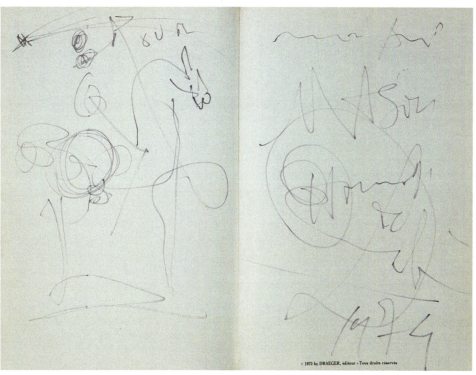

37060   **Salvador Dali.** *Les Dîners de Gala.* Paris: Draeger, [1973]. First French edition. **Inscribed by Dali to New York restaurateur Charles Masson on the white preliminary pages. Also, Dali has drawn in ink a large, loosely-rendered equine figure on the page facing the inscription.** On the blank page 322 someone (presumably Masson) has written six lines of notes concerning the book's signing. Quarto. 320 pages. Lavishly illustrated. Pictorial cloth boards. Ornately designed cookbook, from famed surreal gastronome Salvador Dali. Lavishly illustrated with reproductions of Dali's art and with photographs of the recipes. Near fine book in a lightly worn dust jacket.

Estimate: $1,500-up
Starting Bid: $750

Limited to Eighty-Five Copies Signed by the Artist

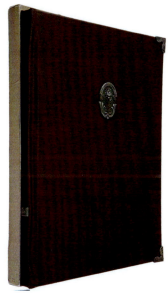

37061   **Leonid Gorban [illustrator].** *The Song of Songs.* Brooklyn: Gorban Press, 1998. First edition, limited to 85 numbered copies, this being number 9, **signed by Gorban.** Quarto. Eight engraved illustrations; eight pages of text engravings. Full morocco over boards. Decorative endpapers. Pewter cornerpieces, small pewter medallion on spine, and a pewter medallion on the front cover. Simple pasteboard slipcase with Gorban Press paper label on front. Fine. Stunning work from the Russian artist.

Estimate: $1,000-up
Starting Bid: $500

Inscribed Volume Of Man Ray's Portraits and Photographs

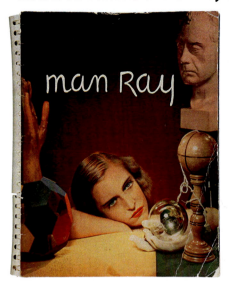 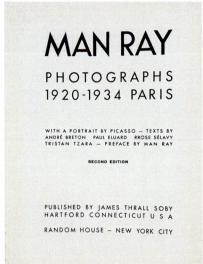

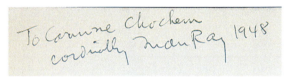

37062   **Man Ray.** *Photographs, 1920-1934 Paris*. With a Portrait by Picasso. Texts by André Breton, Paul Eluard, Rrose Sévaly, Tristan Tzara. Preface by Man Ray. Hartford: James Thrall Soby / New York: Random House, [1934]. Second edition. **Inscribed by Man Ray** to Jewish dancer and painter: **"To Corinne Chochem, Cordially, Man Ray 1948."** Quarto. [6], 104 pages. Illustrated with 104 full-page black and white gravure reproductions of photographs and photograms. Publisher's glossy photograph pictorial front cover with white spiral binding and glossy off-white rear cover. Some light bends to the corners of both covers with rubbing to extremities and minor loss. Rear cover rubbed with minor abrasions. Spiral binding somewhat darkened and broken at one point but intact. Bottom of tabs at binding displaced, top has few detached. Interior clean, except for occasional offsetting from reproductions and inscription. Very minor toning and foxing throughout. A very good copy of a beautifully designed artist's book.

Estimate: $1,500-up
Starting Bid: $750

One of 76 Signed Copies

37063   **Joan Mitchell, lithographs. Nathan Kernan, text.** *Poems*. [Mount Kisco, New York]: Printed and Published by Tyler Graphics Ltd., 1992. First edition, number 38 of 76 copies **numbered and signed by Mitchell and Kernan** on the limitation page. Folio. Eight gorgeous full-page lithographs (two-double-page) by Mitchell. Loose in publisher's handmade paper portfolio with blue title to front cover. Housed in the publisher's maroon cloth drop-down box with title label affixed to front cover. Some light soiling to box. Overall, a fine copy of a rare artist's book.

From the colophon page: "*Poems* is a book of eight Joan Mitchell lithographs illuminating the poetry of Nathan Kernan, with title and colophon pages, paper folio and cloth-covered box. The edition is seventy-six books...All books are signed on the colophon page by the artist and poet with book numbering by the artist."

Estimate: $2,000-up
Starting Bid: $1,000

"The Biggest and Most Expensive Book Production of the 20th Century"

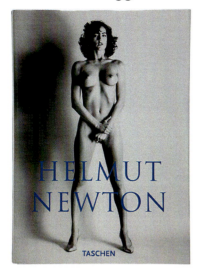
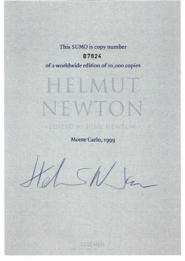

37064   **Helmut Newton.** *SUMO.* Monte Carlo: Taschen, 1999. Edited by June Newton. Deluxe worldwide edition limited to 10,000 copies, of which this is number 07824, **boldly signed by Helmut Newton** on the title page in blue crayon. Elephant folio (28 x 20 inches). 464 pages. Over 400 full-page photographs. Photo pictorial boards, photo pictorial dust jacket. With the Philippe Starck-designed chrome bookstand. Minor rippling to signature page at lower gutter margin. A fine copy, in its original shipping box.

Weighing over 66 pounds, this extremely large and sumptuous volume is — according to publisher Taschen — "the biggest and most expensive book production of the 20th century." An impressive collection of the always arresting — and often controversial — photographs by the provocative and influential Helmut Newton (1920-2004), covering his fashion, celebrity, and nude portrait work. A massive publication.

Estimate: $4,000-up
Starting Bid: $2,000

"We Were Somewhere Around Barstow On The Edge Of The Desert When The Drugs Began To Take Hold."

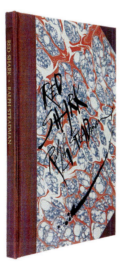

37065   **Ralph Steadman. Signed Lithograph and Limited Edition Book**, including: **[Hunter S. Thompson]. Ralph Steadman. Raoul Duke and Dr. Gonzo Screaming Through the Desert.** A wonderful two-color lithograph depicting the chapter one section title from Thompson's *Fear and Loathing in Las Vegas*, presumably from ***Modern Fiction and Art: Prints by Contemporary Authors***. Lexington, 1999. In excellent condition, with additional hand-painted acrylic accents in yellow and white, and silver paint-pen. The lithograph is printed in black and red, initialed on the lower left and **signed by Steadman** on the lower right in pencil where an embossed watermark resides. Measures 16.75 x 12 inches, while the matted framed piece measures 23.5 x 18.5 inches. [and:] **[Hunter S. Thompson]. Ralph Steadman.** *Red Shark.* [Tucson]:Sylph Publications, 2003. First edition. **One of 100 copies signed by the author, Anna Steadman, Joe Petro II, and Kurt Vonnegut, of which this is copy number 80.** 29 pages. Illustrated with reproductions of drawings and photographs. Half bound in iridescent red cloth over marbled boards with screenprinted titles on front cover and red morocco label with gilt titles on spine. Fine.

Estimate: $1,500-up
Starting Bid: $750

Specially Bound Edition with the Extra Suite of Woodblock Prints by Martin Puryear, Each Signed by the Artist

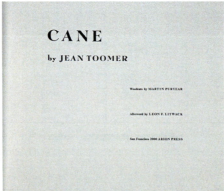

37066   **Jean Toomer. *Cane*.** Woodcuts by Martin Puryear. Afterword by Leon F. Litwack. San Francisco: Arion Press, 2000. First edition, number 30 of 400 copies **signed and numbered by Puryear.** With seven full-page woodcuts bound in and two smaller woodcuts within the text. Text on mouldmade German paper; lithographs on handmade Japanese Kitakata. Specially bound in full brown leather with black titles to the covers and spine. **One of a limited number of copies housed in the special wooden crate-like box created by Puryear. With the extra suite of seven woodblock prints, also numbered 30 of 50, each signed by Puryear.** Minor coffee stain to bottom corner of text, affecting about half of the text and a few lithographs. Otherwise, a near fine copy.

Estimate: $10,000-up
Starting Bid: $5,000

A Monumental Work With Stunning Etchings by Terry Winters, Signed by the Artist

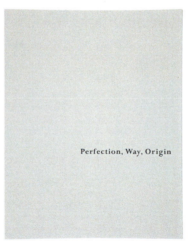

37067   **Terry Winters, etchings. Jean Starobinski, text. *Perfection, Way, Origin*.** Translated by Richard Pevear. [Bay Shore, New York: Universal Limited Art Editions, Inc., 2001]. First edition, number 16 of 38 limited edition copies **signed by Terry Winters and Jean Starobinski** on the limitation page. Large folio. Unpaginated text. With twenty-eight etchings by Winters. Publisher's handmade UICB cream paper boards with blind-stamped titles on the spine. Housed in the publisher's handsome aluminum box with a folder of ten etchings, titled *Set of Ten*, printed on custom handmade Ruscombe Mill paper, **each etching signed and dated by Terry Winters** and each with the publisher's seal blind-stamped to the bottom margin, and also with a bound copy of the French text. Minor scratches and soiling to the aluminum box. Fine condition.

From the colophon: "*Perfection, Way, Origin* comprises this book, a set of ten etchings and a bound copy of the French text enclosed in an aluminum box. The book is 58 pages and includes 28 etchings by Terry Winters for an original text by Jean Starobinski."

Estimate: $10,000-up
Starting Bid: $5,000

Limited Edition, Signed by Illustrator Willy Pogany

37068 **[Willy Pogany, illustrator]. Samuel Taylor Coleridge. *The Rime of the Ancient Mariner.*** London: George Harrap, [1910]. First Pogany edition. **Limited to 525 numbered copies, this being 279, signed by Pogany.** Quarto. Calligraphic letterpress, tipped-in color plates within decorated borders, illustrated and decorated throughout. Light brown polished morocco over boards. Gilt lettering to spine; gilt design and lettering to top board. Top edge gilt. Spine dulled. Extremities rubbed, boards slightly scuffed. An attempt has been made to erase an inked inscription from the front pastedown. Overall, a very good, internally clean and vibrant copy of one of Pogany's most masterful productions.

Estimate: $1,500-up
Starting Bid: $750

Limited Edition, Signed by Rackham

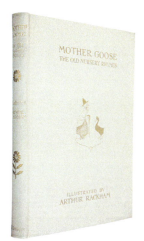
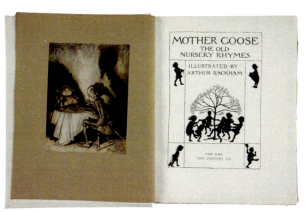
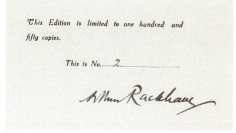

37069 **[Arthur Rackham, illustrator]. *Mother Goose. The Old Nursery Rhymes.*** Illustrated by Arthur Rackham. New York: Century, [1913]. Limited to 150 numbered copies, of which this is number 2, **signed by Arthur Rackham.** Large quarto. xi, [1, blank], 159, [1] pages. Thirteen color plates mounted on brown paper, with descriptive tissue guards, and eighty-five drawings in black and white (one mounted on brown paper, with descriptive tissue guard). Publisher's white cloth with gilt titles and decoration. A few spots of occasional light soiling to binding. Top edge gilt with others untrimmed. Modest toning. Binding cracked at page 80/81. A near fine copy in publisher's perished slipcase.

Estimate: $1,500-up
Starting Bid: $750

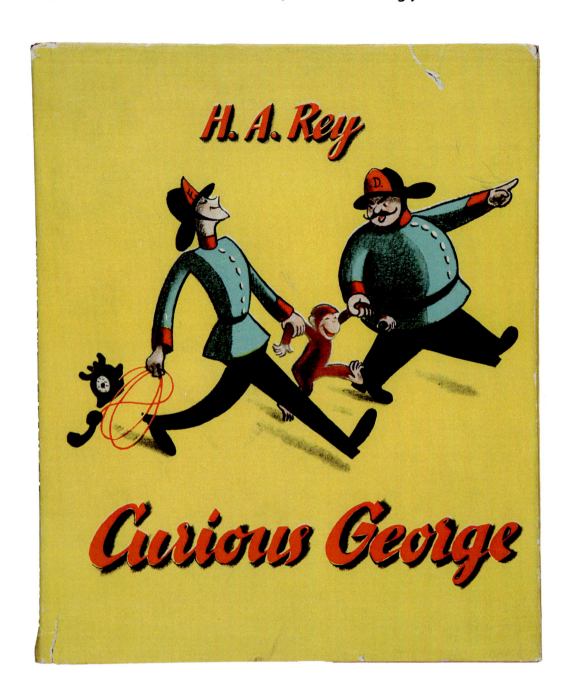

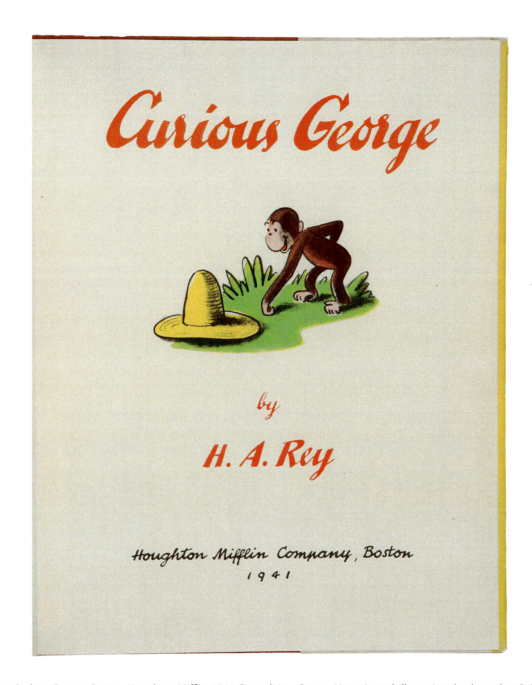

37070 **H. A. Rey. *Curious George*.** Boston: Houghton Mifflin, 1941. First edition. Quarto. Unpaginated. Illustrations by the author. Publisher's brick red cloth with Curious George vignette in black on front board and lettering in black on spine. Illustrated endpapers. Original dust jacket with $1.75 price. A couple of faint scratches to cloth on rear board. Original unrestored dust jacket is rubbed, with a few chips to extremities and spine ends; also with a few short closed tears and shallow creases at edges. Rear flap with Bullock's Wilshire price sticker ($1.75). A remarkably crisp, bright copy in near fine condition. We could only locate one other record of this title in dust jacket selling at auction in the past 35 years, and that was this very copy. Extremely scarce.

A classic children's book, *Curious George* burst upon the scene in 1941, a year after H. A. Rey and his wife Margret (both German Jews) had escaped Paris only hours ahead of the Nazis. The Reys had fashioned makeshift bicycles from spare parts and fled Europe with possessions limited only to clothes, food, and five manuscripts, one of which was *Curious George*.

Featuring one of the most beloved characters in children's literature, *Curious George* has never been out of print, and the story of the curious little monkey continues to delight and entertain children seventy years after its first publication. A superb copy, in the remarkably rare original dust jacket.

Estimate: $15,000-up
Starting Bid: $11,500

With an Original Color Drawing Inscribed and Signed by H. A. Rey

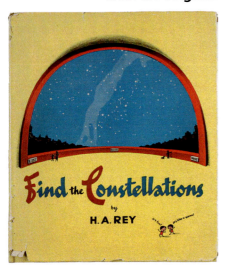 

37071   **H. A. Rey.** *Find the Constellations.* Boston: Houghton Mifflin Company, [1956]. Second printing. **With an original color drawing (in black pen, and yellow & green pencil) by H. A. Rey on the front free endpaper, showing a child gazing through a telescope at yellow highlighted stars in a green sky (finding constellations!). The drawing is inscribed and signed by the author/illustrator, "To Eleanor J. West / with best regards! / H A Rey / Waterville Valley, August 11, 1959."** Octavo. 72 pages. Publisher's yellow cloth with blue titles. Original pictorial dust jacket. Minor shelf wear to the boards. Lightly bumped corners. Text is very clean. Minor soiling and staining to jacket panels. Significant chipping to the jacket edges. Spine spilt approximately three-quarters from bottom to top, with some loss. A very good copy in a somewhat tattered jacket, with a marvelous original color drawing apropos of the title and contents of the book.

Estimate: $1,000-up
Starting Bid: $500

With Two Small Original Drawings of Bunnies by H. A. Rey

 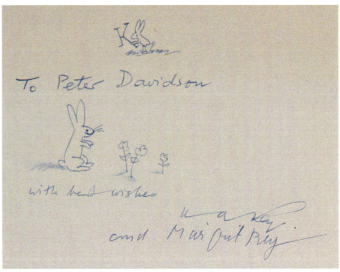

37072   **[H. A. Rey, illustrator].** Margret Rey. *Spotty.* With Pictures by H. A. Rey. [New York]: Harper & Brothers, [1945]. **Inscribed in H. A. Rey's hand and signed by both author and illustrator, "To Peter Davidson / with best wishes / H A Rey / and Margret Rey," interspersed with two small drawings of bunnies, one carrying the letter K and the other standing before a row of flowers,** on the verso of the front free endpaper, all in blue ink. Octavo. Unpaginated. Publisher's blue cloth backstrip over pictorial paper boards. Spine ends chipped and frayed. Board edges noticeably worn. Dust-soiling and a few ink marks in the text. Ownership stamps to the pastedowns and free endpapers. Pencil doodle of a rabbit on rear pastedown. Very good, and rarely, if ever, found with an inscribed drawing.

Estimate: $1,000-up
Starting Bid: $500

The Exceedingly Rare First Printing of Rowling's First Harry Potter Book, with a Signed Photo and Transmittal Autograph Note Signed on Her Own Stationery

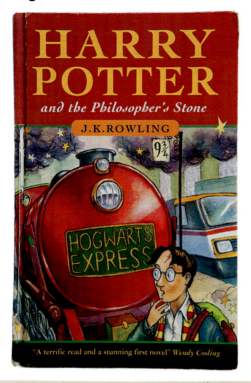

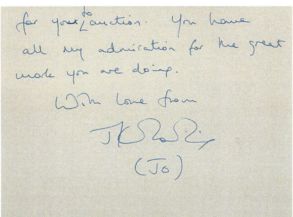

37073   J. K. Rowling. *Harry Potter and the Philosopher's Stone.* [London]: Bloomsbury, [1997]. First edition, first printing, one of 500 copies of the first and rarest of the Harry Potter books, and likely one of approximately 300 copies sent to British libraries. Correct full number line ("10 9 8 7 6 5 4 3 2 1"), "Copyright © Text Joanne Rowling 1997" (rather than "J. K. Rowling"), and "Taylor1997" (rather than "Taylor 1997") on the copyright page, and with "1 wand" appearing twice (first and last) in the list of "Other Equipment" on page 53. Octavo. 223, [1, blank] pages. Publisher's pictorial laminated boards illustrated by Thomas Taylor. Noticeable shelf wear to the binding. Boards rubbed. Spine a bit tender, with several spots of abrasion along the joints. One area along the top of the front joint likely repaired, with the laminate lacking in an area measuring about two and one-half inches and in a small fingernail-size area on the spine. Spine ends bumped and a bit tattered. Corners rubbed and bumped; three exposed. Glue remnants on the front free endpaper, probably from a removed library bookplate. No other library markings present. Text mildly toned around the edges. Substantially over-opened at the title page. A well-thumbed, likely ex-library copy of the rarest Harry Potter book in about very good condition.

Accompanying the book are two unique pieces of Rowlingiana. The first is a black-and-white **Photograph Signed "J K Rowling"** measuring four and one-half inches by six and three-quarters inches. The second item is an **Autograph Note Signed "J K Rowling / (Jo)" on her personal cardstock stationery,** reading "23/1/04 / Dear Adam, / Firstly, I am very [underlined] sorry about / the huge delay in responding to / your letter. I had a baby last / year and took some time off, / hence the vast backlog of mail. / However, here is a signed picture / for you to auction. You have / all my admiration for the great / work you are doing. / With love from / J. K. Rowling / (Jo)." Rowling's note, essentially a transmittal letter for the signed photo here, is written on each side of the card, which measures five and three-quarter inches by four and one-quarter inches, and comes with the original mailing envelope. There is a light horizontal crease to the photo at Rowling's eye level, else both items are in fine condition.

Estimate: $20,000-up
Starting Bid: $10,000

First Edition Cats in First Issue Dust Jackets

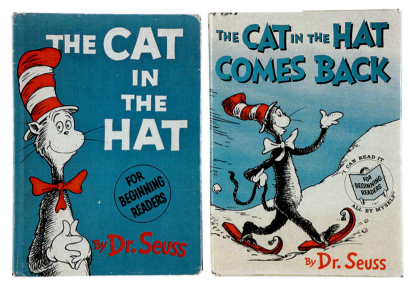

37074   **Dr. Seuss. Two** *Cat in the Hat* **Books**, including: ***The Cat in the Hat.*** [New York]: Random House, [1957]. First edition, first issue, with flat (not glazed) boards, "200/200" on front flap, and no mention of Beginner Books series on rear panel. Publisher's binding and first issue dust jacket. Octavo. 61 pages. A beautiful copy, with only a tiny amount of rubbing to spine ends of binding. Dust jacket with rubbing along folds and extremities; minor chipping to spine ends and to head of flap folds. Near fine. [and:] ***The Cat in the Hat Comes Back***. [New York]: Random House, [1958]. First edition, first printing. Octavo. 63 pages. Glossy printed boards. Original dust jacket with no printed price. Thin strip of what looks to be remnants of adhesive along top and bottom board edges. Very minor wear to jacket. Interior exceptionally clean. Better than very good.

Younger & Hirsch, pp. 26 and 40.

Estimate: $2,500-up
Starting Bid: $1,250

Lavishly Extra-Illustrated

 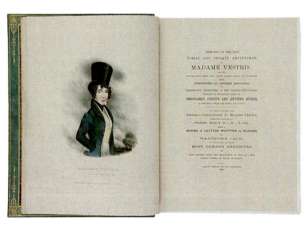

37075   [Extra-Illustrated]. **Madame Vestris.** *Memoirs of the Life, Public and Private Adventures, of Madame Vestris....* London: Printed for the Booksellers, 1839. Quarto. 61 pages. Bound with *Memoirs Concerning Madame Vestris, Collected from Various Sources.* Filled with over 100 engravings (some hand-colored), sheet music, playbills, et cetera. A fine example of the Victorian mania of grangerizing: locating pertinent engravings of individuals, places, and so on, mentioned within a book, and then rebinding the volume with the new material. Madame Vestris, as a popular actress and singer of the time, would have guaranteed a wealth of such material from magazines, playbills, etc. Attractively bound by S. Kaufmann in full teal morocco over boards. Raised bands. Gilt lettering and designs to compartments with scarlet leather inlays. Gilt tooling and scarlet leather inlays to the boards. Inner doublures of decorative paper with ornate gilt-tooled turn-ins. Very moderate shelf wear to the edges of the boards. In simple slipcase. Near fine.

Estimate: $1,500-up
Starting Bid: $750

Preliminary Painting of Cover Art for "The Cricket in Times Square" Signed by Garth Williams

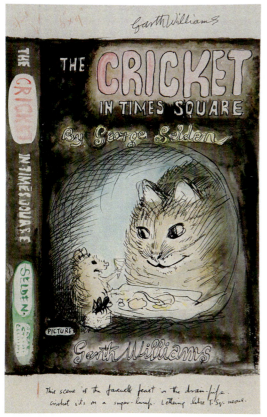

37076   Garth Williams. Original painting and preliminary sketches for the dust jacket design of *The Cricket in Times Square* by George Selden, 1960. Original painting in ink and watercolor/gouache on stiff paper, measuring approximately 10.875 x 6.875 inches. Painting features front cover and spine lettering and design. Williams has written at bottom of sheet: "This scene is the farewell feast in the drain-pipe. Cricket sits on a sugar-lump. Lettering like T. Sq. neons." The verso contains this note in Williams' hand: "Customs declaration item A." (Williams was sending much of his artwork to New York from his home in Mexico.) Also on the back: "Garth: This one, please - Hal. Note: ARIEL BOOKS on spine, *not FSC*. HDV." (Hal Vursell was Williams' editor at Ariel Books, an imprint of Farrar, Straus and Cudahy.) **Signed in full by Garth Williams** on the front. **Also included are six rough sketches**, measuring 10.625 x 8.25 inches. Pencil on paper. A few shallow folds at corners. **All initialed by Williams**. All generally fine. *From the Estate of Garth Williams.*

Estimate: $2,000-up
Starting Bid: $1,000

Original Painting of Alternate Cover Art by Garth Williams

37077   Garth Williams. Original painting for an unused dust jacket design for *The Cricket in Times Square* by George Selden, 1960, featuring Chester Cricket and Tucker Mouse. Ink and watercolor/gouache on stiff paper. One sheet measuring 8.875 x 6 inches. With notations on verso reading "Customs declaration item A" in Williams' hand (Williams was sending much of his artwork to New York from his home in Mexico), and "NOT this one" in an unknown hand, but likely that of H. D. (Hal) Vursell, editor of the juvenile department of Farrar, Straus and Cudahy. Unsigned. In fine condition. *From the Estate of Garth Williams.*

Estimate: $1,000-up
Starting Bid: $500

Two Original Ink Drawings Signed by Garth Williams

37078 **Garth Williams.** Two preliminary drawings for illustrations in *The Cricket in Times Square* by George Selden, 1960: an unused drawing (labeled "22" by Williams) featuring Papa Bellini listening to Chester's musical chirping, eventually replaced by another drawing for what became illustration #20; and an alternate version of illustration #24 featuring Chester Cricket and Tucker Mouse in the drainpipe. Both drawings in ink on stiff paper, both measuring 12.875 x 8.625 inches. A couple of shallow bends outside the image area, and a few minor instances of surface loss to top margin of the latter drawing. The drawing of Papa Bellini has Williams' note in red ink:"Text may be run under this pix. GW." **Both are signed in full by Garth Williams.** Both are generally near fine.

Cricket's author George Selden, was apparently unhappy with Williams' illustration "22" and requested a change. Editor Hal Vursell diplomatically asked Garth Williams if he might consider the author's suggestion of a different approach to the same scene, this time by putting Chester square in the foreground and making the cricket and his music the focal point. Williams obliged. Afterall, as Vursell wrote Williams, " this would emphasize the cricket as musician which, I suppose, is the real point of the book." *From the Estate of Garth Williams.*

Estimate: $1,000-up
Starting Bid: $500

Six Detailed Pencil Drawings, Including a Possible Self-Portrait, All Initialed by Garth Williams

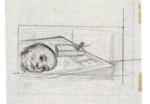

37079 **Garth Williams.** Six preliminary drawings (some of which were not used) for *The Cricket in Times Square* by George Selden, 1960. Pencil on paper. Six sheets (four of which are onionskin) measuring 11 x 8.5 inches, three in landscape format. A couple with shallow folds, a couple with tape stains which appear to have come from the preproduction process. **All initialed by Garth Williams.** All in generally fine condition.

Williams' distinctive soft pencil drawings were always markedly different from his pen and ink book illustrations. These six detailed drawings are perfectly charming and showcase the cute animals and gentle style for which he is, perhaps, best known. The early version of illustration #7 in which Tucker and Harry show Chester Times Square is particularly appealing in its sweetness and warmth. Also of note is the unused drawing with Chester in his matchbox atop a stack of *Time* magazines—surely that is a tongue-in-cheek self-portrait of Garth Williams staring out from the cover. Six delightful drawings from the master of children's illustration. *From the Estate of Garth Williams.*

Estimate: $1,000-up
Starting Bid: $500

The 1505 Greek-Only Edition of Aesop Printed by Aldus Manutius

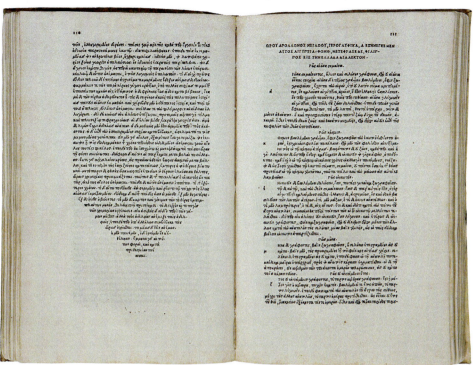

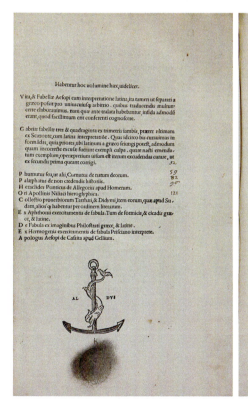

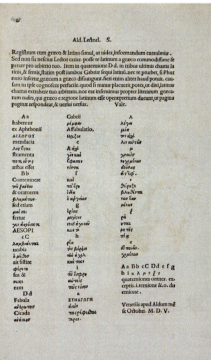

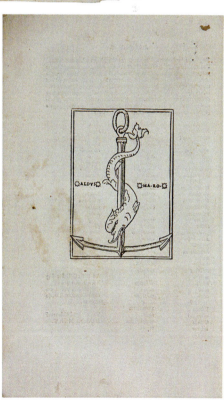

37080   **Aesop.** *Vita et Fabellae Aesopi...Gabriae Fabellae...Collectio Proverbiorum Tarrhaei &c.* [Venice]: Aldus Manutius, [1505]. First Aldine edition, in Greek only. Folio (27.5 x 17.5 cm): a-h^8 i^6 χ^8 λ^8 μ^8 ν^8 ξ^8 o^4; 114 leaves. Full early limp vellum. Woodcut of the famous dolphin and anchor device to first and last leaves. Some edge wear, rubbing and light staining to covers. Hinges a bit tender at the upper gutters. A few small holes to front free endpaper. Black ink library stamp below dolphin and anchor device on A1r obscured. Early marginalia to a good number of leaves. Minor scattered foxing. An excellent copy of the very rare Greek-only Aldine edition of Aesop, which Dibdin described as "among the rarer and more beautiful productions of the Aldine Press." Further, Quaritch's Aldine Collection catalog of 1929 calls this edition "VERY RARE. It is extremely difficult to obtain a fine copy of this book."

Estimate: $7,500-up
Starting Bid: $3,750

Uncorrected Galley Proofs Inscribed by the Author, With an Autograph Letter from Daniel Webster

First Appearance in English of the Complete *Decameron*

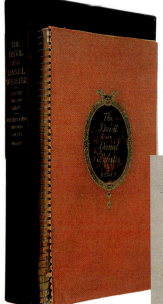

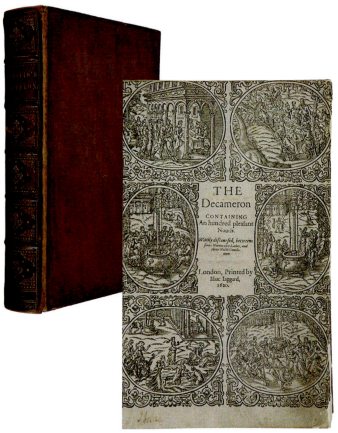

37081 **Stephen Vincent Benét. Author's Own Copy of the Uncorrected Galley Proofs for *The Devil and Daniel Webster*.** Weston, Vermont: The Countryman Press, 1937. Uncorrected galley proofs. **Inscribed by the author on the first page.** Octavo. Unpaginated. Spiral bound with salmon cloth front board with black and gold vignette. Some wear to the binding holes on the boards, else very good. Offered in a black cloth chemise and slipcase. The slipcase has a beautiful morocco spine label with titles stamped in gilt.

Presentation copy inscribed by the author on his 41st birthday: **"For [...]/ with very good wishes from/ Stephen Vincent Benét/ [illegible] July 22, 1939."** A period engraved portrait of Daniel Webster is mounted on the inner left flap of the chemise to which has been affixed **Webster's clipped signature: "Danl Webster/ U.S. Senate."** Adding further interest to this exceptional lot is a **two-page Daniel Webster autograph letter signed "D. W."** The letter is dated March 28, 1850. Webster writes in part: "The letter is admirable — too good, too good — I do not deserve the one hundredth part of what it says."

Estimate: $1,000-up
Starting Bid: $500

37082 **Giovanni Boccaccio. [*The Decameron*]. *The Modell of Wit, Mirth, Eloquence, and Conversation*.** London: Isaac Jaggard for Mathew Lownes, 1625-1620. Second edition of Volume I, first edition of Volume II. Two small folio volumes in one. Illustrated with woodcuts. Early binding in full calf over boards. Professionally rebacked with the original backstrip retained. Hinges reinforced. Lacking first and final blanks in both volumes. Two engraved title pages bound at the front, one dated 1620, the other, 1625; both title pages have been restored and mounted on paper, one is missing a four inch by four inch portion of the upper corner. Restoration to the first two leaves, with some minor loss to the text. A page from a dealer catalog is tipped to the front pastedown. Some slight water damage to the five final leaves; also, ink notations in an early hand to the recto of the final leaf. An attractive, tight copy in very good condition of the first appearance in English of this cornerstone of European literature.

Up to this point Boccaccio was well known in England. Several of the stories had been translated and published with other texts. But it wasn't until 1620 when the "first practically complete edition appeared, translated inaccurately, but very splendidly, apparently from the French version of Antonione Le Macon. Isaac Jaggard published it, in folio in two parts, with woodcuts, and the title bore no translator's name" (Hutton). Mixed edition sets such as this are not uncommon. As there have been no records of a second edition of the second volume, it is assumed that Jaggard printed a larger run of the first edition of volume two in anticipation of a second edition.

Edward Hutton, *Giovanni Boccaccio*, p. 315. Pforzheimer 71 & 72.

Estimate: $1,500-up
Starting Bid: $750

Three Signed Dan Brown Novels, Including His First Book

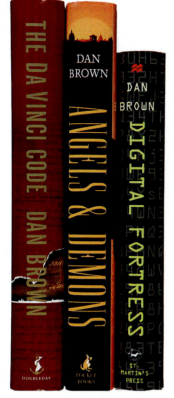  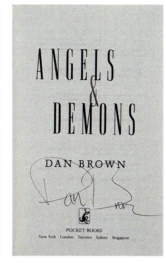 

37083   **Dan Brown. Three Signed First Editions**, including: *Digital Fortress.* New York: St. Martin's Press, [1998]. Crease to front free endpaper. Brown's first book. [and:] *Angels & Demons.* New York: Pocket Books, [2000]. Remainder mark to bottom edge. [and:] *The Da Vinci Code.* New York: Doubleday, [2003]. All copies first editions, first printings. **Each is signed by Brown on the title page.** All in publisher's bindings and dust jackets. All fine.

Estimate: $1,500-up
Starting Bid: $750

The Olympia Press First Edition

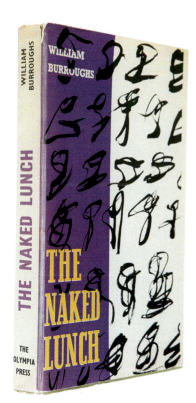

37084   **William S. Burroughs.** *The Naked Lunch.* Paris: Olympia Press, [1959]. First edition, first issue, with "Francs: 1,500" on rear cover and on dust jacket. Mass market-sized paperback with wraparound dust jacket. 225 pages. Jacket has some mild toning to edges and a small tear at the top front edge near the spine. Neat rubberstamp on rear wrapper: "New Price NF 18." A near fine copy.

One of the most influential and lasting works of literature to emerge from the Beat period. A beautiful copy of this infamous and provocative book.

Estimate: $1,500-up
Starting Bid: $750

First Edition of "Alice" Printed in America

37085 **Lewis Carroll.** *Alice's Adventures in Wonderland.* Illustrated by John Tenniel. Boston: Lee and Shepard, 1869. First edition printed in America. Octavo. 192 pages. Publisher's green pebbled cloth with gilt titles and decoration. All edges gilt. Minor rubbing with some light abrading to extremities. A couple of soft bumps to fore-edge of boards. Mild toning and thumbing to pages with some lightly scattered foxing to preliminary pages. Overall, an about near fine copy.

Estimate: $1,500-up
Starting Bid: $750

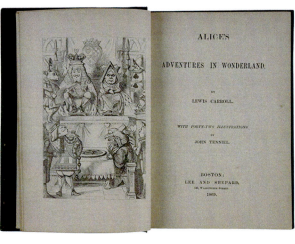

Early Edition of *The Courtier's Manual*

37086 **[The Courtier's Manual].** *The Courtier of Counte Baldessar Castilio.* Divided into foure Bookes. Verie Necessarie and profitable for young gentlemen and gentlewomen, abiding in Court, Palace, or Place. Translated into English By Tho. Hobby. London: Thomas Creede, 1603. Fourth edition. Modern full leather with ornate gilt-stamped device and gilt ruling on both covers. Four raised bands with gilt decoration and ruling. All edges stained red. Woodcut ornamental device and initials on title page. Set in Gothic type with shoulder notes. Missing initial blank A1. Front pastedown and three preliminaries have been added, as has one terminal leaf and rear pastedown. Title page has been backed with a contemporary page. Last two pages of text have been restored with some loss. Minor chipping to page edges at front and rear. Toning to page edges. Bookseller's ticket on front pastedown. Pages trimmed with minor handwritten notes on title page. Very good.

Estimate: $2,000-up
Starting Bid: $1,000

The First Complete Don Quixote in English

37087 **Miguel de Cervantes Saavedra.** *The History of the Valorous and Witty Knight Errant, Don Quixote of the Mancha.* Written in Spanish by Michael Cervantes: and now Translated into English. London: Edward Blount, 1620. First volume, second edition; second volume, first edition. Two octavo volumes. [22], 572, [4]; [18], 276, 279-504. [2]. Facsimile engraved title page to Volume I, which lacks the full title. Volume II has the full title, but lacks the engraved title. Bound in modern full calf over boards. Raised bands. Gilt lettering to spines. All edges gilt. Inked name of previous owner. Slight dampstaining to Volume I, which is missing some of the gilt to the edges. Ex-library rubberstamp (dated 1830) to first page of the translator's preamble. Closed tear to page 487 of Volume II. Overall a handsome set in very good condition of the complete Don Quixote first appearance in English.

Estimate: $15,000-up
Starting Bid: $7,500

"I was neat, clean, shaved and sober, and I didn't care who knew it. I was everything the well-dressed private detective ought to be."

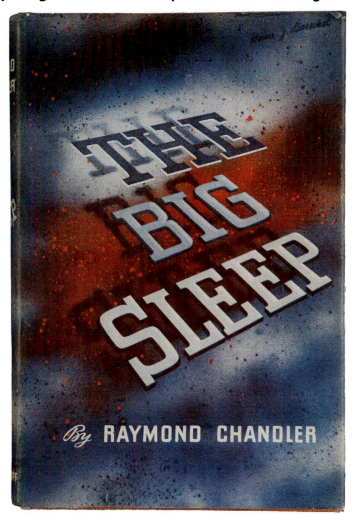

37088 **Raymond Chandler. *The Big Sleep.*** New York: Alfred A. Knopf, 1939. First edition, first printing, of the author's first book. Octavo (7.375 x 5 inches). [8], 277, [1], [2, blank] pages. Publisher's brownish orange V cloth (smooth) decoratively stamped and lettered in dark gray blue on front cover and spine. All edges trimmed. Top edge stained dark blue. Original color pictorial dust jacket by Hans J. Barschel. Spine very slightly darkened, minor rubbing to corners and spine extremities, some browning to endpapers from pastedown glue. Jacket with a short closed tear at lower corner of rear panel, reinforced with tissue on the verso, and a few additional repairs at the edges of the flap folds. The rear panel and spine of the jacket are very slightly browned. A very attractive copy.

"'Down these mean streets a man must go who is not himself mean, who is neither tarnished nor afraid....He is the hero; he is everything. He must be a complete man and a common man and yet an unusual man.' This is the Code of the Private Eye as defined by Raymond Chandler in his 1944 essay 'The Simple Act of Murder.' Such a man was Philip Marlowe, private eye, an educated, heroic, streetwise, rugged individualist and the hero of Chandler's first novel, *The Big Sleep*. This work established Chandler as the master of the 'hard-boiled' detective novel, and his articulate and literary style of writing won him a large audience, which ranged from the man in the street to the most sophisticated intellectual. Marlowe subsequently appeared in a series of extremely popular novels, among them *The Lady in the Lake, The Long Goodbye,* and *Farewell, My Lovely*" (Elizabeth Diefendorf, editor, *The New York Public Library's Books of the Century*, p. 112).

Selected as one of *Time Magazine's* All-Time 100 Novels, with the following review: "'I was neat, clean, shaved and sober, and I didn't care who knew it. I was everything the well-dressed private detective ought to be.' This sentence, from the first paragraph of *The Big Sleep*, marks the last time you can be fully confident that you know what's going on. The first novel by Raymond Chandler, who at the time was a 51-year-old former oil company executive, is a mosaic of shadows, a dark tracery of forking paths. Along them wanders Philip Marlowe, a cynical, perfectly hard-boiled private investigator hired by an old millionaire to find the husband of his beautiful, bitchy wildcat daughter. Marlowe is tough and determined, and he does his best to be a good guy, but there are no true heroes in Chandler's sun-baked, godforsaken Los Angeles, and every plot turn reveals how truly twisted the human heart is."

Bruccoli, *Chandler,* A1.1.a.

Estimate: $10,000-up
Starting Bid: $5,000

Signed by Agatha Christie

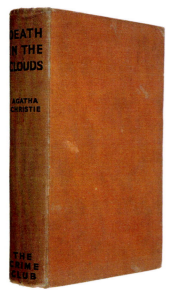
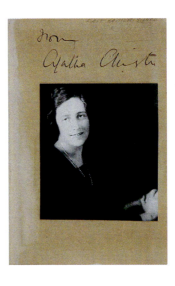
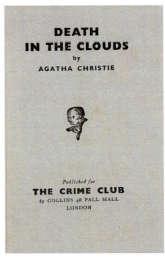

37089   **Agatha Christie.** *Death in the Clouds.* London: Published for The Crime Club by Collins, 1935. First edition. **Signed by the author.** Modern photograph of the author affixed to the front free endpaper. Octavo. 252 pages, [4] advertisements. Publisher's orange cloth with titles printed in black on the spine. Slight fading to spine panel with light soiling to the boards. Minor wear to the extremities with a slight slant to text block. Light scattered foxing to the contents, else very good.

A delightful Hercule Poirot mystery in which the Belgian detective must solve a murder mystery while on a flight from Paris to Croydon.

Estimate: $1,500-up
Starting Bid: $750

Limited to Only Ten Copies, with Original Watercolors and Ink Drawings

37090   **Charles Paul de Kock.** *Sister Anne.* Boston: Frederick J. Quinby, [1902]. Bibliomaniac edition, limited to 10 copies. Octavo. 141 pages. Publisher's full red morocco with floral iris onlay in gilt and morocco. Decorated morocco doublures and full morocco free endpapers. Engraved frontisportrait by Jacques Reich and hand-illuminated title page and chapter initials. Vellum pages. **Illustrated with original watercolors by Albert de Ford Pitney (two), G. A. Williams, Walter Russell, two original pen and ink drawings by E. Boyd Smith, and two original pen and ink drawings by W. M. Crocker.** Occasional light foxing. Front hinge cracked after second free endpaper. Area of soiling to verso of second free endpaper. Housed in publisher's matching book-backed box with some rubbing and scuffing. An overall near fine example of this lavish production.

Estimate: $2,000-up
Starting Bid: $1,000

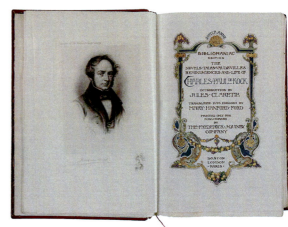

Beautiful, Ornate Bindings by the Harcourt Bindery, with Original Art, Including Original Etchings Signed by John Sloan

37091 Charles Paul De Kock. Three Volumes from the Romainville Edition of the Works of Charles Paul De Kock, including: *The Child of My Wife*, *Andre - The Savoyard* (Volume I only), *The Damsel of the Three Skirts*. Letter T of 26 copies. Octavo. Full green morocco bindings by the Harcourt Bindery, with floral gilt and morocco onlays on the covers, tall raised bands on spines, full morocco doublures and endleaves elaborately tooled in gilt, green, blue, and red. Top edges gilt, other edges untrimmed. Hand-illuminated initial letters, head-pieces, and tailpieces throughout. *The Child of My Life* illustrated by W. J. Sinnott (two original pen and ink drawings), C. White (two original etchings), and Louis Meynelle (two original pen and ink drawings). *The Damsel* illustrated in its entirety by Louis Meynelle with four pen and ink drawings, an original watercolor, an original etching (in two states), and four photogravures from drawings by Meynelle (in two states). *Andre* illustrated in its entirety by John Sloan with two original etchings (each in two states, one state signed), an original etching in color (in two states, one state signed), four original pen and ink drawings in the text, and four photogravures (each in two states), with two signed. Minor wear and soiling to boards. Spines darkened. Front cover of *The Damsel* darkened, as well. Hinges cracked on two volumes. Marginal dampstain to a few leaves in *The Child of My Wife*. Internally clean, and overall in very good condition.

Estimate: $3,000-up
Starting Bid: $1,500

The First Two Sherlock Holmes Books

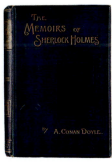

37092 Arthur Conan Doyle. First Editions of the First Two Sherlock Holmes Books, including: **The Adventures of Sherlock Holmes.** London: George Newnes, 1892. First edition, first issue with misprint of "Violent Hunter" for "Violet Hunter" on page 317, line 23. Large octavo. 317 pages. Illustrated by Sidney Paget. First state binding with no name on the street sign in the front cover illustration. All edges gilt. Floral endpapers. Minor soiling and edge wear to boards; wear to very tips of corners. Front hinge cracked. Occasional foxing. Ink gift inscription dated 1893; ink name to title page. Very good. [and:] **The Memoirs of Sherlock Holmes.** London: George Newnes, 1894. First edition. Large octavo. 279 pages. Illustrated by Sidney Paget. Dark blue illustrated cloth over beveled boards with titles and illustration in gilt and black. All edges gilt. Floral endpapers. Binding slightly cocked. Wear to extremities; dampstain to rear board. Very good.

"The initial twelve tales were collected between covers as *The Adventures of Sherlock Holmes*, published in England and America in 1892; and eleven of the second twelve [...] as *The Memoirs of Sherlock Holmes*, published in 1894. If any reader be prepared to name two other books that have given more innocent but solid pleasure, let him speak now — or hold his peace!" (Haycraft 50).

DeWaal 520 & 596. Green and Gibson, A10a and A14a. Haycraft 50.

Estimate: $2,500-up
Starting Bid: $1,250

With Leaves Dating from 1240 to 1923, Including Koberger, Froben, Barker, Baskerville, Bruce Rogers, and Others

37093 **[Antiquarian Book Leaves].** Otto F. Ege. *Original Leaves from Famous Books. Eight Centuries 1240 A. D. - 1932 A. D.* [Cleveland School of Art, circa 1950]. Regular edition, number 17 of 110 limited edition sets containing twenty-five matted original leaves, with descriptive labels, encased in a heavy buckram portfolio with gilt-stamped leather front cover label. Annotated Chronological Index and publisher's folding prospectus laid in. Wear and bowing to portfolio. Minor abrading to the title label. Minor edge toning to some mats, else fine condition.

The leaves included are from the following works: St. Jerome, *Vulgate Bible*, manuscript on vellum, France, 1240; Aristotle, *Nichomachean Ethics*, manuscript on paper, Germany, 1365; Livy, *History of Rome*, Italian manuscript in cursive bookhand, 1436; Voragine, *The Golden Legend*, Antonio de Strata, Venice, Italy, 1480; Dante, *Divine Comedy*, Petrus de Piasio, Venice, Italy, 1491; Schedel, *Nuremberg Chronicle*, Anton Koberger, Nuremberg, 1493; *The Justinian Code*, Thielman Kerver, Paris, 1512; Pliny, *Natural History*, Johann Froben, Basle, 1525; Erasmus, *Adages*, Jerome Froben, Basle, 1528; Vesalius, *Anatomy*, Johannes Oporinus, Basle, 1555; Petrarch, *Sonnets and Canzoni*, Gabriel Giolito, Venice, 1559; Hippocrates, *Writings*, Lucantonio Giunta, Venice, 1585; Gerard, *History of Plants*, John Norton, London, 1597; Hakluyt, *Voyages*, Robert Barker, 1598-1600; Chaucer, *Works*, Adam Islip, London, 1602; Cervantes, *Don Quixote*, Juan de la Cuesta, Madrid, 1608; *The King James Bible - Authorized Edition*, Robert Barker, London, 1611; Bacon, *The Advancement of Learning...*, John Haviland, London, 1638; Shakespeare's Fourth Folio (*The Tragedy of Macbeth*, leaf 3D3, pages 42-43), H. Herringman, E. Brewster, and R. Bentley, London, 1685; Johnson, *Dictionary*, W. Strahan, London, 1755; Virgil, *Poems*, John Baskerville, Birmingham, 1757; Montaigne, *Essays*, Designed by Bruce Rogers, Printed by Riverside Press, Cambridge, 1902-1904; Milton, *Paradise Regained, Samson Agonistes and Other Poems*, Doves Press, London, 1905; Boccaccio, *The Decameron*, The Ashendene Press, Chelsea, 1920; Homer, *Iliad and Odyssey*, Bremer Press, Munich, 1923.

Estimate: $3,000-up
Starting Bid: $1,500

Limited Edition Signed by William Faulkner

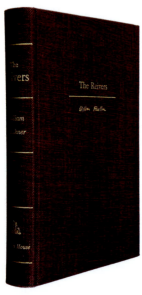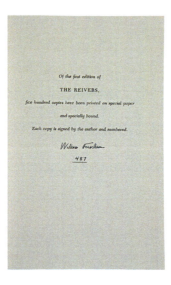

37094 **William Faulkner.** *The Reivers. A Reminiscence.* New York: Random House, [1962]. First edition, first printing. Number 487 of 500 limited edition copies printed on special paper, specially bound, and **signed by Faulkner** on limitation page. Octavo. 305 pages. Original crimson cloth with gilt titles. Clear acetate dust wrapper. Top edge stained red. Minimal shelf wear. Pencil marks to rear free endpaper, else fine.

Estimate: $1,500-up
Starting Bid: $750

The Snopes Trilogy — Three Limited Editions Signed by William Faulkner

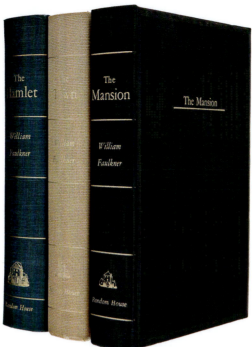

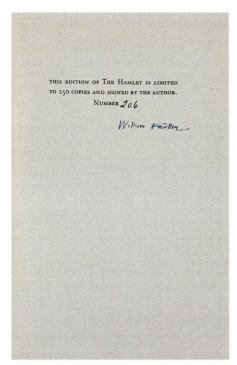

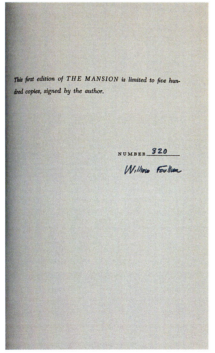

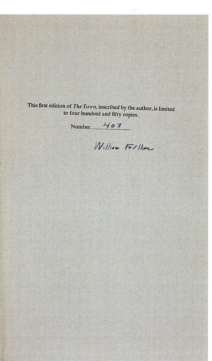

37095 **William Faulkner. Signed Limited Editions of The Snopes Trilogy,** including: *The Hamlet.* New York: Random House, 1940. Number 206 of 250 limited edition copies **signed by William Faulkner** on the limitation page. Octavo. 421 pages. Publisher's three-quarter green cloth over light green paper boards with gilt spine titles. Top edge gilt. In original glassine dust jacket. Minimal shelf wear. Some wear and loss of the glassine. A fine copy. [and:] *The Town.* New York: Random House, [1957]. Number 403 of 450 limited edition copies **signed by Faulkner** on the limitation page. Octavo. 371 pages. Publisher's tan cloth with gilt spine titles and facsimile gilt signature on front board. Top edge red. Minor edge wear. Bookplate to front pastedown. Fine condition. [and:] *The Mansion.* New York: Random House, 1959. Number 320 of 500 limited edition copies **signed by Faulkner** on the limitation page. Octavo. 436 pages. Publisher's black cloth over beveled boards with gilt titles. Top edge blue-green. Blue marbled endpapers. Minimal edge wear. One corner crease (page 177/178). Tiny ink mark to bottom of fore-edge. A crisp copy in fine condition. Each limited edition is housed in a custom red half morocco slipcase and red cloth chemise.

Estimate: $10,000-up
Starting Bid: $5,000

Rare First Edition, First Issue of Fielding's Classic

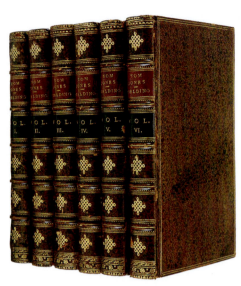 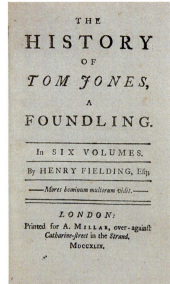

37096   Henry Fielding. *The History of Tom Jones, A Foundling.* London: Printed for A. Millar, 1749. First edition, first issue. One of a first printing run of only 2,000 copies with errata leaf in Volume I, the errata uncorrected, and all cancels and final blanks (K12 in Volume I and R12 in Volume III) as noted in Rothschild 850. Six sixteenmo volumes. Nineteenth-century full mottled calf with red and black morocco spine labels lettered in gilt inside five raised bands. Gilt dentelles. Marbled endpapers. All edges gilt. Housed in a custom black cloth slipcase. Mild shelf wear with some rubbing to the joints. Volume I rebacked with the spine laid down, and a few other volumes with very minor repairs to joints. Previous owner's armorial bookplates affixed to the front pastedowns of each volume. Pages somewhat toned, but overall a clean, fresh copy in very good condition.

"[*Tom Jones*] is generally regarded as Fielding's greatest, and as one of the first and most influential of English novels" (Drabble, 988).

Grolier English 48. Randall and Winterich, 1200.

Estimate: $4,000-up
Starting Bid: $2,000

First Edition, First Printing

37097   F. Scott Fitzgerald. *The Beautiful and Damned.* New York: Charles Scribner's Sons, 1922. First edition, first printing. Octavo. [x], 450 pages. Publisher's green B cloth (linen-like grain) with blind-stamped front cover titles and gilt spine titles. Original second issue dust jacket with the title of the book on the front cover in black. A tight, square copy with minor soiling to the boards, light wear to the extremities, and slight fading to the spine cloth. Ownership signature and gift inscription to front endpapers. Chipping to spine and flap fold ends of the jacket, affecting "THE" in the title and the "S" in "SCRIBNERS" on the spine. Two short splits along the flap folds, the longer of which measures three inches. Significant brown tape repairs to jacket edges, which have bled through to the front of the jacket. Very good. Bruccoli A 8.I.a.

Estimate: $2,000-up
Starting Bid: $1,000

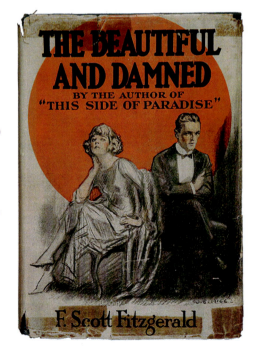

Inscribed by Fitzgerald as "This story of a Europe that is no more."

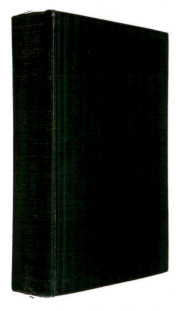

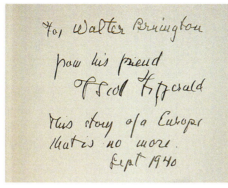

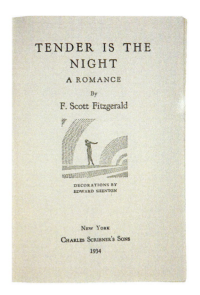

37098   **F. Scott Fitzgerald.** *Tender is the Night.* A Romance. New York: Charles Scribner's Sons, 1934. First edition, third printing ("Devereux" on page 320, line 17). **Inscribed by Fitzgerald on the front free endpaper: "For Walter Bruington / from his friend / F Scott Fitzgerald / This story of a Europe / that is no more. / Sept 1940."** With in-text decorations by Edward Shenton. Octavo. [x], 408 pages. Publisher's dark green cloth, with single-ruled blind border on front cover and gilt spine titles. Minor edge wear to the boards and corners. Light scuffing to the spine cloth. Spine gilt faded. A very good copy with a bright and clean textblock. Bruccoli A 14.I.c

Estimate: $6,000-up
Starting Bid: $3,000

First James Bond Novel

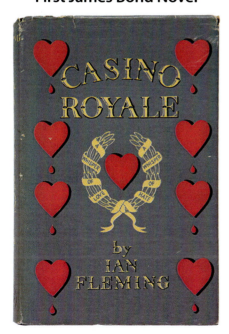

37099   **Ian Fleming.** *Casino Royale.* London: Jonathan Cape, [1953]. First edition. second printing. Octavo. 218 pages. Book has just a slight lean and minimal foxing to the endpapers. Dust jacket has chipping to top edge, with tape stains on the verso; staining to the rear panel. Two bookseller tickets to front endpapers. Very good.

Estimate: $1,500-up
Starting Bid: $750

First Edition of the Fourth James Bond Book

37100   **Ian Fleming.** *Diamonds Are Forever.* London: Jonathan Cape, [1956]. First edition, first printing. Octavo. 257 pages. Publisher's binding and dust jacket. Modest rubbing to cloth extremities. Minor foxing to pages edges and endpapers. Name and date to front free endpaper. Light restoration to jacket. Overall near fine.

Estimate: $1,500-up
Starting Bid: $750

Uncorrected Proof of the Ninth James Bond Novel, In the Scarce Proof Dust Jacket

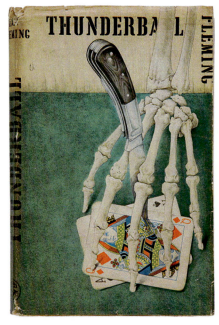
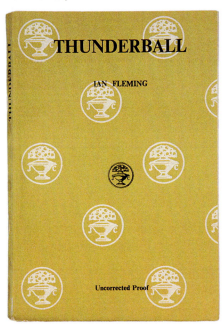

37101 **Ian Fleming.** *Thunderball.* London: Jonathan Cape, [1961]. Uncorrected proof of the first edition. Twelvemo. 254 pages. Publisher's green printed wrappers. **In the rare proof state dust jacket.** Spine cocked, creased, and stained. A couple of creased leaves, and minor spotting to the lower margin of a few pages after page 201. Spine ends of the dust jacket tattered. Top edge of jacket creased, as the jacket is noticeably taller than the book. Overall, a very good copy of a scarce James Bond proof copy, in the scarcer proof state dust jacket.

Estimate: $1,500-up
Starting Bid: $750

Superb Archive of Correspondence From Various California Writers

37102 **Edward Dubois Flint. The Author's Archive of Letters, Articles, and Related Material Concerning His Book** *The Garden Patch*, **1913.** 9.25 x 10.5 inches. Fifty-eight album pages contained in a tooled leather Arts and Crafts-style binder designed by Ethel Shearer of San Francisco. Fine condition.

A fabulous archive which includes pages of professional newspaper reviews of Flint's *The Garden Patch* as well as many more personal reviews sent to the author's Los Gatos, California home from intimates such as Jack London, Luther Burbank, and Edwin Markham. The album contains many wonderful examples including a one-page **typed letter by Jack London** dated August 3, 1914 with a stamped signature, a one-page **typed letter signed by Luther Burbank** dated January 18, 1913, Flint's original registry of copyright for the book with the Library of Congress; **an original poem titled "The Praise of Poverty" written directly in the book by American poet Edwin Markham**; and many short pieces and poems written by the author. Included are letters of congratulation from **President Wilson** on White House letterhead (signed by his secretary) and from **Henry Ford** on his personal letterhead and signed by his secretary. Shearer's binder is a work of art featuring a hand-tooled vine framing the title, with a delightful vignette of hand-colored vegetables below. A wonderful archive and a personal California history in a wonderful hand-made binding.

Estimate: $1,000-up
Starting Bid: $500

Beautiful Signed Limited Set Of Bret Harte's Works, with Twelve Signed Plates, Including One Plate Signed by Frederic Remington

 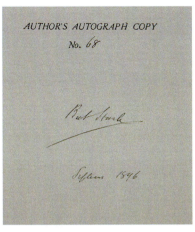 

37103 **Bret Harte.** *The Writings of Bret Harte.* Boston and New York: Houghton, Mifflin, [1896]-1914. Autograph edition. One of 350 numbered copies, of which this is number 68, **signed and dated by Bret Harte.** Volume XXI: *The Life of Bret Harte* **signed by author Henry C. Merwin.** Twenty-one octavo volumes. Numerous photogravure frontispieces, vignette titles, and plates after drawings and paintings by Mary Hallock Foote, Eric Pape, Frederic Remington, et al., **twelve of which are signed, including the plate by Frederic Remington.** Three-quarter red morocco over cloth with gilt-stamped titles and decorations on spine. Five raised bands with six ruled compartments. Top edge gilt, others uncut. Some shelf wear and rubbing to extremities, particularly at corners. Toning to page edges. A near fine set.

Estimate: $1,500-up
Starting Bid: $750

First Edition, First State

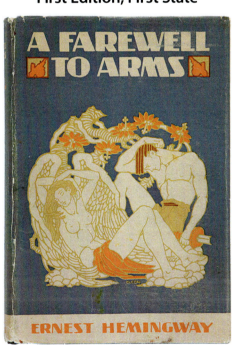

37104 **Ernest Hemingway.** *A Farewell To Arms.* New York: Charles Scribner's Sons, 1929. First edition, first state with "Katharine Barclay" misspelling on front inner flap, and without the legal disclaimer on page [x], as called for. Octavo. 355 pages. Publisher's smooth black cloth with gold paper labels, lettered and ruled in black. Top and bottom edges trimmed; fore-edge untrimmed. Lightly rubbed extremities. Offsetting to front endpapers, probably due to a clipping being laid in at one time. Very mild toning throughout. Dust jacket is moderately soiled and rubbed with a minor amount of loss at corners. A very good copy, much better than typically encountered. Hanneman, p. 24.

Estimate: $2,500-up
Starting Bid: $1,250

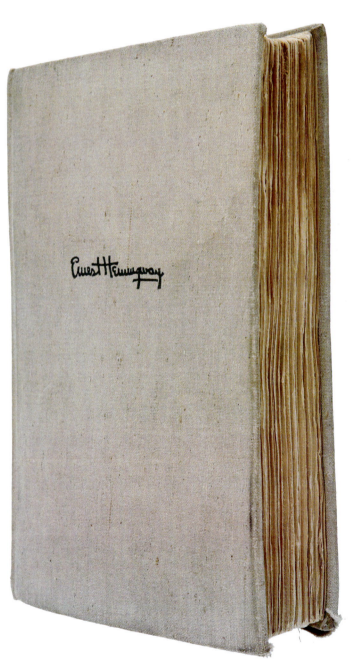

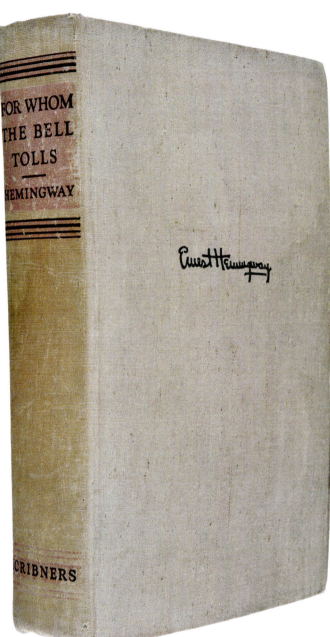

For Popsie and Frankie
Steinhart from their friend
and neighbor this copy of the 15
original edition copies of this book
Best always
Ernest Hemingway.

FOR WHOM
THE BELL TOLLS

By

E R N E S T
H E M I N G W A Y

NEW YORK
CHARLES SCRIBNER'S SONS
1940

37105 Ernest Hemingway. *For Whom the Bell Tolls.* New York: Charles Scribner's Sons, 1940. First edition. **Presentation copy, inscribed by Hemingway on the front free endpaper: "For Popsie and Frankie / Steinhart [Hemingway's neighbors in Havana] from their friend / and neighbor this copy of the 15 / original edition copies of this book / Best always / Ernest Hemingway."** Octavo. [x], 471, [1, blank] pages. Publisher's full oatmeal cloth with the front cover stamped in black and the spine stamped in red and black. **This copy is a bit taller than the trade edition, with uncut edges.** Fairly heavy dark soiling and dampstaining to cloth. Spine darkened. Minor smearing to a few words in the inscription. Noticeable spotting and staining throughout the text, mostly limited to the margins. A very good copy.

"An advance issue of 15 copies, which measure 8 5/8 x 5 3/4, were bound uncut in the same cloth as the first edition" (Hanneman A18a, p. 52).

Estimate: $20,000-up
Starting Bid: $10,000

Jonson's *Workes*

37106 Ben Jonson.
The Workes of Benjamin Jonson. [and:] ***The Workes of Benjamin Jonson The Second Volume***, *Containing These Plays, Viz. 1 Bartholomew Fayre. 2 The Staple of Newes. 3 The Divell is an Asse.* London: Richard Bishop; Richard Meighen, 1640. Second edition of Volume I, first edition of Volume II. Two folio volumes. [10], 668, 228; [12], 88, [2], 93-170, [1], 163-292, 79, 70-122, 133-155, [1], 75, [1], 159, [1], 132 pages. Though some pages numbered incorrectly, text appears complete. Volume I includes: *Every Man In His Humour; Every Man Out of His Humour; Cynthias Revels; Poetaster; Sejanus; Volpone; Epicoene; The Alchemist; Catiline; Epigrammes; The Forrest; Part of the King's Entertainment; Masques.* Volume II includes: *Bartholmew Fayre; The Divell is an Asse; Under-Woods; The Magnetick Lady; A Tale of a Tub; The Sad Shepherd; The Staple of News; Masques; Horace, His Art of Poetrie; The English Grammar;* and *Timber.* Contemporary full speckled calf, rebacked to style with original spine labels laid down. Chipping and abrading to boards. Hinges cracked. Bookplate and portion of pastedown from Volume I crudely excised. Volume I with engraved title page reinforced along fore-edge. Light chipping to preliminary pages of both volumes. Mild toning and scattered foxing to pages, with an occasional notation or small tear. An important set in about very good condition.

ESTC S112456 and S111824.

Estimate: $3,000-up
Starting Bid: $1,500

First Edition of Joyce's *Portrait of the Artist as a Young Man*

37107 James Joyce. *A Portrait of the Artist as a Young Man.*
New York: B. W. Huebsch, 1916. First edition. Octavo. 299 pages. Publisher's binding with mild rubbing to cloth extremities and a very slight lean to spine. Top edge lightly sunned and dusted. Small stain to top edge, modestly affecting textblock. Spine darkened and some small spots of soiling to front board. Lacking front free endpaper. Contemporary clippings affixed to front pastedown and adjacent flyleaf, causing offsetting. Mild offsetting to rear endpapers and faint toning to pages. A very good copy.

Estimate: $1,500-up
Starting Bid: $750

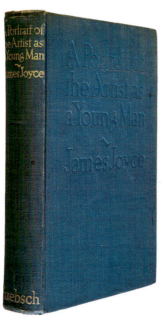

One of 750 First Editions from Shakespeare & Co. on Handmade Paper

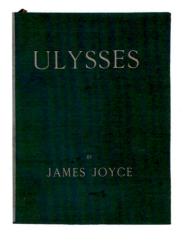
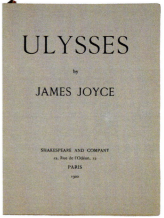

37108 James Joyce. *Ulysses.*
Paris: Shakespeare and Company, 1922. First edition. Number 540 of 750 numbered copies on handmade paper, out of a total edition of 1,000 copies. Quarto (9.125 x 7.25 inches; 232 x 184 mm.). [8], 732, [1, colophon], [3, blank] pages (final blank leaf affixed to rear wrapper). "Printed for Sylvia Beach by Maurice Darantiere at Dijon, France" (colophon). Modern antique-style half marbled sheep, ruled in blind, over marbled paper over boards. Spine ruled in blind in six compartments with five gilt-decorated raised bands and two burgundy leather labels ruled and lettered in gilt. Top edge marbled, others uncut, marbled endpapers. Front and rear covers of the original blue printed wrappers (without the flaps) have been bound in. Spine of custom leather binding is faded and rubbed, especially at extremities, the marbled paper blistered slightly on the covers. A few small stains to the front wrapper, some slight discoloration and a couple of scuff marks to the rear

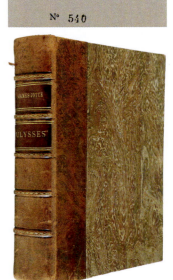

wrapper. Small faint blue stain on the lower edge. Text slightly browned, intermittent faint dampstain to the outer margin and to the rear wrapper and rear endpapers, some very occasional minor marginal soiling or staining. Pages 201/202 and 203/204 poorly opened at the outer edge. Previous owner's ink signature, dated 1970, on verso of front free endpaper. A very good copy.

Of the 1,000 copies of the first edition, 100 were on Dutch handmade paper (measuring 23.7 x 19.5 cm.) numbered from 1 to 100 and signed by Joyce, 150 were on vergé d'Arches paper (measuring 26.2 x 20.1 cm.) numbered from 101 to 250, and 750 were on handmade paper (measuring 23.7 x 18.5 cm.) numbered from 251 to 1000. The last two formats were not issued signed.

Estimate: $10,000-up
Starting Bid: $5,000

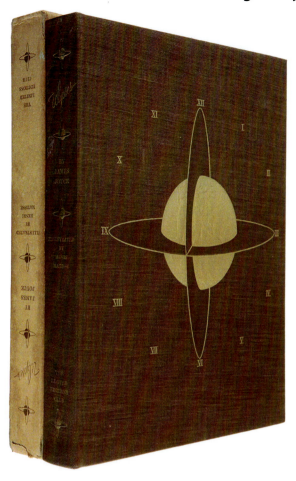

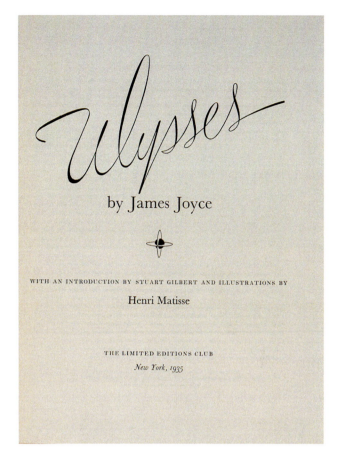

THIS EDITION OF JAMES JOYCE'S ULYSSES
CONSISTS OF FIFTEEN HUNDRED COPIES
MADE FOR THE MEMBERS OF
THE LIMITED EDITIONS CLUB
THE ILLUSTRATIVE ETCHINGS AND DRAWINGS
HAVING BEEN CREATED ESPECIALLY
FOR THIS EDITION BY
HENRI MATISSE
THE EDITION WAS DESIGNED BY GEORGE MACY
AND PRINTED AT THE PRINTING-OFFICE OF
THE LIMITED EDITIONS CLUB, THIS COPY BEING
NUMBER 596
SIGNED BY Henri-Matisse

37109   James Joyce. Henri Matisse, illustrator. *Ulysses*. With an introduction by Stuart Gilbert and illustrations by Henri Matisse. New York: The Limited Editions Club, 1935. The first illustrated edition of *Ulysses*, number 596 of 1,500 numbered copies **signed by the artist, Henri Matisse.** Quarto. [xvi], [2], 363, [1, blank], [2, limitation leaf], [4, blank] pages. Twenty-six plates, consisting of six soft-ground etchings, printed by hand, and twenty lithographic drawings, made as studies for the etchings, printed on thin colored papers. Original brown buckram embossed in gold on front cover and spine from a design by LeRoy H. Appleton. Top edge sprinkled brown, others uncut. Housed in the publisher's printed cardboard slipcase with light soiling, wear around the edges, and a partial split along the bottom. Very minor shelf wear to boards. A couple of small white stains to spine, and one to front cover. Small areas of thumbsoiling to a few leaves. A near fine copy.

The Artist & the Book 197. LEC bibliography 71. Slocum and Cahoon A22.

Estimate: $4,000-up
Starting Bid: $2,000

Inscribed, Signed, and Dated First Edition of King's First Novel

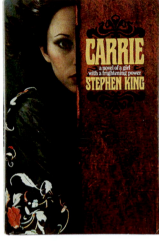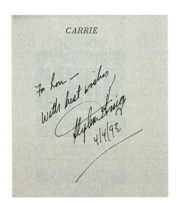

37110 **Stephen King.** *Carrie.* New York: Doubleday & Company, Inc., 1974. First edition, first impression, with code "P6" in gutter of page 199. **Inscribed, signed, and dated by King on the half-title page.** Octavo. 199 pages. Maroon cloth with spine stamped in gilt. Black endpapers. Deckled fore-edge. Very minimal rubbing to publisher's dust jacket. A fine and bright copy of King's first novel.

Estimate: $1,500-up
Starting Bid: $750

All Signed by Stephen King

37111 **Stephen King.** *The Dark Tower* **Series, Volumes I-IV Signed Firsts**, including: *The Gunslinger*; *The Drawing of the Three*; *The Waste Lands*; *Wizard and Glass*. [New York]: Viking, [2003]. First American Illustrated trade editions. **Signed by the author.** Four octavo volumes. Illustrated by Michael Whelan, Phil Hale, Ned Dameron, and Dave McKean respectively. Publisher's bindings and dust jackets. Light shelf wear. Minor bleed to top and bottom edge of Volume I. Else near fine.

Estimate: $1,500-up
Starting Bid: $750

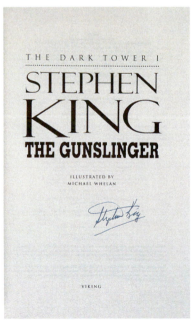

Signed Limited Edition Additionally Inscribed and Signed by King

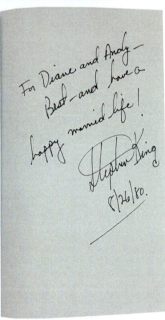

37112 **Stephen King.** *Firestarter.* Huntington Woods: Phantasia, 1980. First edition, number 656 of 725 limited edition copies **signed by King** on the limitation page. **Additionally inscribed by the author.** Octavo. 428 pages. Publisher's binding and dust jacket. Slipcase somewhat scuffed. Slight rippling to the top of the jacket. Otherwise, near fine.

Estimate: $1,000-up
Starting Bid: $500

Inscribed by Stephen King

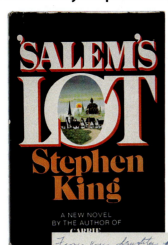

**37113   Stephen King.
'Salem's Lot.** Garden City:
Doubleday, 1975. First
edition. **Inscribed by
the author.** Octavo. 439
pages. Publisher's binding
and dust jacket. Original
second state dust jacket (clipped and the $7.95 price inset at the top of
the front flap). Shelfwear to the book and jacket, particularly at spine
and edges. Some toning to rear panel with minor tape stain and a few
small tears. Generally very good.

Estimate: $1,500-up
Starting Bid: $750

Inscribed First Edition

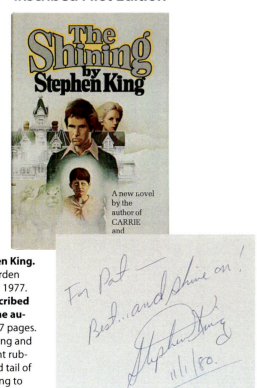

**37114   Stephen King.
The Shining.** Garden
City: Doubleday, 1977.
First edition. **Inscribed
and dated by the au-
thor.** Octavo. 447 pages.
Publisher's binding and
dust jacket. Slight rub-
bing to head and tail of
spine. Light toning to
flaps. Remainder spray on
bottom edge. Otherwise,
near fine.

Estimate: $1,500-up
Starting Bid: $750

Limited and Signed Edition

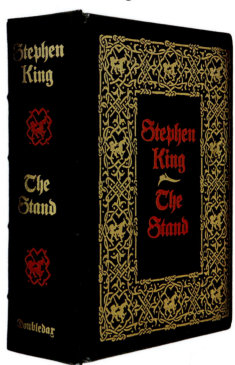

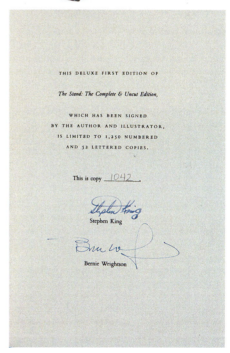

37115   Stephen King. The Stand. New York: Doubleday, 1990. Deluxe,
limited edition. Number 1,042 of 1,250 numbered copies **signed by
the author and the illustrator**, Bernie Wrightson, on the limitation
page. Octavo. 1,237 pages. Publisher's full black calf binding with red
titles, gilt decorations, and four raised bands on the spine. All edges
gilt. Protected by the original glassine and housed in a red satin-lined
black wooden case, as issued. Gilt lightly rubbed where the fore-edge
meets the top edge and bottom edges, as the book fits very snugly into
the wooden case. Some wrinkling and wear to the glassine wrapper. A
side panel strip of the lid to the case has broken and been repaired with
glue. A near fine copy of a desirable King collectable.

Estimate: $1,500-up
Starting Bid: $750

Frieda Lawrence Inscribed Limited Edition "with gay and sad memories."

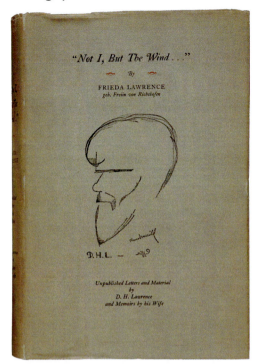

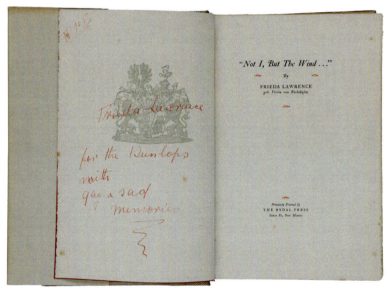

37116   Frieda Lawrence. Fantastic Frieda and D. H. Lawrence Lot, including: *Not I, But the Wind..."* Santa Fe: The Rydal Press, 1934. First edition limited to 1,000 hand-numbered copies of which this is copy number 106. **Inscribed by the author in red ink** *"Frieda Lawrence/ for the Dunlops/ with/ gay and sad/ memories"* and with an undated Christmas card laid in which reads "With many good/ Wishes/ Frieda Lawrence/ remembering/ long ago!" Octavo. 311 pages. Illustrated. Grey cloth boards with natural cloth backstrip. Titles printed on a paper label affixed to the spine. Fore-edge untrimmed. Boards are slightly soiled with moderate wear at the extremities. Contents have only a hint of light scattered foxing. Complete with the original dust jacket which is toned along the spine panel. A rare book offered in a custom made cloth chemise and half-morocco slipcase. [and:] **Willard Johnson, editor. *The Laughing Horse*, May - 1924.** Santa Fe: Owned and copyrighted by James T. Van Rensselaer, Roy Chanslor, and Willard Johnson. Octavo. Unpaginated. Red wrappers printed in black with cover art by Gerald Cassidy. With a bend in the vertical center, else near fine. The issue is offered in a half-morocco folded box with titles stamped in gilt on the spine. **Includes a letter from D. H. Lawrence titled "Dear Old Horse" on pages three through six. The issue also includes a poem by Mabel Dodge Luhan titled "The Ballad of a Bad Girl" with an illustration by D. H. Lawrence captioned "The Bad Girl in the Pansy Bed." [and:] Horn Snuff Container Given to Willard Johnson by Frieda Lawrence.** Willard Johnson was the editor of *The Laughing Horse*, a literary magazine published in Santa Fe, New Mexico. He was a close friend of the Lawrences and helped Frieda, in particular with many of her publishing projects after her husband's death. This horn snuff box measures about 3" in length and is pictured on an included photograph, resting on the title page of *The First Lady Chatterley* with the inscription **"'To the Holy Ghost'/ of the enterprise/ Willard/ from/ Frieda."** (The inscribed copy is held in the archives of UCLA). The horn snuff container has a fancy script "R" carved below a crown. It is said that it had been given to Frieda by her distant cousin, Baron Manfred von Richthofen, the famous "Red Baron," German aviator extraordinaire of WWI. Fine condition.

Estimate: $1,500-up
Starting Bid: $750

Rare D. H. Lawrence First Edition Limited to Only 100 Copies

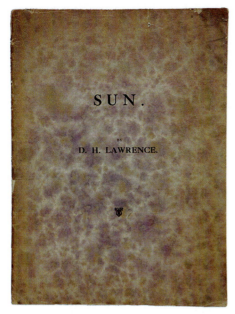 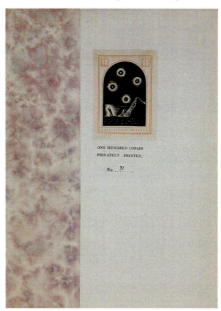

37117   **D. H. Lawrence.** *Sun.* London: E. Archer [Privately printed], September, 1926. First edition privately printed and limited to 100 hand-numbered copies of which this in number 71. Octavo. 20 pages. Decorative paper wrappers. Titles printed in black on the front cover. Top edge untrimmed; all others trimmed. Rockwell Kent-designed bookplate neatly mounted on the inside cover, just above the limitation. With modest chipping at the extremities, toning along the edges of the wrappers and pages, else a near fine copy.

Estimate: $1,500-up
Starting Bid: $750

Limited Edition signed by D. H. Lawrence, One of Only 150 Copies

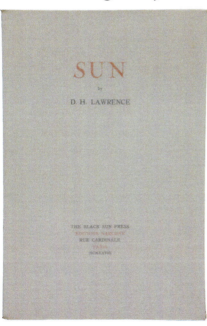 

37118   **D. H. Lawrence.** *Sun.* Paris: The Black Sun Press, 1928. First unexpurgated edition, limited to 150 copies on Holland Van Gelder Zonen to be sold at the Bookshop of Harry Marks, New York. There were an additional 15 copies printed on Japanese vellum but they were not signed. **Boldly signed "D. H. Lawrence" on a slip tipped in and centered on the half-title page.** Octavo. 38 pages. With a color illustration by the author used as the frontispiece. Cream paper wrappers printed in black and red on the cover. Top edge trimmed, all others untrimmed. A fine, bright copy with the original glassine wraps and housed in the original gold foil folder with pink ribbon ties. Contents with scattered light foxing.

It is said that Harry and Caresse Crosby of The Black Sun Press sent Lawrence as payment three pieces of gold in a snuff box that had once belonged to the Queen of Naples.

Estimate: $1,500-up
Starting Bid: $750

Ninety-Two Signed Limited First Editions from The Lord John Press, with Many Limited to Only Twenty-Six Lettered Copies Matched for Subscriber "B"; and Many of the Numbered Editions for Subscriber "2"

37119 [Lord John Press]. Ninety-Two Books Published by Lord John Press Between the Years 1977 and 2000, including: **John Updike.** *Hub Fans Bid Kid Adieu.* 1977. One of 26 copies. [and:] **Donald Barthelme.** *Here in the Village.* 1978. Limited to 50 numbered copies, this # 4. [and:] **Ray Bradbury.** *Twin Hieroglyphs that Swim the River Dust.* 1978. 26 copies. [and:] **John Cheever.** *The Day the Pig Fell into the Well.* 1978. 26 copies. [and:] **John Cheever.** *The Day the Pig Fell into the Well.* 1978. Unbound, unsigned signatures. Penciled to the half-title: "#2 of 4 unbound signatures [signed] Herb Yellin." [and:] **James Dickey.** *The Enemy from Eden.* 1978. 26 letter copies. Inscribed by Gardner on the half-title, also with a sketch by him of an elephant.[and:] **John Hawkes.** *The Universal Fears.* 1978. 26 copies. [and:] **Joyce Carol Oats.** *The Step-Father.* 1978. 26 copies. [and:] **John Updike.** *From the Journal of a Leper.* 1978. 26 copies. [and:] **John Barth.** *Todd Andrews to the Author.* 1979. 50 copies, this # 43. [and:] **Ray Bradbury.** *The Attic Where the Meadow Grows.* 1979. 75 copies, this # 69. [and:] **William Everson, Gary Snyder, Philip Levine, Clayton Eshleman & Jerome Rothenberg.** *Out of the West.* 1979. 350 copies. [and:] **John Gardner.** *Vlemk the Box-Painter.* 1979. 100 copies, this # 69. Original sketch by the author. [and:] **John Gardner.** *Vlemk the Box-Painter.* 1979. Advance proof. Wraps. Original sketch by the author. [and:] **John Gardner.** *Vlemk the Box-Painter.* Trade edition. Original sketch by the author. [and:] **William Gass.** *The First Winter of My Married Life.* 1979. 26 copies. [and:] **Ross MacDonald.** *A Collection of Reviews.* 1979. 50 copies, this # 18. [and:] **Joyce Carol Oates.** *Queen of the Night.* 1979. 50 copies, this # 40. [and:] **Walker Percy.** *Questions They Never Asked Me.* 1979. 50 copies, this# 23. [and:] **John Updike.** *Talk From the Fifties.* 1979. 75 copies, this # 69. [and:] **Ray Bradbury.** *The Last Circus & the Electrocution.* 1980. 100 copies, this # 69. [and:] **Ray Bradbury.** *The Last Circus & the Electrocution.* 1980. Proof copy. Wraps. [and:] **Ray Bradbury.** *The Last Circus & the Electrocution.* 1980. Yellow and red dust jacket. [and:] **Ray Bradbury.** *The Last Circus & the Electrocution.* 1980. Yellow and black dust jacket. Original drawing by the author. [and:] **Gerald Ford.** *A Vision for America.* 1980. 100 copies, this # 69. [and:] **Gerald Ford.** *A Vision for America.* 1980. 500 copies. [and:] **Ken Kesey.** *The Day After Superman Died.* 1980. 50 copies, this # 8. [and:] **Norman Mailer.** *Of a Small and Modest Malignancy, Wicked and Bristling with Dots.* 1980. 100 copies, this # 69. [and:] **Norman Mailer.** *Of a Small and Modest Malignancy, Wicked and Bristling with Dots.* 1980. 300 copies. [and:] **James Purdy.** *Proud Flesh.* 1980. 50 numbered copies, this # 19. [and:] **John Updike.** *People One Knows.* 1980. 100 copies, this # 69. [and:] **Eudora Welty.** *Acrobats in a Park.* 1980. 100 copies, this # 69. [and:] **John Ashbery, Galway Kinnell, W. S. Merwin, L. M. Rosenberg, and Dave Smith.** *Apparitions.* 1981. 50 copies, this # 25. [and:] **Gerald Ford.** *Global Security.* 1981. Miniature. 100 copies, this # 69. [and:] **Ursula K. Le Guin.** *Gwilan's Harp.* 50 copies, this # 30. [and:] **Edna O'Brien.** *James and Nora.* 1981. 26 copies. [and:] **John Barth.** *The Literature of Exhaustion and Literature of Replenishment.* 1982. 100 copies, this # 69. [and:] **John Barth.** *The Literature of Exhaustion and the Literature of Replenishment.* 1982. 300 copies. [and:] **Samuel Beckett.** *Ill Seen Ill Said.* 1982. 26 copies. [and:] **Ray Bradbury.** *The Love Affair.* 1982. 100 copies, this # 69. [and:] **Robert Coover.** *The Convention.* 1982. 50 copies, this # 2. [and:] **Günter Grass.** *Kinderlied.* 1982. 50 copies, this # 2. [and:] **Robert B. Parker.** *Surrogate.* 1982. 50 copies, this # 2. [and:] **John Updike.** *The Beloved.* 1982. 100 copies, this # 2. [and:] **Laura (Riding) Jackson.** *Some Communications of Broad Reference.* 1983. 26 copies. [and:] **Ursula K. Le Guin.** *In the Red Zone.* 1983. 50 copies, this # 2. [and:] **John Bart.** *Don't Count on It.* 1984. 50 copies, this

2. [and:] **Thomas Berger.** *Granted Wishes.* 1984. 26 copies. [and:] **Raymond Carver.** *If It Please You.* 1984. 26 copies. [and:] **Harry Crews.** *2 by Crews.* 1984. 26 copies. [and:] **James Crumley.** *The Muddy Fork.* 1984. 50 copies, this # 2. [and:] **William Everson.** *Renegade Christmas.* 1984. 26 copies. [and:] **Gerald Ford.** *Churchill Lecture.* 1984. 100 copies, this # 14. [and:] **Joyce Carol Oates.** *Luxury of Sin.* 1984. 26 copies. [and:] **Robert B. Parker.** *The Private Eye in Hammett and Chandler.* 1984. 50 copies, this # 2. [and:] **John Updike.** *Jester's Dozen.* 1984. 50 copies, this # 13. [and:] **Robert B. Parker.** *Parker on Writing.* 1985. 75 copies, this # 69. [and:] **Eudora Welty.** *In Black and White.* 1985. 100 copies, this # 69. [and:] **Michel Tournier.** *Un Jardin à Hammamet.* 1986. 26. [and:] **Garry Trudeau.** *Rap Master Ronnie.* 1986. 26 copies. [and:] **John Updike.** *A Soft Spring Night in Shillington.* 1986. 50 copies, this # 2. [and:] **Ray Bradbury.** *Death Has Lost Its Charm For Me.* 1987. 26 copies. [and:] **Joyce Carol Oates.** *The Time Traveler.* 1987. 26 copies. [and:] **Walker Percy.** *The State of the Novel.* 1987. 200 copies. [and:] **Reynolds Price.** *House Snake.* 1987. 26 copies. [and:] **Dennis Etchison [editor].** *Lord John Ten.* 1988. 75 copies, this # 69. [and:] **Gerald Ford.** *The Tenth Convention.* 1988. Miniature. 150 numbered copies, this # 69. [and:] **John Updike.** *Getting the Words Out.* 1988. 50 copies, this # 2. [and:] **Ray Bradbury.** *The Climate of Palettes.* 1898. miniature. 26 copies. [and:] **Stephen King.** *Dolan's Cadillac.* 1989. 26 copies. [and:] **Ross Thomas.** *Spies, Thumbsuckers, etc.* 1989. 50 copies, this # 3. [and:] **Bruce Francis.** *Scenic Route.* 1990. 26. [and:] **Dan Simmons.** *Entropy's Bed at Midnight.* 1990. 100 copies, this # 69. [and:] **John Updike.** *Mites & Other Poems in Miniature.* 1990. Miniature. 26 copies. [and:] **Harry Crews.** *Madonna at Ringside.* 1991. 26 copies. [and:] **Louise Erdrich and Michael Dorris.** *Route 2.* 1991. 26 copies. [and:] **Elmore Leonard.** *Notebooks.* 1991. 50 copies, this # 2. [and:] *Lord John Signatures.* 1991. 26 copies. [and:] **James Lee Burke.** *Texas City, 1947.* 1992. 26 copies. [and:] **Norman Mailer.** *How the Wimp Won the War.* 1992. 26 copies. [and:] **Dan Simmons.** *Children of Night.* 1992. 26 copies. [and:] **Dan Simmons.** *The Hollow Man.* 1992. 26 copies. [and:] **Dan Simmons.** *Summer Sketches.* 1992. 26 copies. [and:] **William Gibson.** *Virtual Light.* 1993. 1993. 26 copies. [and:] **Thomas McGuane.** *Sons.* 1993. 26 copies. [and:] **John Updike.** *Concerts at Castle Hill.* 1993. 50 copies, this # 2. [and:] **Louise Erdrich.** *The Bingo Palace.* 1994. 26 copies. [and:] **John Casey.** *Supper at the Black Pearl.* 1995. 26 copies. [and:] **Ray Bradbury.** *Witness and Celebrate.* 2000. 26 copies. [and:] **Ray Bradbury.** *Witness and Celebrate.* 2000. **Inscribed by Herb Yellin.** Not signed by Bradbury. [and:] **John Updike.** *Humor in Fiction.* 2000. 26 copies.

A near-comprehensive collection of books published by the Lord John Press. Each is signed by the author, unless otherwise noted. All are limited editions. Those indicated above as being limited to 26 copies are the lettered editions and each one is designated by the letter "B." All volumes are near fine to fine.

Herb Yellin created the Lord John Press in 1977 and begin publishing first editions by his favorite living authors in autographed, limited editions. The books and broadsides coming out of this Northridge, California operation were soon in demand from discerning book lovers and collectors. The authors ranged from Eudora Welty to Stephen King, from William Gibson to Samuel Beckett. These truly beautiful, artfully designed books serve as a impressive legacy of the diverse and colorful literature in the last quarter of the twentieth century.

Estimate: $15,000-up
Starting Bid: $13,000

First English Edition Inscribed by Maugham

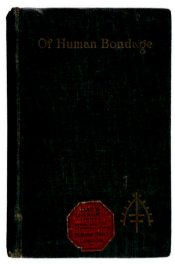 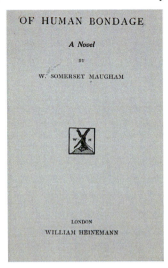 

37120 **W. Somerset Maugham.** *Of Human Bondage.* London: William Heinemann, 1915. First English edition printed from stereotype plates made from the American first issue type, with the misprint on page 257. **Inscribed by the author** on the front free endpaper. Octavo. 648 pages with 18 pages of advertisements printed on cheaper paper and inserted at the back. Publisher's blue cloth with titles stamped in gilt. Housed in a green cloth chemise and matching slipcase. Boards soiled and rather worn, especially at the extremities. Small London library label affixed at the bottom of the front board. Some offsetting to the preliminary pages, otherwise internally clean and in good condition.

A curiously signed presentation copy inscribed by Maugham in San Francisco twenty-one years after the book's publication. It reads: "**For Leon Gelbe/ W. Somerset Maugham/ writes his name/ in San Francisco/ on March 11, 1936.**"

Estimate: $1,500-up
Starting Bid: $750

Cormac McCarthy's Epic Trilogy, All Signed

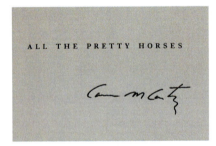 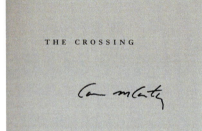 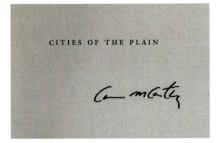

37121 **Cormac McCarthy. The Border Trilogy, including**: *All the Pretty Horses; The Crossing; Cities of the Plain.* New York: Alfred A. Knopf, 1992, 1994, 1998. First editions. **Each volume signed by the author**, all on the half title page. Three octavo volumes. Publisher's black cloth over black paper boards with front covers and spines stamped in gilt. Original pictorial dust jackets. Light rubbing to jackets. Fine copies.

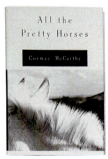 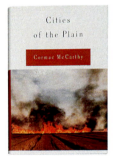

Cormac McCarthy's almost mythic trilogy - a startling and powerful modern classic of the Southwest that propelled McCarthy to international mainstream literary acclaim - is comprised of three stand-alone novels. *All the Pretty Horses*, the National Book Award-winning first novel in the trilogy, is now a staple on high school reading lists, and is, perhaps, McCarthy's most popular work. A beautiful first edition set of the Trilogy, with all volumes signed.

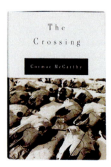

Estimate: $3,000-up
Starting Bid: $1,500

First American Edition of *Moby-Dick*

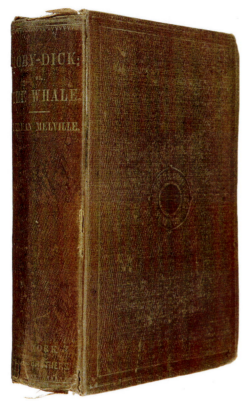
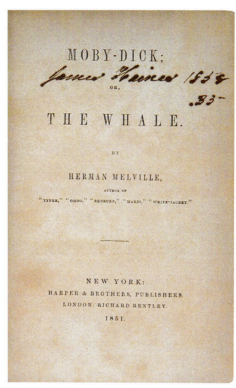

37122   **Herman Melville. *Moby-Dick; or, The Whale.*** New York: Harper & Brothers, 1851. First American edition. Octavo. xxiii, [1, blank], 634, [1, "Epilogue"], [1, blank], [6, ads], [4, blank] pages. BAL first binding of publisher's drab purple-brown "A" cloth. Covers stamped in blind with a heavy rule frame and publisher's circular device at center, spine decoratively stamped and lettered in gilt, original orange coated endpapers. Double flyleaves at front and back. Some moderate scattered foxing or browning, as usual. Covers rather worn with rubbed extremities. Shelf wear to edges with exposed boards at bumped corners and near joints. Spine sunned with slight fraying at ends and along the joints. The fabric along the joints is starting to separate. Binding slightly cocked. Endpapers rather browned with hinges strong. Inked name of previous owner to title page. Small bookseller ticket to rear pastedown. A handsome, unsophisticated copy of Melville's greatest achievement, and arguably the greatest novel in American literature.

"[Melville's] great book, *Moby Dick*, was a complete practical failure, misunderstood by the critics and ignored by the public; and in 1853 the Harpers' fire destroyed the plates of all of his books and most of the copies remaining in stock [only about sixty copies survived the fire]... Melville's permanent fame must always rest on the great prose epic of *Moby Dick,* a book that has no equal in American literature for variety and splendor of style and for depth of feeling" (*Dictionary of American Biography* XII, pp. 522-526).

"*Moby Dick* is the great conundrum-book. Is it a profound allegory with the white whale the embodiment of moral evil, or merely the finest story of the sea ever written?" (Grolier, *100 American*).

BAL 13664. Grolier, *100 American*, 60.

Estimate: $15,000-up
Starting Bid: $7,500

**An Inscribed First Edition, First Printing of "Gone with the Wind,"
as Well as Three Typed Letters Signed "Peggy" by Mitchell
and a Ticket Stub from the 1939 Film Premiere in Atlanta**

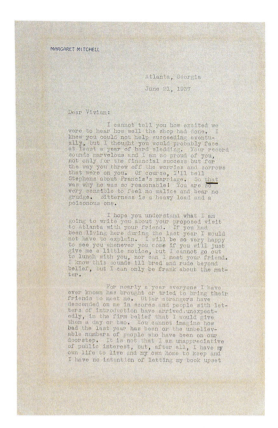

MARGARET MITCHELL

Atlanta, Georgia
June 21, 1937

Dear Vivian:

I cannot tell you how excited we
were to hear how well the shop had done. I
knew you could not help succeeding eventually, but I thought you would probably face
at least a year of hard sledding. Your record
sounds marvelous and I am so proud of you,
not only for the financial success but for
the way you threw off the worries and sorrows
that were on you. Of course, I'll tell
Stephens about Francis's marriage. So that
was why he was so reasonable! You are so
very sensible to feel no malice and bear no
grudge. Bitterness is a heavy load and a
poisonous one.

I hope you understand what I am
going to write you about your proposed visit
to Atlanta with your friend. If you had
been living here during the last year I would
not have to explain. I will be so very happy
to see you whenever you come if you will just
give me a little notice, but I cannot go out
to lunch with you, nor can I meet your friend.
I know this sounds ill bred and rude beyond
belief, but I can only be frank about the matter.

For nearly a year everyone I have
ever known has brought or tried to bring their
friends to meet me. Utter strangers have
descended on me in scores and people with letters of introduction have arrived unexpect-
edly, in the firm belief that I would give
them a day or two. You cannot imagine how
bad the last year has been or the unbelievable numbers of people who have been on our
doorstep. It is not that I am unappreciative
of public interest, but, after all, I have my
own life to live and my own home to keep and
I have no intention of letting my book upset

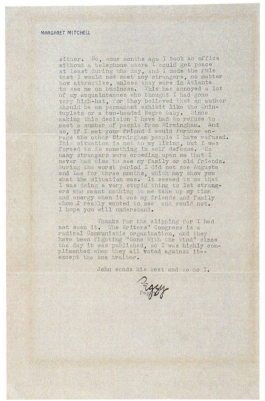

MARGARET MITCHELL

either. So, some months ago I took an office
without a telephone where I could get peace
at least during the day, and I made the rule
that I would not meet any strangers, no matter
how attractive, unless they were in Atlanta
to see me on business. This has annoyed a lot
of my acquaintances who thought I had gone
very high-hat, for they believed that an author
should be on permanent exhibit like the Quintuplets or a two-headed Negro baby. Since
making this decision I have had to refuse to
meet a number of people from Birmingham. And
so, if I met your friend I would further en-
rage the other Birmingham people I have refused.
This situation is not to my liking, but I was
forced to do something in self defense. So
many strangers were crowding upon me that I
never had time to see my family or old friends.
During the worst period I did not see Augusta
and Lee for three months, which may show you
what the situation was. It seemed to me that
I was doing a very stupid thing to let strangers who meant nothing to me take up my time
and energy when it was my friends and family
whom I really wanted to see and could not.
I hope you will understand.

Thanks for the clipping for I had
not seen it. The Writers' Congress is a
radical Communistic organization, and they
have been fighting "Gone With the Wind" since
the day it was published, so I was highly com-
plimented when they all voted against it--
except the one traitor.

John sends his best and so do I.

Peggy

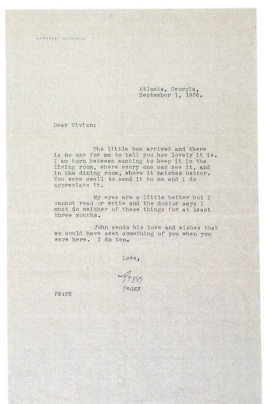

MARGARET MITCHELL

Atlanta, Georgia
November 14, 1939

Dear Vivian:

Forgive the haste of this letter.
I just want to thank you for your sweet letter
and your good wishes. Everything has been topsyturvey and all atwit here in Atlanta since the
date of the premiere was announced, and I do not
see how John and I will be able to draw a breath
until after the affair is over. Every civic and
social organization plans to give a party around
that time and our phone rings like mad all day
long. No announcement has been made yet about
when the tickets will go on sale and what price
will be charged. Everyone believes I know the
answers to these questions, so they telephone me
and I know no more than anyone else. Many thous-
and reservations have already been sent in, some
of them coming from as far-off places as Canada
and Mexico; the theatre seats nineteen hundred;
so you can imagine what a scramble is going on.
The main purpose of this letter is for you to
tell Mrs. Crowder to make her hotel reservations
as quickly as possible. People have been reserv-
ing hotel rooms for the last week and, as there
are to be several conventions in town at the same
time, rooms are fading rapidly. I am glad you
are going to stay with Augusta so you'll be sure
of a place to sleep.

If I do not see you at this time
please overlook it. With the Macmillan publishing company coming down here in a body and Mr.
Selznick and his stars, too, I expect to be tied
up.

Herschel Brickell is in Jackson,
Mississippi, or Natchez at present, working on
his book about the history of Natchez.

Love,

Peggy

MARGARET MITCHELL

Atlanta, Georgia,
September 1, 1936.

Dear Vivian:

The little box arrived and there
is no use for me to tell you how lovely it is.
I am torn between wanting to keep it in the
living room, where every one can see it, and
in the dining room, where it matches better.
You were swell to send it to me and I do
appreciate it.

My eyes are a little better but I
cannot read or write and the doctor says I
must do neither of these things for at least
three months.

John sends his love and wishes that
we could have seen something of you when you
were here. I do too.

Love,

Peggy

PM:FH

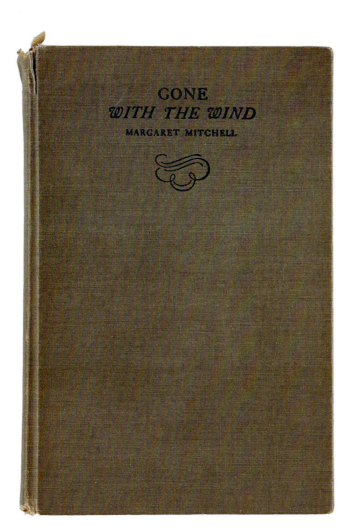

37123 **Margaret Mitchell.** *Gone with the Wind.* New York: Macmillan, 1936. First edition, first printing with "Published May, 1936" on copyright page and no note of other printings. **Inscribed by Margaret Mitchell on front free endpaper: "To Vivian Latady with much love from Margaret Mitchell / Dec. 3, 1936 / Atlanta, Ga."** Octavo. 1,037 pages. Original gray cloth decoratively stamped and lettered in blue on front cover and spine. Front hinge cracked; binding loose. Wear to head and tail of spine. Cloth nicked at head of spine and splitting and fraying at top of both joints. A near very good copy.

Also, with **Three Typed Letters Signed by Margaret Mitchell (who has signed them "Peggy"), addressed to "Vivian" [Latady]**, including: **Atlanta, September 1, 1936.** She thanks her friend Vivian for a gift and tells her about her bout of severe eye strain: "My eyes are a little better but I cannot read or write and the doctor says I must do neither of these things for at least three months." One page. [and:] **Atlanta, June 21, 1937.** The bulk of the letter concerns Mitchell's apology that she would not be able to meet Vivian's friend. She goes into great detail of the utter chaos of her life since the publication of her book and how she had made a promise to herself that she would no longer meet any strangers. "This has annoyed a lot of my acquaintances who thought I had gone very high-hat, for they believed that an author should be on permanent exhibit like the Quintuplets or a two-headed Negro baby." Two pages. [and:] **Atlanta, November 14, 1939.** Mitchell describes the frenzy of the December 15th Atlanta premiere of *the Gone with the Wind* film: "Everything has been topsyturvey and all atwit here in Atlanta since the date of the premiere was announced...." She encourages Vivian's friend to book a hotel room as soon as possible since "rooms are fading rapidly." All letters are on Mitchell's stationery with her name printed at top, each sheet measuring 10.875 x 7.125, with the usual folds. All are in near fine condition; the 1937 letter has some toning around the edges.

Also included is a **ticket stub from the Atlanta premiere of** *Gone with the Wind,* **at the Loew's Grand Theatre on Dec. 15, 1939.** Ticket has an illustrated vignette showing Rhett and Scarlett in an embrace with Tara in the background. Ticket has been torn in half. 2.25 x 3.75 inches. Fine.

Estimate: $7,000-up
Starting Bid: $3,500

The Beloved American Novel, Signed by the Author

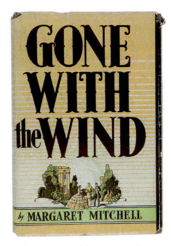

37124   **Margaret Mitchell.** *Gone with the Wind.* New York: The Macmillan Company, 1936. First edition, second issue, with "Published June, 1936" on copyright page; in the second issue dust jacket, with "$3.00" price in lower corner of front flap and with "Gone with the Wind" in first column on rear panel. **Signed by Mitchell** on the front free endpaper. Octavo. 1,037 pages. Original gray cloth decoratively stamped and lettered in blue on front cover and spine. Very minimal rubbing to cloth at extremities. Tiny nick to head of spine. With Atlanta bookseller's ticket to rear pastedown. Dust jacket in much better condition than is normally encountered, with a few chips along the edges and a couple of short tears. A very nice copy in better than very good condition.

By the end of 1936, over a million copies of *Gone with the Wind* had sold, and Margaret Mitchell's life had been turned upside down-only a couple of weeks after publication of the book she wrote her publisher that "life has been so much like a nightmare." By the end of the year she was unable to handle the crush of autograph-seekers, and she politely refused to sign any more copies of the book after December of 1936 (she declined, even, to sign a copy for her brother!). The person who managed to get this book signed was one of the lucky few.

Estimate: $6,000-up
Starting Bid: $3,000

Wonderful Copy of Pynchon's Classic

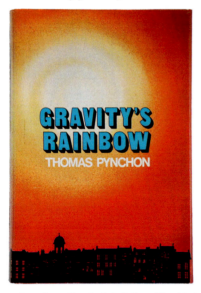

37125   **Thomas Pynchon.** *Gravity's Rainbow.* New York: Viking, [1973]. First edition, first printing. Octavo. 760 pages. Publisher's binding and dust jacket. Modest foxing to spine cloth. Hinges slightly shaken. Endpapers shows mild foxing and offsetting with foxing to page edges. Modest toning and rubbing to jacket extremities. Overall near fine.

Estimate: $1,500-up
Starting Bid: $750

Pynchon's First Book

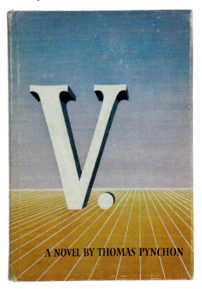

37126   **Thomas Pynchon.** *V.* Philadelphia: Lippincott, [1963]. First edition, first printing. Octavo. 492 pages. Publisher's binding and first issue dust jacket without reviews on rear panel. Darkening to top edges of boards with soft bumping to spine ends and upper corner of rear board. A few spots of soiling to fore-edge. Jacket is lightly rubbed and edge worn with a few tiny chips and tears. Portion of rear inner flap, running from slightly above center of fore-edge and down through tail of rear fold, has been torn off and reattached with tape to verso. Overall very good.

Estimate: $1,500-up
Starting Bid: $750

Beautiful Set of Rabelais

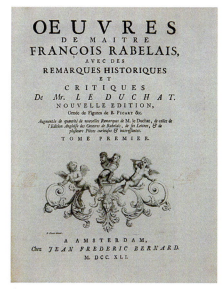 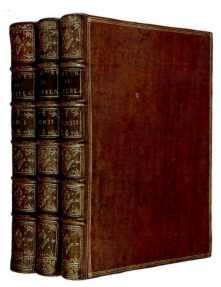

37127   **François Rabelais**. *Oeuvres de Maitre François Rabelais, avec des Remarques Historiques et Critiques de Mr. Le Duchat*. Amsterdam: Jean Frederic Bernard, 1741. Nouvelle edition. Three quarto volumes. Half-title leaf, engraved half-title leaf, full title leaf, [1-4] avertissement du libraire, preface [I]-XXXVI, [1]-526 pages; half-title leaf, frontispiece leaf, full title leaf, [I]-XXXIV, [3]- 383 pages; half-title leaf, engraved frontispiece leaf, full title leaf, [i-ii] avertissement du libraire, engraved author portrait leaf, [i-vi] La Vie, La Lettres half-title, dedication, [1]-154, section title leaf, [157]-218, section title leaf, [3]- 150 pages, [1-20] table des matieres, [1-2] clef de Rabelais, [1-13] table des matieres. Lavishly Illustrated with full-page half-titles, three fold-out engravings of Rabelais' residence and one fold-out map; seventeen full-page engravings by Picart, Tanje, and Bernaerts with numerous engraved chapter titles, initials, vignettes, and decorative devices throughout. Bound in full polished calf with triple fillet borders and gilt-tooled board edges. Five raised bands on spine with gilt-stamped floral decorations and compartment ruling. Red and brown morocco labels on spine with gilt-stamped titles and ruling. All edges stained red. Marbled endpapers with armorial bookplate on front pastedown. Faded ownership initials to title pages. Minor foxing and offsetting in all volumes. A near fine set of a beautiful edition.

Estimate: $2,000-up
Starting Bid: $1,000

Signed Limited Ayn Rand

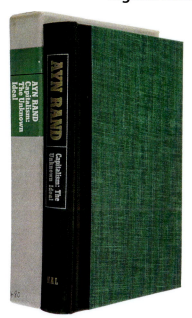 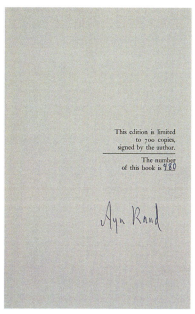

37128   **Ayn Rand**. *Capitalism: The Unknown Ideal*. [New York]: NAL, [1966]. First edition, limited to 700 numbered copies of which this is 480. **Signed by Rand.** Octavo. Publisher's binding and slipcase. Lacking front free endpaper. Slipcase is toned with minor rubbing and a touch of abrading to paper label. Very good.

Estimate: $1,500-up
Starting Bid: $750

Signed First Edition of Ayn Rand

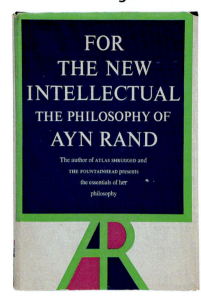

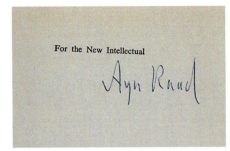

37129   Ayn Rand. *For the New Intellectual: The Philosophy of Ayn Rand.* New York: Random House, [1961]. First edition, first printing. **Signed by Rand** on half-title page. Octavo. 242 pages. Publisher's binding and dust jacket. Softly bumped on upper corner of front board. Minor toning to end-papers and page edges. Front hinge cracking. Light wear to jacket with edge toning and a few small chips to extremities. About near fine.

Estimate: $1,500-up
Starting Bid: $750

Beautiful Original Illustrations by Will Vawter

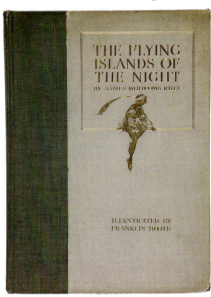

37130   [Will Vawter, Two Original Illustrations]. James Whitcomb Riley. *The Flying Islands of the Night.* Indianapolis: Bobbs-Merrill, [1913]. Later edition. Quarto. 124 pages. **Illustrated with 16 color plates by Franklin Booth, each with descriptive tissue guard. Additionally, Will Vawter has provided two wonderful original illustrations. A pair of dancing Gnomes done in watercolors on the recto of frontispiece and a grasshopper done in pin and ink on dedication page.** Publisher's binding with minor rubbing and darkening to extremities, and with abrading to corners. Inscription on front free endpaper. Front hinge cracking at title page. Faint soiling to rear pastedown. Very good.

Estimate: $1,500-up
Starting Bid: $750

First Edition of Shakespeare's Collected Poems

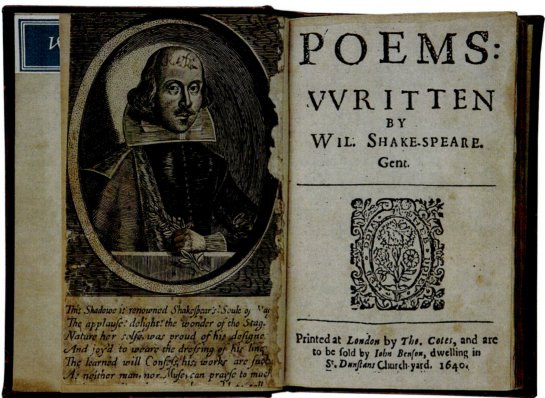

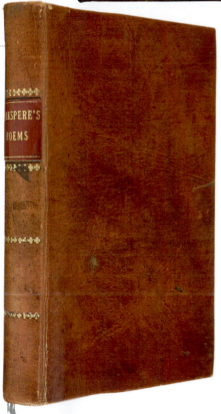

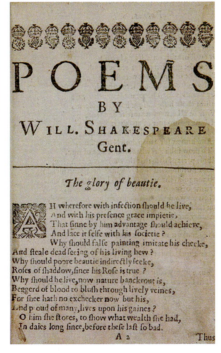

37133 **William Shakespeare.** *Poems Written by Wil. Shakespeare. Gent.* Printed at London by Tho. Cotes, and are to be sold by John Benson, dwelling in St. Dunstans Church-yard, 1640. First edition. Small octavo (5 x 3 inches). 104 leaves, plus engraved portrait frontispiece of the poet by William Marshall after Martin Droeshout. There are two title pages (both in fine facsimile, and with five other facsimile leaves in the text: B8, C3, F4-5, and the final leaf M4), each identical and with the printer's woodcut device. Between these title pages are three short preliminary texts: a "note to the reader" by Benson, and two poems by Leonard Diggens and John Warren. The frontispiece has been restored and tipped in. Later full calf over boards. Title label to spine with gilt lettering. Some damp-staining to the first dozen leaves. Pages have been aggressively trimmed, cramping the text. Some inked marginalia in an early, neat hand on five pages. Overall, a very good, bright copy.

Thomas Thorpe first published Shakespeare's sonnets in 1609. They didn't see publication again until 1640. This edition is essentially the second edition of the sonnets, and the first edition of Shakespeare's collected poems. There has been much mention by scholars about the manner in which John Benson arranged, edited, retitled, even omitted some of the sonnets. This Benson edition remained as something of an authority until Edmond Malone's scholarship of the 1770s.

ESTC S106377. Pforzheimer 880.

Estimate: $20,000-up
Starting Bid: $10,000

Six Signed Salman Rushdie Books

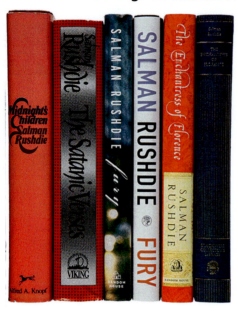
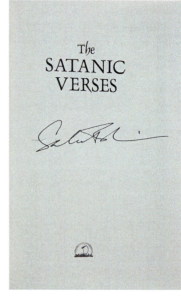

37131   **Salman Rushdie. Six Books,** including: *Midnight's Children.* New York: Alfred A. Knopf, 1981. First American edition. **Signed by the auth**
on the title page. Octavo. 446 pages. Maroon cloth over gray boards. Very mild yellowing and rubbing to the dust jacket, the front flap has a crease
where it has been folded. Near fine. [and:] *The Satanic Verses.* New York: Viking, 1989. Later printing. **Signed by the author** on the title page. Octa
547 pages. Black cloth over black boards. Dust jacket. Fine. [and:] *Fury.* London: Jonathan Cape, 2001. First edition. **Signed by the author** on the t
page. Octavo. 259 pages. Black cloth over boards. Dust jacket. Fine. [and:] *Fury.* New York: Random House, 2001. First American edition. **Signed by**
the author on the title page. Octavo. 259 pages. Dust jacket. Fine. [and:] *The Enchantress of Florence.* London: Jonathan Cape / Blackwell Collecto
Library, [2008]. First deluxe edition, **limited to 100 numbered copies, this being number 89, signed by the author.** Octavo. 359 pages. Blue
cloth over cream boards. No dust jacket issued. Publisher's slipcase. Fine. [and:] *The Enchantress of Florence.* New York: Random House, [2008].Firs
American edition. **Signed by the author** on the title page. Octavo. 355 pages. Dust jacket. Fine.

Estimate: $1,500-up
Starting Bid: $750

First Edition of Salinger's Classic

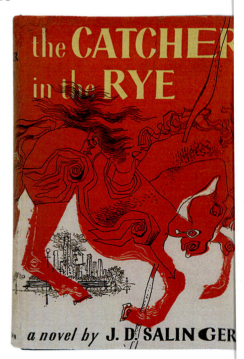

37132   **J. D. Salinger.** *The Catcher in the Rye.* Boston: Little, Brown and Company, 1951. First
edition stated, in first issue dust jacket with Salinger portrait on back panel. Octavo. 277 pages.
Publisher's black cloth with gilt titles to spine. Gilt dulled. Faint foxing to fore-edge; light thumb-
soiling to bottom edge. Offsetting and toning to endpapers, more prominent to rear pastedown.
Dust jacket has been professionally restored. Minor toning to spine and rear panel of jacket. Near
fine.

Estimate: $3,000-up
Starting Bid: $1,500

Steinbeck's Scarce Signed *Saint Katy*

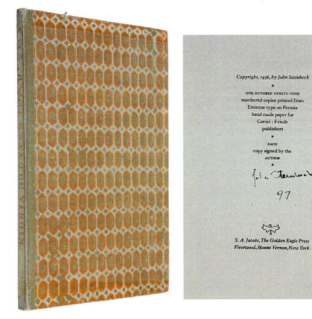

37134   **John Steinbeck. *Saint Katy the Virgin*.** New York: Covici Friede, [1936]. First edition, one of 199 numbered copies **signed by the author**, of which this is number 97. Twelvemo. 25 pages. Original gold cloth backstrip, stamped in red, over gold, white and peach printed boards. With original glassine cover. Extremities slightly rubbed, small dent at the top of the boards. Glassine has small tears at both ends with a bit of loss, else a near fine example. This copy contains the "Merry Christmas" slip, originally issued with this title.

Goldstone & Payne A6a.

Estimate: $2,500-up
Starting Bid: $1,250

One of the Most Important Poetry Works of the Twentieth Century

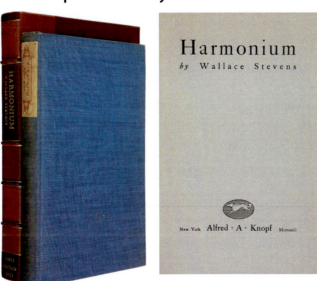

37135   **Wallace Stevens. *Harmonium*.** New York: Alfred A. Knopf, 1923. First edition, third binding state, one of 715 copies printed in 1926. Octavo. 140 pages. Original blue cloth with titles printed in red on a yellow paper label mounted to the spine. Slight toning to spine panel, with a former owner's name written neatly in ink on the front free endpaper, otherwise with trivial shelf wear and in near fine condition. Housed in a custom half-morocco slipcase with titles stamped in gilt on two labels on the spine.

Harmonium was Stevens' first collection of poetry published at the late age of 44. Some of his most famous poems are included here, such as "The Emperor of Ice-Cream," a poem on the banality of funeral ceremonies, "The Snow Man," and "Sunday Morning."

Edelstein, A1.a. Connolly, *One Hundred Modern Books*, 46.

Estimate: $1,000-up
Starting Bid: $500

Tennyson's First Appearance In Print

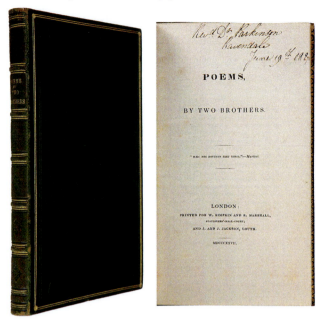

37136 **[Alfred and Charles Tennyson].** *Poems, by Two Brothers.* London: W. Simpkin and R. Marshall, 1827. First edition. Octavo. xii, 228 pages with advertisement leaf following title. Bound in full morocco with blindstamped devices and double-rule gilt borders to covers. Five raised bands with gilt ruling and titles with blindstamped devices to spine. All edges gilt. Gilt outer edges and inner dentelles with marbled endpapers. Some rubbing to boards and discoloration to spine Bookplate to front pastedown with ownership signature on title. Scattered foxing throughout. Very good.

Alfred Tennyson wrote these poems in conjunction with his brother Frederick when they were between the ages of fifteen and eighteen years old. This volume contains original advertisements dated 1827 verifying this fact. Of the poems in this book, about one-third were identified as being by Alfred, this being noted in the second edition published in 1893.

Estimate: $2,000-up
Starting Bid: $1,000

Laid-In Note of Tennyson

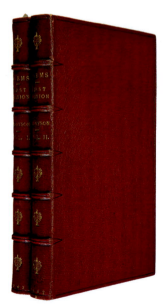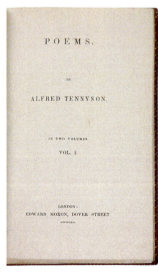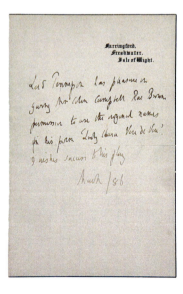

37137 **Alfred Tennyson.** *Poems.* London: Edward Moxon, 1842. First edition. **Handwritten note by the author laid in.** Two twelvemo volumes. vii, 233 pages; vii, 231 pages. Bound by Riviere in full red leather with five raised bands, gilt spine titles, decorations and date. Top edges gilt and gilt fillets. Blue endpapers with rich inner dentelles. Joints and covers lightly rubbed. Light staining at the rear page edges of Volume Two. Bookplates at the preliminaries of each volume. Otherwise very good**.**

Laid-in note in Tennyson's hand granting playwright Colin Campbell Rae Brown permission to use his original names mentioned in the poem "Lady Clara Vere de Vere" in Brown's play "Vere de Vere" on page 155 of Volume One.

Estimate: $1,500-up
Starting Bid: $750

Tolkien's Classic

37138   J. R. R. Tolkien. *The Hobbit, or There and Back Again.* London: George Allen & Unwin, [1937]. First edition, second impression. Octavo. 310 pages. With illustrations by the author. Publisher's green cloth with black designs and lettering. Map endpapers. Publisher's green stain to top edge. Binding slightly cocked, rear board bowed. Some foxing to cloth, with occasional puckering. Top stain mottled; foxing to fore-edge and bottom edge. A few leaves with thin brown stain to bottom edge, with minimal intrusion onto pages. Some pages with mild foxing and with shallow bends; one leaf wrinkled. Inconspicuous British bookstore sticker to front pastedown. Original dust jacket is price-clipped, with "Second Impression" at bottom of front flap. Jacket has a few chips, particularly to the base of the spine, a few short tears, some mild foxing, and moisture waves to front panel. An about very good copy.

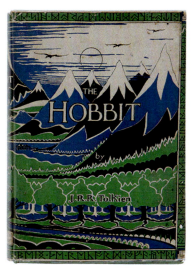

The first impression to contain Tolkien's color illustrations. 2,300 copies of the second impression were printed, 423 of which were destroyed in the bombing of London in 1940.

Estimate: $5,000-up
Starting Bid: $2,500

First Edition of *Huckleberry Finn*

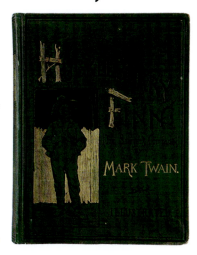

37139   Mark Twain. *Adventures of Huckleberry Finn (Tom Sawyer's Comrade).* New York: Charles L. Webster and Company, 1885. First edition with the following first issue points, per BAL: "Him and another Man" with "88" on p. [13]; "with the was" instead of "with the saw" on p. 57; and frontispiece with "Heliotype Printing Company" and visible tablecloth. Also, "Huck Decided" instead of "Huck Decides" under "Chapter VI" on p. [9], a first issue point per MacDonnell (*Firsts*, p. 31); p. 283 on a stub. Octavo. 366 pages. Portrait frontispiece. Text illustrations by E. W. Kemble. Publisher's full green pictorial cloth, stamped and lettered in gilt and black. Laid in is an early photograph postcard of Twain with his name in Cyrillic. Bumped corners. Professionally recased retaining original boards and backstrip. Hinges reinforced. Some slight dampstaining to lower corner of pastedown through table of contents. Some minor tape-staining to rear free endpaper. Overall, a very good, clean copy, showing some professional conservation work.

BAL 3415. Kevin MacDonnell in *Firsts*, September 1998 - Vol. 8, No. 9, "Huck Finn, Among the Issue Mongers," pages 29-35.

Estimate: $1,500-up
Starting Bid: $750

Four Rabbit Angstrom Books

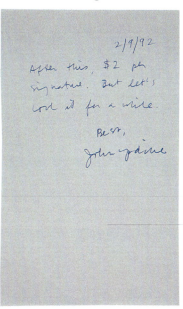
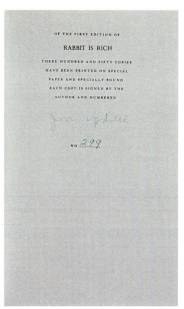

37140   John Updike. Four Novels, including: *Rabbit, Run.* New York: Alfred A. Knopf, 1960. First edition. **Updike inscription laid-in.** Some staining to the top board. Moderately chipped damp-stained dust jacket with tape stains to the flaps. Inked name of former owner on front free endpaper. Overall, very good. [and:] *Rabbit Redux.* New York: Alfred A. Knopf, 1971. First edition. Light wear to the upper edge of the dust jacket. Near fine. [and:] *Rabbit is Rich.* New York: 1981. First deluxe edition, **limited to 350 numbered copies, this being 299, signed by the author.** Dust jacket. Publisher's slipcase. Fine. [and:] *Rabbit at Rest.* New York: Alfred A. Knopf, 1990. First edition. Dust jacket. Fine.

Estimate: $1,500-up
Starting Bid: $750

The Exceedingly Rare True First American Edition
of *Twenty Thousand Leagues Under the Seas*

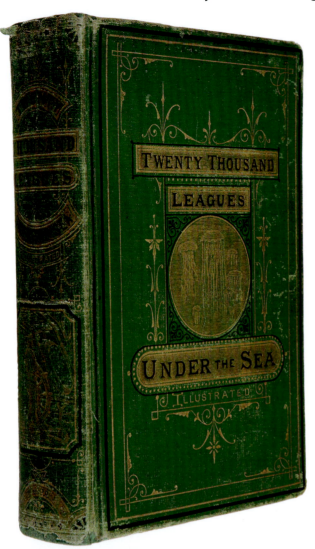

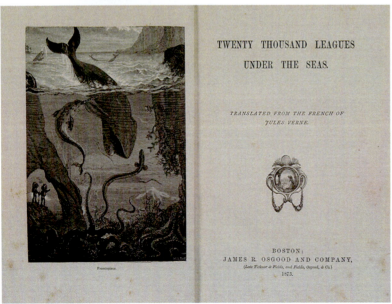

37141   Jules Verne. *Twenty Thousand Leagues Under the Seas.* Boston: James R. Osgood, 1873. The true first American edition. One of only a small number of copies extant (perhaps fifty copies or less). Octavo. viii, 303 (with "The End" on page 303). With 109 full-page plates inserted throughout, including two maps, as called for. Publisher's green cloth with front cover ruled in black and gilt. Paneled in gilt and lettered in black with gilt borders, with centered gilt device of jellyfish. Spine decoratively stamped in gilt and black, with the misprint "Sea" instead of "Seas." Rebacked with the original spine laid down and later green cloth reinforcing chipped original spine edges. Edges rubbed with some wear. Covers somewhat soiled and rubbed. Spine rubbed. Original endpapers present. Some moderate occasional foxing in text. Tape repairs in text to pages 81 and 95 with a few occasional marginal tears in text. Still, a very good copy of this rarity, most copies of which burned in the Great Boston Fire of 1872.

This copy has a special provenance evidenced by a penciled signature on the recto of the frontispiece. The name "John Mead Howells" is penciled in, and refers to William Dean Howells' son, who was a noted architect at the beginning of the twentieth century. The name in the book here is either John Mead's ownership signature or, more likely, William Dean Howells handwriting, signing the book to identify it as his son's or as a gift to him. An exceedingly rare book with a unique provenance.

Estimate: $7,000-up
Starting Bid: $5,500

Set of Signed Vonneguts

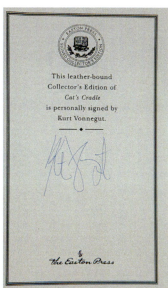

37142   Kurt Vonnegut, Jr. Nineteen Signed Leatherbound Editions, including: Six Signed First Editions and Thirteen Signed Editions. Norwalk: The Easton Press and Franklin Center: Franklin Library, [1990-2005]. Leather-bound editions, six of which are firsts. **All are signed by the author.** Publisher's full leather with gilt-stamped decoration and ruling to front and rear cover and gilt-stamped titles and decoration to spine. All edges gilt. Ribbon marker. All near fine.

Signed first editions: ***Bagombo Snuff Box***; ***Fates Worse Than Death***; ***Hocus Pocus***; ***Look at the Birdie***; ***Timequake***; ***While Mortals Sleep***.

Signed editions: ***Bluebeard***; ***Breakfast of Champions***; ***Cat's Cradle***; ***Galápagos***; ***God Bless You, Dr. Kevorkian***; ***God Bless You, Mr. Rosewater***; ***A Man Without a Country***; ***Mother Night***; ***Player Piano***; ***Slapstick***; ***Slaughterhouse-Five***; ***The Sirens of Titan***; ***Welcome to the Monkey House***.

Estimate: $2,000-up
Starting Bid: $1,000

First Edition of *The Time Machine*

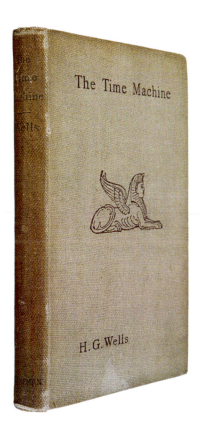

37143   H. G. Wells. *The Time Machine*. London: William Heinemann, 1895. First British edition (the American edition of the book preceded the British edition by a few weeks). Octavo. 152 pages, plus 16 pages of advertisements. Original gray cloth. First state cloth 'B1' binding (Currey). Decorative cover design and lettering stamped in purple. Spine darkened, mild soiling and rubbing to boards. Some foxing to the endpapers. Slightly cocked binding. A very good, tight, copy.

Currey, page 524. Hammond B1. Wells 4.

Estimate: $2,000-up
Starting Bid: $1,000

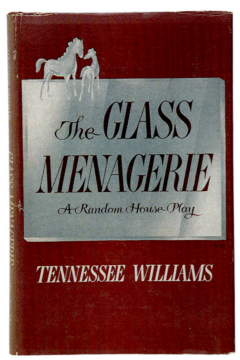

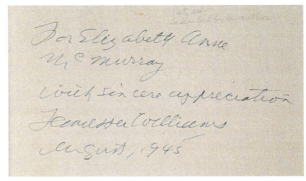

37144   **Tennessee Williams.** *The Glass Menagerie.* New York: Random House, [1945]. First edition, first printing. **Inscribed by Williams on front free endpaper, "For Elizabeth Anne / McMurray / with sincere appreciation / Tennessee Williams / August, 1945".** Octavo. 124 pages. Publisher's red cloth with modest wear to extremities and a small area of faint soiling to upper corner of front board. Mild toning to pages with a few tiny spots of scattered foxing to endpapers. Light wear to extremities of jacket with minor foxing to rear panel and a bit of sunning to spine. Included are two typed letters signed by prominent ABAA booksellers to a previous owner attesting to the authenticity of William's inscription and with mailing envelopes. Near fine. A lovely inscribed copy of this high spot in American theater.

Estimate: $1,500-up
Starting Bid: $750

END OF SESSION ONE

SESSION TWO

Heritage Live!™, Internet, Fax, and Mail Only Session
Wednesday, September 14, 2011 | 3:00PM CT | Dallas | Lots 37145 – 37428

A 19.5% Buyer's Premium ($14 minimum) Will Be Added To All Lots
To view full descriptions, enlargeable images and bid online, visit HA.com/6058

SPECIAL INTERNET BIDDING FEATURE

Online proxy bidding ends at HA.com two hours prior to the opening of the live auction. Check the Time Remaining on individual lots for details. After Internet proxy bidding closes, live bidding will take place through Heritage Live™, our bidding software that lets you bid live during the actual auction. Your secret maximum will compete against those bids, and win all ties. To maximize your chances of winning, enter realistic secret maximum bids before live bidding begins. (Important note: Due to software and Internet latency, bids placed through Live Internet Bidding may not register in time and those bidders could lose lots they would otherwise have won, so be sure to place your proxy bids in advance.)

37145 **Hubert Howe Bancroft.** *The Works of Hubert Howe Bancroft.* San Francisco: A. L. Bancroft, 1883-1890. First editions. Thirty-nine octavo volumes. Numerous maps, including many that fold out. Publisher's sheep with black gilt-lettered morocco spine labels. All edges marbled. General shelf wear to boards and extremities. Joints tender or partially split on some volumes with the majority being rebacked with original spines reattached. Some hinges reinforced. Scattered minor toning throughout the set, primarily to endpapers. Overall, a very good set of a monumental work. Graff 155. Howell 50. Howes B91.

Est.: $800-up
Start Bid: $400

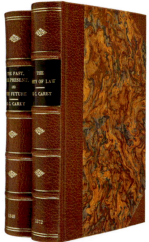

37146 **H. C. Carey. Two First Editions, Uniformly Bound,** including: *The Past, the Present, and the Future.* Philadelphia: Carey & Hart, 1848. First edition. Octavo. 472 pages (front blank, reckoned in the pagination, not present). [and:] *The Unity of Law; As Exhibited in the Relations of Physical, Social, mental, and Moral Science.* Philadelphia: Henry Carey Baird, 1872. First edition. Octavo. xxiv, 433, [1, blank], 24 [publisher's catalog], pages (missing the blank between the text and publisher's catalog). Uniformly bound in modern three-quarter morocco over marbled paper boards with gilt titles and decorative gilt stamping in compartments with four raised bands. Minor spotting to a few leaves in each book. Text edges dust-soiled. Near fine. Two works from a prominent economist who was once described as "the most original American political economist before Veblen."

Est.: $600-up
Start Bid: $300

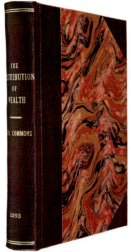

37147 **John R. Commons.** *The Distribution of Wealth.* New York: Macmillan and Co., 1893. First edition. Octavo. x, [2, Chart of Human Faculties], 258, [24, publisher's catalog] pages. Modern three-quarter crimson leather over marbled boards. Black ink college library stamp to title page and page 33. Embossed blindstamp from the Library Company of Philadelphia to the title page, page 129, and page 257. Some bottom corners of the text very lightly bumped. Otherwise, a near fine copy. Commons was a very influential economist, most notably regarding the concept of collective action.

Est.: $600-up
Start Bid: $300

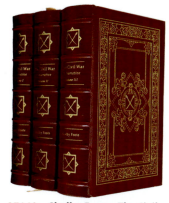

37148 **Shelby Foote.** *The Civil War. A Narrative.* Norwalk: The Easton Press, 1986. First Easton Press edition. **Signed by the author.** Three octavo volumes. Full red morocco. Mild scuffing to the bottom gilt edges. Near fine.

Est.: $600-up
Start Bid: $300

37149   John Charles Fremont. *Memoirs of My Life.* Chicago: Belford, Clarke, 1887. First edition. Quarto. 655 pages. Publisher's decorated cloth with light rubbing and abrading to extremities. A few small scuffs and stains to binding. Address label to front pastedown. Hinges slightly shaken. Engraved frontispiece with tissue guard and engraved plates. Folding map at rear. Minor foxing to fore-edge with a few lightly abraded edges. Very good.

Est.: $1,000-up
Start Bid: $500

37150   Godey's Lady's Book. Philadelphia: Louis A. Godey, 1835-1866. Eleven non-consecutive volumes. Numerous illustrations and engravings throughout, some hand-colored. Bound in contemporary fashion with typical shelfwear, foxing, and offsetting to images. Occasional loss to spines and corners. All volumes generally very good.

Est.: $600-up
Start Bid: $300

37151   [Ulysses. S. Grant]. *Personal Memoirs of U. S. Grant.* New York: Charles L. Webster, 1885-1886. First edition. Two octavo volumes. 584; 647 pages. Publisher's deluxe half-leather with gilt embossed seals to boards. General light rubbing with some abrading to extremities. Front free endpaper of Volume 1 cracking at gutter. Pages with minor toning. A very good set in this desirable binding.

Est.: $600-up
Start Bid: $300

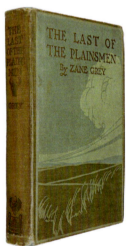

37152   Zane Grey. The Last of the Plainsmen. New York: Outing Publishing, 1908. First edition. **Signed by Grey and C. J. "Buffalo" Jones** on front free endpaper. Octavo. 314 pages. Publisher's binding, recased with original cloth laid down. General rubbing to cloth with light sunning and abrading to extremities. Front hinge reinforced. **Signed images of Grey and Jones mounted to pastedowns.** Period clippings affixed to preliminary pages. Frontispiece detached with clippings to recto. Ex-library with moderate evidence. Housed in a custom clamshell box with library pocket. Good.

Est.: $600-up
Start Bid: $300

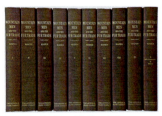

37153   LeRoy Hafen. *The Mountain Men and the Fur Trade of the Far West.* *Biographical Sketches of the Participants by Scholars of the Subject and with Introductions by the Editor.* Spokane: Arthur H. Clark, 2000-2004. Second printing, in an edition of 500 copies. Ten octavo volumes. Publisher's full brown cloth with gilt spine titles. Small stamped ownership seal to front free endpaper. Otherwise, near fine.

Est.: $600-up
Start Bid: $300

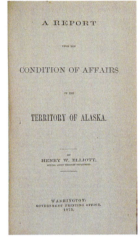

37154   [Hannibal Hamlin]. *Seal Fisheries in Alaska, 44th Congress, First Session, House of Representatives, Ex. Doc. No. 83* [bound with:] *A Report Upon the Condition of Affairs in the Territory of Alaska.* Washington: Government Printing Office, 1875-1876. **Signed "H. Hamlin" and with his "Library of Hannibal Hamlin" stamp on the title page.** Octavo. 201; 277 pages. Beautiful three-quarter morocco over marbled boards. Titles stamped in gilt between five raised bands on the spine. Marbled endpapers. All edges marbled. Fine condition.

Est.: $600-up
Start Bid: $300

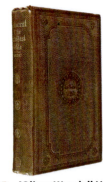

37155   [Oliver Wendell Holmes]. *The Autocrat of the Breakfast-Table.* Boston: Phillips, Sampson, 1858. First edition, first issue. **Autograph letter signed from Holmes** to publisher and dated 1867 tipped to front free endpaper. Octavo. 373 pages. Publisher's binding with abraded extremities. Spine ends lightly chipped. Front hinge cracking. Engraved half-title page. Catalog entries affixed to front pastedown. Very good.

Est.: $600-up
Start Bid: $300

37156   Herbert Hoover. *The Ordeal of Woodrow Wilson.* New York: McGraw-Hill, [1958]. First edition, limited to 500 numbered copies of which this is 388. **Signed by Hoover.** 318 pages. Publisher's binding and slipcase. Fine copy in a lightly rubbed and toned slipcase.

Est.: $600-up
Start Bid: $300

37157   Douglas MacArthur. *Reminiscences.* New York: McGraw-Hill, [1964]. First edition, limited to 1750 numbered copies of which this is 457. **Signed by MacArthur.** Octavo. 438 pages. Publisher's binding and slipcase. Minor rubbing and bumping to slipcase with one edge split. Near fine.

Est.: $600-up
Start Bid: $300

37158   David McCullough. Five Signed First Editions, including: *The Johnstown Flood.* [and:] *The Great Bridge.* [and:] *The Path Between the Seas.* [and:] *Mornings on Horseback.* [and:] *Truman.* All in near fine or better condition, all in dust jackets.
Est.: $600-up
Start Bid: $300

37159   John Muir. *The Mountains of California.* New York: The Century Co., 1894. First edition. Twelvemo. [iv], ix-[xvi], 381 pages. With fifty-three illustrations, many of them full-page, reckoned in the pagination. Publisher's light green cloth with gilt titles and decorative stamping in green and gilt. Top edge gilt. Minor edge wear. Some soiling to boards. Corners lightly rubbed. Some foxing, heaviest at endpapers. Bookplate to front pastedown. A tight, square copy in very good condition. Number 56 of the Zamorano 80.
Est.: $600-up
Start Bid: $300

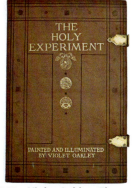

37160   Violet Oakley. *The Holy Experiment.* *A Message to the World from Pennsylvania.* [Philadelphia: Printed by the Author], 1922. Number 262 of 500 limited edition copies. Elephant folio. Unpaginated. With twenty (of twenty-two) lithographic plates of the author's mural work at the Senate Chambers of the State Capitol of Harrisburg, Pennsylvania (missing plates one and two). Publisher's brown leather titled in gilt and ruled and tooled in dark brown. Inside covers gilt. Minor wear to folder and interior text, else very good.
Est.: $600-up
Start Bid: $300

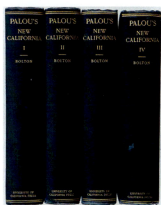

37161   Fray Francisco Palóu. *Historical Memoirs of New California*. Berkeley: University of California Press, 1926. Sesquicentennial edition. Four octavo volumes. Publisher's full blue cloth with gilt spine titles and ruling. Covers worn, rubbed at spine and turned corners. Light foxing, particularly to top edge. Bookplates to two volumes. Generally, all very good.
Est.: $600-up
Start Bid: $300

37162   Theodore Roosevelt. *The Rough Riders.* New York: Charles Scribner's Sons, 1899. First edition. **Signed by the author.** Octavo. 298 pages. Illustrated. Publisher's cloth with gilt-stamped titles and device on front cover and titles on spine. Top edge gilt, others uncut. Covers and extremities rubbed with small stains. Spine has minor loss at ends with staining. Front hinge beginning with rear weak. Very light toning to page edges. Generally very good.
Est.: $1,000-up
Start Bid: $500

37163   Theodore Roosevelt. *The Works of Theodore Roosevelt*. New York: Charles Scribner's Sons, 1906. Elkhorn Edition. One of 1,000 numbered copies, of which this is number 871. Twenty-three octavo volumes. Publisher's full burgundy buckram with paper spine title labels. Top edges gilt, others uncut. Shelfwear to boards and spines, with a few being torn at the head. Spine labels have some light staining and discoloration. Generally, a very good set.
Est.: $600-up
Start Bid: $300

37164   Hunter S. Thompson. *Fear and Loathing: On the Campaign Trail '72.* [San Francisco]: Straight Arrow Books, [1973]. First edition, first printing. **Signed by Thompson.** Octavo. 506 pages. Publisher's binding and dust jacket. Minor rubbing and abrading to cloth extremities with a slight spine lean. Jacket is lightly rubbed and edge worn with several small tears. Modest sunning to spine. Very good.
Est.: $600-up
Start Bid: $300

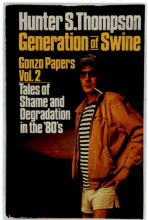

37165   Hunter S. Thompson. *Generation of Swine.* New York: Summit Books, [1988]. First edition, first printing. **Signed by Thompson.** Octavo. 304 pages. Publisher's binding and dust jacket. Mild toning to jacket with a touch of wear to tail of spine. Fine.
Est.: $600-up
Start Bid: $300

37166   Hunter S. Thompson. *Kingdom of Fear.* New York: Simon & Schuster, [2003]. First edition, first printing. **Signed by Thompson.** Octavo. 354 pages. Publisher's binding and dust jacket. Minor rubbing to jacket extremities. Near fine.

Est.: $600-up
Start Bid: $300

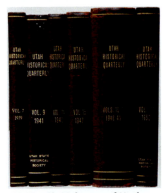

37167   Six Volumes of *Utah State Historical Society.* Salt Lake City: Utah State Historical Society, 1939-1950. Bound editions. Six octavo volumes. Illustrated with numerous plates and fold-out maps. Full leatherette with gilt-stamped titles on front and spine. General shelf wear and rubbing to extremities. Some have bookplates, stamps or owner's signature. Otherwise, very good.

Est.: $600-up
Start Bid: $300

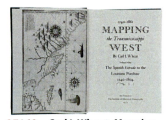

37168   Carl I. Wheat. *Mapping the Transmississippi West, 1540-1861.* [Storrs-Mansfield: Maurizio Martino, n.d.]. Reprint edition, limited to 350 copies. Five quarto volumes bound in six. Numerous folding maps and illustrations. Publisher's green buckram with gilt spine titles and ruling. Light rubbing to boards. Otherwise, near fine.

Est.: $600-up
Start Bid: $300

37169   Rigobert Bonne (1727-1795). A wonderful hand-colored engraving from *Atlas de Toutes les Parties Connues du Globe Terrestre...* by Raynal and Bonne. Geneva: 1780. Entitled *Le Nouveau Mexique, Avec La Partie Septentrionale De L'Ancien, ou De La Nouvelle Espagne*, the map depicts the Southwest with Baja California, Northern Mexico, Texas, Louisiana, and their waterways. In excellent condition with minor offsetting and fold lines. Visible area of print measures 8.75 x 12.5 inches, matted and framed to a measurement of 15.5. x 21.75 inches.

Est.: $600-up
Start Bid: $300

37170   John Thomson. Map of America. One large double-page hand-colored map: plate No. 52 depicting the North and South Americas, from Thomson's *New General Atlas.* Edinburgh: 1816. Generally in very good condition with some minor foxing, a few small edge tears, some of which are reinforced with tape on reverse. Light dampstaining at bottom of reverse with a repair measuring 1.25 x 2 inches at the British Isles. Measures 21.25 x 23.75 inches.

Est.: $600-up
Start Bid: $300

37171   Victor Levasseur. *Amérique Septentrionale.* A beautifully hand-colored engraving depicting North America with supplemental illustrations in the decorative margins. From *Atlas National Illustré des 86 Departments et des Possessions De La France.* Paris: c. 1860. Some very light toning and crinkling to edges with dampstaining to bottom half of the margins, only somewhat affecting border. Otherwise, very good. Measures approximately 14 x 20.5 inches.

Est.: $600-up
Start Bid: $300

37172   John Thomson. Maps of *Spanish North America.* Two large double-page hand-colored maps: plate No. 58 depicting Mexico, plate No. 59 Central America, from Thomson's *New General Atlas.* Edinburgh: 1816. In very good condition with some minor foxing and spotting throughout, a few small edge tears, and toned edges. Folded and reinforced as issued. Measures 21.25 x 28.75 inches.

Est.: $600-up
Start Bid: $300

37173   Roy Chapman Andrews. *The New Conquest of Central Asia. A Narrative of the Explorations of the Central Asiatic Expeditions in Mongolia and China, 1921-1930.* New York: American Museum of Natural History, 1932. First edition. 678 pages. Numerous photographic reproductions. Three fold-out maps at rear. Publisher's orange cloth with black titles and ruling to front cover and spine. Some shelfwear to boards and corners with slight sunning to spine. Very good.

Est.: $600-up
Start Bid: $300

37174   Thomas Baines.
Explorations in South-West Africa.
*Being an Account of a Journey
in the Years 1861 and 1862 from
Walvisch Bay, on the Western Coast,
to Lake Ngami and the Victoria
Falls.* London: Longman, Green,
Longman, Roberts, and Green,
1864. First edition. 535 pages.
Chromolithograph frontispiece
with numerous engravings and
three fold-out maps. Modern binding of gray over green cloth with
paper label on spine. Frontis loose
at foot. Overall, a near fine copy.
Est.: $600-up
Start Bid: $300

37175   C. G. Bruce. *Twenty Years
in the Himalaya.* London: Edward
Arnold, 1910. First edition. Octavo.
335 pages. Sixty illustrations and
a folding map. Publisher's full
red cloth over boards with gilt-
stamped titles and ruling to spine.
Rubbing to extremities. Spine
somewhat faded. Slightly cocked.
Some light foxing throughout,
primarily to page edges. Embossed
stamp to front free endpaper and
Rowland Ward sticker to front
pastedown. A very good copy of a
scarce volume.
Est.: $600-up
Start Bid: $300

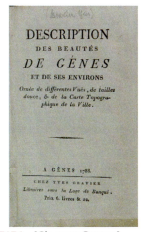

37176   [Giacomo Brusco].
*Description Des Beautés de Génes
et de ses Environs.* Genoa: Chez
Yves Gravier, 1788. Later printing of the 1781 edition. Octavo.
268 pages. Sixteen of seventeen
engraved plates called for (lacking plate opposite p. 12), most of
which are folding. Contemporary
mottled leather binding. Marbled
endpapers. Titles and floral vignettes stamped in gilt on the
spine. Moderate wear, particularly
to extremities. One plate almost
detached. Otherwise, very good.
Est.: $1,000-up
Start Bid: $500

37177   H. Capello and R. Ivens.
*From Benguella to the Territory
of Yacca. Description of a Journey
into Central and West Africa.*
London: Sampson Low, Marston,
Searle, & Rivington, 1882. First
edition. Two octavo volumes. lii,
395; xv, 350, 32 [publisher's cata-
log] pages. Engraved illustrations
throughout both volumes. Three
folding maps (two of which with
taped repairs at the folds). Original
light brown pictorial cloth bindings
with titles stamped in gilt. Some
minor repairs to bindings, with
new endpapers. Text block slightly
cocked. Library stamps throughout. Otherwise, a very good copy
of this scarce work.
Est.: $600-up
Start Bid: $300

37178   John Hunt. *The Ascent
of Everest.* [London]: Hodder
and Stoughton, 1953. Second
impression. **Signed by the au-
thor, Edmund Hillary, George
Lowe, Charles Wylie, Michael
Westmacott, John Jackson,
Alfred Gregory, George Band,
Michael Ward and three others**.
Octavo. 299 pages. Illustrated.
Publisher's binding with dust
jacket. Boards show shelfwear and
at corners. Light foxing to edges.
Price-clipped jacket has wear, par-
ticularly at edges. Otherwise, very
good.
Est.: $1,000-up
Start Bid: $500

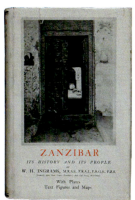

37179   W. H. Ingrams. *Zanzibar.*
Its History and its People. London:
H. F. & G. Witherby, [1931]. First
edition. Octavo. 527 pages.
Numerous illustrations and two
maps. Publisher's red cloth with
blindstamped borders with gilt-
stamped titles and ruling on spine.
Dust jacket. Top edge gilt. Boards
retouched with paint. Rubbed dust
jacket has small tears. Generally
very good.
Est.: $600-up
Start Bid: $300

37180   W. Edward Oswell.
*William Cotton Oswell. Hunter
and Explorer. The Story of His Life
with Certain Correspondence and
Extracts From the Private Journal
of David Livingstone, Hitherto
Unpublished.* London: William
Heinemann, 1900. First edition.
Two octavo volumes. [i]-xxiv, [1]-
267 pages; [i]-xi, [1]-289 pages.
Frontispiece portraits, maps, and
illustrations. Publisher's buckram
with gilt-stamped titles on spine.
Pages uncut. Spines faded. Spines
somewhat cocked. Page edges
slightly toned. Shelf wear. Very
good.
Est.: $800-up
Start Bid: $400

37181   Theodore Roosevelt.
**Four Hunting and Travel
Volumes**, including: *American
Big-Game Hunting.* Edinburgh:
David Douglas, 1893. Scottish
edition. [and:] *Hunting Trips of a
Ranchman: Sketches of Sport on the
Northern Cattle Plains.* New York:
G. P. Putnam's Sons, 1899. Later
edition. [and:] *Outdoor Pastimes
of an American Hunter.* New York:
Charles Scribner's Sons, 1905.
Later edition. [and:] *Through the
Brazilian Wilderness.* New York:
Charles Scribner's Sons, 1914. First
edition. All books generally very
good in publisher's bindings.
Est.: $600-up
Start Bid: $300

37182 **Captain L. Sitgreaves.** *Report of an Expedition Down the Zuni and Colorado Rivers.* Washington: Beverley Tucker, Senate Printer, 1854. First edition, second printing. Octavo. 198 pages plus numerous engraved inserted plates, as follows: twenty-three ethnographic plates, six plates of mammals, five ornithological plates, twenty-one reptile plates, three fish engravings, and twenty-one botanical plates. Lacking map at rear, with only remnants present in the gutter. Chipping and sunning to spine cloth, with a vertical tear near the tail extending almost all the way across the spine. Moderate wear to cloth edges. Corners bumped. Spotting to text edges. Scattered foxing, including to some plates. Ownership inscription to front free endpaper. Good.

Est.: $600-up
Start Bid: $300

37183 **John Hanning Speke.** *Journal of the Discovery of the Source of the Nile.* Edinburgh: William Blackwood, 1864. Second edition. Octavo. xxxi, [1], 658 pages. Contemporary full leather by Bickers and Son. Engraved frontispiece and plates. Folding map at rear. Minor rubbing and scuffing to binding with front board and free endpaper detached. Lightly sunned spine with some offsetting to front board. School award bookplate. Textblock clean with mild toning to page edges. Very good.

Est.: $1,000-up
Start Bid: $500

37184 **[Henry M. Stanley].** *The American Testimonial Banquet to Henry M. Stanley In Recognition of His Historic Achievements in the Cause of Humanity Science & Civilization and a Greeting to His Chief Officers...May 30 1890.* London: Privately printed, 1890. First edition. Large octavo. Original blind stamped full calf over beveled boards with an American eagle atop a shield emblazoned with "Stanley" with floral devices in each corner. Twelve stiff gilt-edge cardboard pages with both text and six silver gelatin mounted photographic portraits mounted in blind stamped mats. Silk covered hinges. Decorative endpapers. Moderate crazing to the leather with modest wear at the extremities. Spine re-backed. Externally very good condition with fine contents and photographs.

Est.: $800-up
Start Bid: $400

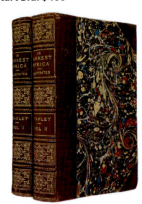

37185 **Henry M. Stanley.** *In Darkest Africa.* New York: Charles Scribner's Sons, 1890. Two octavo volumes. Many illustrations. Map pocket to each volume. Three folding maps. Half morocco over marbled boards. All edges gilt. Some scuffing to the extremities. Overall, a clean copy in very good condition.

Est.: $600-up
Start Bid: $300

37186 **Henry M. Stanley.** *In Darkest Africa.* New York: Charles Scribner's Sons, 1890. First American edition. Two octavo volumes. Three folding maps in the rear pockets. Brown half morocco over marbled boards. All edges gilt. Lightly rubbed edges. Mild toning throughout. An attractive, very good set of Stanley's great adventure across the African continent.

Est.: $1,000-up
Start Bid: $500

37187 **Three Books on Africa's Waterways**, including: **S. W. Baker.** *Exploration of the Nile Tributaries of Abyssinia...* Hartford: O. D. Case, 1868. First edition. [and:] **David and Charles Livingstone.** *Narrative of an Expedition to the Zambesi and Its Tributaries; and of the Discovery of the Lakes Shirwa and Nyassa.* 1858-1864. London: John Murray, 1865. First edition. [and:] **Frank Oates.** *Matabele Land and The Victoria Falls.* London: Kegan Paul, Trench, and Co., 1889. Second edition. All volumes generally very good.

Est.: $600-up
Start Bid: $300

37188 **[Henry St. John Bolingbroke].** *Letters on the Spirit of Patriotism: on the Idea of a Patriot King: and on the State of Parties, at the Accession of King George the First.* London: Printed for A. Millar, 1749. First authorized edition. Octavo. xii, 9-251 pages. Later three-quarter brown leather over marbled boards with gilt floral stamping on the spine in compartments with five raised bands, and a gilt-lettered black morocco spine title label. Marbled endpapers. All edges stained black. Minor abrading to the binding. Mostly unobtrusive minor foxing and spotting. Very good. Written for private circulation in 1738 for the benefit of Frederick, Prince of Wales, and later distributed in an edited edition until Bolingbroke bought up these unauthorized copies and had them burned. He edited this edition and had it printed in 1749.

Est.: $600-up
Start Bid: $300

37189 **[Chinese Block Book].** **Chinese Wood Block Book Featuring Illustrations of Objects in the Book of Odes.** [Tokyo: n.d., 20th C.]. Three volumes [10 by 7.25 inches] with approximately thirty-six accordion-folded leaves in each volume. Complete in seven chapters in three volumes (Vol. I: Chap. 1-2; Vol. II: Chap. 3-4; Vol. III: Chap. 5-7). Stab sewn bindings of blue patterned paper, mounted label printed in black on the covers.

Est.: $600-up
Start Bid: $300

37190 [Chinese Calligraphy]. **Original Rubbings from Engraved Stones.** [N.p.: n.d., 20 C.]. Calligraphy by Yan Lugong, [13.75 by 6.75 inches] with thirty-two individual panels on sixteen accordion-folded leaves. Ownership seal in red. Bound between cedar boards with manuscript paper label somewhat perishing and also labeled directly on the wood in calligraphy.

Est.: $600-up
Start Bid: $300

37191 [Chinese History]. **Calligraphic Manuscript Record of Daling. A Local History or Gazetteer of Daling, Present-Day Guangdong Province.** [N.p.: 1916]. Calligraphy by Han Houlin [copyist, with his seals in red ink], this is a brush and ink manuscript edition complete in two large octavo volumes [11.25 by 7.25 inches] of fifty-two and forty accordion-folded leaves.

Est.: $600-up
Start Bid: $300

37192 [Chinese Manuscript]. **Calligraphic Manuscript of Chinese Divination Manual with Moving Volvelles.** Subjects include Astrology and Palmistry among others. [N.p.: n.d., mid to late 19th C.]. Calligraphy by an unknown copyist, this is a brush and ink manuscript [10 by 6.5 inches] of approximately fifty-two accordion-folded leaves. Stab sewn binding of hand-made paper. Soiled and rubbed.

Est.: $1,000-up
Start Bid: $500

37193 [Chinese Philosophy]. **Chinese Wood Block Printed Book of Chinese Philosopher and Sage, Mencius (f. 4th Century BC).** [N.p., n.d., 19th-20th C.]. Two volumes [12 by 8 inches] with eighty-four and seventy-two accordion-folded leaves. Chapters 5-6 and 11-12 of a larger work. Stab sewn binding of calligrapher's waste or practice paper over orange paper wrappers, labeled in black ink on the covers on mounted label.

Est.: $600-up
Start Bid: $300

37194 [Chinese Philosophy]. **Calligraphic Manuscript of Chinese Philosophy. Questions and Answers from Master Cold Cliff (Zheng Wei Shu, B. 1543; D. 1621).** [N.p.: n.d., early 20th C.]. Calligraphy by an unknown copyist, this is a brush and ink manuscript [11.75 by 8.25 inches] of forty-eight accordion-folded leaves. Stab sewn binding of hand-made paper (calligrapher's waste), paper title label in black ink mounted on the cover.

Est.: $600-up
Start Bid: $300

37195 [Chinese Poetry]. **Calligraphic Manuscript of Various Tang Dynasty Poets [7th to 10th C.].** [N.p.: n.d., ca. 1910]. Kaishu-style calligraphy by Han Houlin [copyist, with his seals in red ink], this is a brush and ink manuscript edition complete in two octavo volumes [10 by 6 inches] of thirty-six accordion-folded leaves per volume.

Est.: $600-up
Start Bid: $300

37196 *Chronicon Preciosum: or, an Account of English Money, the Price of Corn and Other Commodities, For the last 600 Years.* London: Printed for Charles Harper, 1707. First edition. Small octavo. [xiv], 181 pages, plus Index and 5 pages of ads. Modern half leather over marble paper boards. Occasional foxing and mild dampstaining. A near fine, tight copy. With the octagonal "Museum Britannicum" rubber stamp throughout, indicating that this book once belonged to Sir Hans Sloane (1660-1750) whose entire collection was bequeathed to the state and which became the foundation for the British Museum.

Est.: $600-up
Start Bid: $300

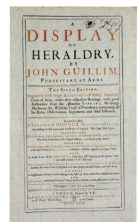

37197 **John Guillim.** *A Display of Heraldry.* London: Printed by T. W. for R. and J. Bonwicke and R. Wilkin, 1724. [10], 20, 460 pages. Folio. Many engravings. Recased to style, retaining original calf boards and backstrip. Binding scuffed and bumped. Hinges reinforced. Armorial bookplate. Overall, a very good, tight, square copy.

Est.: $600-up
Start Bid: $300

37198 **John Maynard Keynes.** *Essays in Biography.* London: Macmillan, 1933. First edition. Octavo. 318 pages. Eight plates. Publisher's binding. Somewhat rubbed at extremities. Corners slightly bumped. Lightly toned edges. Owner's signature. Very good. [and:] **John Maynard Keynes.** *How to Pay for the War.* A *Radical Plan for the Chancellor of the Exchequer.* London: Macmillan, 1940. First edition. Octavo. 88 pages. Publisher's printed paper over boards. Wear to extremities. Price removed on front with abrasion. Slight bubbling to pastedowns. Mild toning. Bookseller's ticket. Otherwise, very good.

Est.: $600-up
Start Bid: $300

37199 **John Stuart Mill. Three Works**, including: *Principles of Political Economy.* Boston: Charles C. Little & James Brown, 1848. First American edition. Two small quarto volumes. [and:] *The Positive Philosophy of Auguste Comte.* Boston: William V. Spencer, 1866. First American edition. [and:] *The Subjection of Women.* New York: D. Appleton, 1869. Early edition. All generally very good.

Est.: $600-up
Start Bid: $300

37200 **Sylvanvs Morgan**. *The Sphere of Gentry*: Deduced from the Principles of Nature, an Historical and Genealogical Work, of Arms and Blazon; in Four Books... London: William Leybourn, 1661. First edition. Folio. [xviii], [1]-120, [ii], 1-118, [119]-121, 4-119, [i], 1-116 pages, [19] index. Additional illustrated title page; Numerous plates including frontispiece on verso of title page, head and tail pieces, initials, and full-page heraldic engravings. Contemporary calf binding rebacked over boards ruled in blind. Spine has five raised bands blindruled with gilt-titled morocco label. Heavily worn covers with some exposure to corners. Hinges starting. Toning and chipping to pastedowns, preliminaries, terminals and page edges. Some light offsetting to text and illustrations. Slightly trimmed. Generally very good.

Est.: $600-up
Start Bid: $300

37201 **Walter Scott**. *The Border Antiquities of England and Scotland*; Comprising Specimens of Architecture and Sculpture, and Other Vestiges of Former Ages, Accompanied by Descriptions, Together with Illustrations of Remarkable Incidents in Border History and Tradition, and Original Poetry. London: Longman, Hurst, Rees, Orme, and Brown, 1814. First edition. Large paper edition, with plates on Indian paper. Two quarto volumes. [i]-cxxvii, [1]-92 pages; [93]-209, [i]-cii pages. Two engraved title pages with ninety-three engraved plates. Bound in half white leather over white cloth with black spine titles. Top edge gilt. Rubbed boards have light soiling with shelfwear and bumped bottom corners. Light foxing throughout. Minor dampstaining to head of rear pages of volume one. Very good.

Est.: $600-up
Start Bid: $300

37202 **Two First Edition Books About Gold**, including: **Michel Chevalier**. *On the Probable Fall in the Value of Gold*. New York: D. Appleton, 1859. First American edition. Octavo. 211 pages. Publisher's binding with minor rubbing to cloth extremities. Sunning to spine and offsetting to front board. Mild toning to pages with light foxing to preliminary pages. [and:] **Alexander von Humboldt and Francois Grimaudet**. *The Fluctuations of Gold and The Law of Payment*. New York: Cambridge Encyclopedia, 1900. First edition. Octavo. 45, 76 pages. Publisher's binding with lightly rubbed extremities. Both volumes in very good or better condition.

Est.: $600-up
Start Bid: $300

37203 *Testamenti Veteris Biblia Sacra Sive Libri Canonici Priscae Judaeorum Ecclesiae a Deo Traditi Latini Recens Ex Hebraeo Sacti*. London: Excudebat Henricus Midletonus, impensis .W. N[orton], M. D. LXXXV [1585]. Octavo. [14], 173, [3]; 230 [i.e. 234], [2]; 160; 251, [1]; 144, 209-224; [20], 424 pages. Nineteenth century half-leather, rubbed and abraded, with spine perishing and boards detached. Lacking rear free endpaper. Textblock appears trimmed, slightly affecting a few headers and page numbers. Notations to title page and occasionally throughout. Heavily abraded preliminary pages, marginally affecting text of final leaf. General mild toning to pages with a few abraded corners and fore-edges. Good candidate for rebinding in fair condition.

Est.: $600-up
Start Bid: $300

37204 *The New Testament of our Lord and Savior Jesus Christ*. In Sgau Karen. Maulmain: American Mission Press, 1850. Second edition. Octavo. Contemporary full sheep with gilt ruling and faded gilt-stamped titles on spine. Front hinge broken with rear starting. Spine cracked with loss at tail. Boards and extremities well worn with corners exposed. Endpapers loose at foot. Library stamp to preliminary and title page. Significant dampstaining with soiling to preliminaries and terminals. Toning and bowing at page edges. A good copy of an scarce early edition.

Est.: $600-up
Start Bid: $300

37205 **Andream Carolum**. *C. B. D. Memorabilia Ecclesiastica seculi á Nato Christo Decimi Septiimi, Juxta Annorum Seriem Notata, et Convenienti Ordine Digesta...* Tubingae: Johannis Georgii Cotte, 1697-1698. Two square quarto volumes. 1 blank leaf, title leaf, [4, 5, 4], 1-1188 pages, [18, 74, 69], 5 blank; 1 blank leaf, title leaf, [2], 1-456 pages, title leaf, secondary title leaf, 4, [1], 1 blank, 1-942 pages, 17 index, 43 index, 24 apologeticus, 51 index rerum et materium, 1 blank, 2 erratorum, 2 blank. Bound in full vellum with yapp edges and exposed exterior bands at gutters. Hand-painted titles and decoration at head of spines. Pages trimmed with all edges black. Covers rather rubbed and soiled with wear. Turn-ins have knocked up pastedowns with some paper loss and worming. Very minor worming to preliminaries and titles of Volume One. Some light foxing to page edges. Occasional minor pencil marking to margins, not affecting the text. Very good or better copies of a scarce book.

Est.: $600-up
Start Bid: $300

37206 **Liturgical Calendar Page From a French Book of Hours Listing the Saints' Days to Be Observed For the Month of January, Ca. 1465**. 5 x 7 inches. Vellum. Single columns on the recto and verso in Gothic liturgical book script. Slight toning at edges. Fine.

Est.: $600-up
Start Bid: $300

37207 **Manly P. Hall.** *Lectures on Ancient Philosophy. An Introduction to the Study and Application of Rational Procedure.* Los Angeles: The Hall Publishing Company, 1929. First edition. **Signed by the author.** Quarto. 471 pages. Full brown morocco over boards. Front joint splitting. Scuffing the chipping to extremities. Over all, a very good, bright copy.

Est.: $600-up
Start Bid: $300

37208 **Charles G. Herbermann, et al, editors.** *The Catholic Encyclopedia. An International Work of Reference on the Constitution, Doctrine, Discipline, and History of the Catholic Church.* New York: Robert Appleton Company, [1907]. Sixteen large quarto volumes, plus the slightly smaller supplemental volume (1922). Publisher's three-quarter tan leather over coarse grain cloth with gilt spine titles and blind-stamping in compartments inside five raised bands. Top edges gilt. Some abrading to the leather of some volumes. Some corners exposed. Minor shelf wear otherwise. Some spotting to cloth of the supplemental volume. A sturdy, substantial, near fine set.

Est.: $600-up
Start Bid: $300

37209 **[Illuminated Manuscript]. Illuminated Manuscript Leaf from a Book of Hours.** [Northern France, n.d., ca. 1475]. Manuscript on vellum, two sides with sixteen lines of text on each, with six one-line initials in colors and gold on the recto, and five one-line initials in colors and gold on the verso , with fine foliated border to one side of text in colors. Pigments are likely mineral, probably cinnabar, malachite, and lapis, and both gold ink and gold leaf are utilized. Latin text from the penitential psalms.

Est.: $600-up
Start Bid: $300

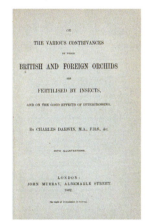

37210 **Charles Darwin.** *On the Various Contrivances by Which British and Foreign Orchids are Fertilised by Insects....* London: John Murray, 1862. First edition, first issue. Octavo. vi, 365, [1] pages, plus 32-page publisher's advertisements dated December, 1861. Illustrations throughout, one folding plate. Original gilt-stamped plum cloth. Approximately top two inches and bottom two inches of spine perished; extremities worn. Hinges cracked. Final leaf of publisher ads detached but present. Good. Scarce.

Est.: $600-up
Start Bid: $300

37211 **R. Lydekker.** *The Great and Small Game of Europe, Western & Northern Asia, and America. Their Distribution, Habits, and Structure.* London: Rowland Ward, 1901. **One of five hundred numbered copies signed by the publisher, of which this is number 9.** Quarto. 445 pages. Eight hand-colored plates with numerous reproductions and illustrations. Publisher's green cloth with gilt-stamped titles and ruling to front cover and spine. Shelf wear to extremities with rubbed spine and corners. Some light foxing to a few plates. Armorial bookplate on front pastedown and blindstamp to front free endpaper. A very good copy of a scarce volume by the the famed British Naturalist.

Est.: $1,000-up
Start Bid: $500

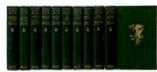

37212 **John Muir.** *The Writings of John Muir.* Boston and New York: Houghton Mifflin, [1916-1924]. Sierra edition. Ten octavo volumes. With illustrations throughout. Publisher's full green cloth with gilt-stamped poppies decoration on front and title with ruling to spine. Top edge gilt. Covers and extremities somewhat rubbed, mostly at spines and corners. Very good.

Est.: $600-up
Start Bid: $300

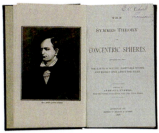

37213 **Americus Symmes.** *The Symmes Theory of Concentric Spheres.* Louisville: Bradley & Gilbert, 1878. [bound with:] **[Robert Paltock].** *The Life and Adventures of Peter Wilkins a Cornish Man.* London: George Routledge and Sons, [n.d.]. Octavo. Buckram over boards. Rubber stamp of previous owner. Very good.

Est.: $600-up
Start Bid: $300

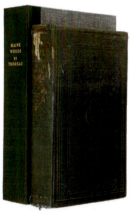

37214 **Henry D. Thoreau.** *The Maine Woods.* Boston: Ticknor and Fields, 1864. First edition, first issue with 24-page catalogue at rear dated April, 1864. Publisher's textured cloth with blind-stamped borders and centered wreath on both covers. Gilt spine titles. Custom clamshell case with leather spine and gilt titles. Boards rubbed with dampstaining affecting faded top third, making the cloth a bit soft in the area, and affecting the endpapers. Spine has some loss at title, near joints, and at foot. Minor foxing and toning. Text has occasional offsetting. Generally very good.

Est.: $600-up
Start Bid: $300

37215 **Three Books on the Western Canadian and Alaskan Wilderness**, including: **Harry A. Auer.** *Camp Fires in the Yukon.* Cincinnati: Stewart & Kidd Company, 1916. First edition. Thomas Martindale's copy. [and:] **John P. Holman.** *Sheep and Bear Trails. A Hunter's Wandering in Alaska and British Columbia.* New York: Frank Walters, 1933. **One of seventy-five numbered copies signed by the author, of which this is number 63.** [and:] **Charles Sheldon.** *The Wilderness of the Upper Yukon...* New York: Charles Scribner's Sons, 1911. First edition. All volumes very good in publisher's bindings.

Est.: $800-up
Start Bid: $400

37216 **Major G. H. "Andy" Anderson.** *African Safaris.* Kenya: Privately Printed, [c. 1946]. First edition. Octavo. xvi, 173 pages. Illustrated (lacking three plates). Publisher's green cloth with titles printed in white on the front board and spine. Binding soiled with scattered insect spotting. Contents sound. Some rubbing and abrading to spine cloth. A good copy of this scarce work.

Est.: $600-up
Start Bid: $300

37217 **Peter Hathaway Capstick.** *The Capstick Collector's Library,* including: *Death in the Lonely Land; Death in the Silent Places; The Last Ivory Hunter; Safari: The Last Adventure; Peter Capstick's Africa; Sands of Silence; Maneaters; Death in the Dark Continent; Last Horizons; Death in the Long Grass.* Lyon: The Derrydale Press, [1990]. **One of 500 specially bound sets for Safari Club International's Silver Anniversary Special Edition. One of 2,500 numbered copies signed by the author, of which this is number 2,097.** Ten octavo volumes. Illustrated by Dino Paravano. Publisher's full blue leather with silver and red titles and decorative stamping to front cover and spine. All edges silver. Near fine.

Est.: $600-up
Start Bid: $300

37218 **R. R. M. Carpenter.** *Game Trails From Alaska to Africa.* N.p.: Privately printed, [1944]. First collected edition limited to 50 numbered copies, of which this is number 37. **Inscribed.** Octavo. Two parts in one volume. xii, 180; 56 pages. Thirty-nine photographic plates and two maps. Original light brown full morocco with gilt device on the front board and gilt-stamped spine titles. Joints modestly worn with some fading to spine. Contents bright with hinges starting. Else a handsome copy in very good condition.

Est.: $600-up
Start Bid: $300

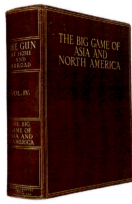

37219 **D. Carruthers, P. B. Van Der Byl, R. L. Kennion, J. G. Millais, H. Frank Wallace, Ford G. Barclay.** *The Gun at Home and Abroad: The Big Game of Asia and North America.* London: The London & Counties Press Association, Ltd., 1915. One of 500 copies produced as part of a set, of which this is number 349. Large quarto. 433 pages. Frontispiece, thirteen plates, and numerous other illustrations. Full leather with gilt-stamped titles and ruling to front cover and spine. Top edge gilt. Other edges uncut. Shelfwear to extremities. Light toning to page edges. Very good.

Est.: $600-up
Start Bid: $300

37220 **Douglas Carruthers.** *Unknown Mongolia. A Record of Travel and Exploration in North-West Mongolia and Dzungaria.* London: Hutchinson & Co., 1913. First edition. Two octavo volumes. xviii, 318; x, 319-659 pages. With 168 illustrations, panoramas and diagrams, and six maps of which four are fold-out. Publisher's blue cloth with gilt-stamped titles. Top edges gilt. Light shelfwear and slightly toned spines. Slight scattered foxing throughout and contemporary gift inscription in each volume. Else very good condition.

Est.: $600-up
Start Bid: $300

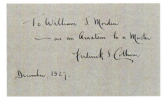

37221 **Frederick S. Colburn.** *The Unbelievable Game Country.* [N.p.]: Privately Printed, 1927. First edition. **Inscribed by the author to William J. Morden.** Large quarto. 181 pages. Numerous photographic reproductions and a map. Blue paper boards with gilt-stamped front title and blindstamped archer with white parchment spine and gilt tiles and ruling. Uncut fore-edge and bottom edge. Boards slightly rubbed with exposed boards at corners. Endpapers show glue shadow. Page edges lightly toned. Morden's bookplate. Generally near fine.

Est.: $800-up
Start Bid: $400

37222 **Henry Zouch Darrah.** *Sport in the Highlands of Kashmir. Being a Narrative of an Eight Months' Trip in Baltistan and Ladak, and a Lady's Experiences in the Latter Country; Together With Hints for the Guidance of Sportsmen.* London: Rowland Ward, 1898. First edition. Octavo. xviii, 506 pages. With fifty-two illustrations, two folding maps, as called for, in pocket mounted to the inside rear cover. Publisher's burgundy cloth with gilt spine titles and white front titles. Re-backed with a portion of the original spine laid down. Light shelf wear to boards. Contents sound. Near fine.

Est.: $600-up
Start Bid: $300

37223 **Elim Demidoff, Prince San Donato.** *Hunting Trips in the Caucasus.* London: Rowland Ward, 1898. First edition. Octavo. 319 pages. With ninety-six illustrations and map. Publisher's light blue cloth with titles stamped in gilt. Light browning to spine and boards with modest soiling. Contents bright, crisp and in very good condition.

Est.: $600-up
Start Bid: $300

37224 **R. H. W. Dunlop.** *Hunting in the Himalaya.* London: Richard Bentley, 1860. First edition. Octavo. 318 pages. Illustrated with four tinted lithographs. One folding map. Original brown cloth with vignette stamped in gilt on the front board and titles stamped in gilt on the spine. Rebound with new endpapers, else a fine copy.

Est.: $600-up
Start Bid: $300

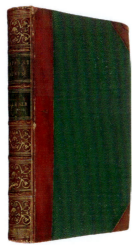

37225 **Henry Faulkner.** *Elephant Haunts: Being a Sportsman's Narrative of the Search for Doctor Livingstone, with Scenes of Elephant, Buffalo, and Hippopotamus Hunting.* London: Hurst and Blackett, 1868. First edition. Octavo. 325 pages. Half red calf over faux green morocco boards. Five raised bands, six compartments, two morocco labels, with gilt stamping, ruling and titles to spine. Marbled endpapers and boards. Shelfwear to spine and covers with bumped corners. Light foxing to preliminaries and terminals. Few small tears to text. Very good.

Est.: $1,000-up
Start Bid: $500

37226 **Major W. Robert Foran.** *Kill: or Be Killed. The Rambling Reminiscences of an Amateur Hunter.* London: Hutchinson & Co., 1933. First edition. Octavo. 320, [12, publisher's catalog] pages. Illustrated with photographs by the author and others. Original black cloth with titles stamped in gilt on the spine. Boards with only modest shelf wear. Contents with some slight toning. Else fine.

Est.: $600-up
Start Bid: $300

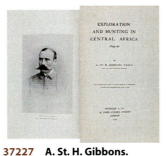

37227 **A. St. H. Gibbons.** *Exploration and Hunting in Central Africa 1895-96.* London: Methuen & Co., 1898. First edition. Octavo. Octavo. xi, 408, 48 [publisher's catalog] pages. With eight full-page illustrations by C. Whymper, twenty-five photographs and a folding map. Publisher's blue cloth with gilt titles and decorative stamping. Boards worn at the extremities, spine panel slightly blistered. Contents with light scattered foxing and toned endpapers. Fold-out map has long closed tear where it connects to the binding, though still attached. Gift inscription. Generally very good.

Est.: $600-up
Start Bid: $300

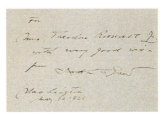

37228 **J. C. Grew.** *Sport and Travel in the Far East.* Boston: Houghton Mifflin Company, 1910. First edition. **Inscribed by the author to Mrs. Theodore Roosevelt, Jr.** and with latter's bookplate on the front pastedown. Octavo. 264 pages. Illustrated. Publisher's blue-green cloth with gilt titles and black decorative stamping. In a modern cloth covered slipcase. Fine.

Est.: $600-up
Start Bid: $300

37229 **Zane Grey. Two Books on Fishing,** including: *Tales of the Angler's Eldorado, New Zealand.* New York: Harper & Brothers, 1926. Very good in worn dust jacket. [and:] *Tales of Swordfish and Tuna.* 1927. A fine copy, lacking the dust jacket. Both first editions.

Est.: $600-up
Start Bid: $300

37230 **Captain William Cornwallis Harris.** *The Wild Sports of Southern Africa; Being the Narrative of a Hunting Expedition from the Cape of Good Hope, through the Territories of the Chief Moselekatse, to the Tropic of Capricorn.* London: Henry G. Bohn, 1852. Fifth edition. Octavo. 359 pages. Twenty-six hand-colored plates, including the frontispiece and vignette title page. Folding map at rear. Half bound in green morocco with gilt ruling over animal print cloth. Blindstamped device to front cover. Five raised gilt-tooled bands with six ruled compartments with gilt stamping and titles on spine. Marbled endpapers and page edges. Tissue guards present. Some shelfwear. Hinges somewhat exposed. Overall, a beautiful illustrated edition.

Est.: $600-up
Start Bid: $300

37231   Captain William Cornwallis Harris. *The Wild Sports of Southern Africa.* London: William Pickering, 1841. Third edition. Octavo. Octavo. xvi, 359, [1, publisher's ad] pages. Twenty-six hand-colored plates and one map. Three-quarter green leather over marbled paper boards with five raised spine bands and gilt titles and rules in compartments. Marbled endpapers. All edges gilt. Light foxing to the preliminary pages, else a handsome copy in fine condition.

Est.: $800-up
Start Bid: $400

37232   Alphons Hoch, editor. *International Sport: North American Big Game Hunters.* London and Munich: Houbard & Co., [1963-64]. Edition de luxe, one of two hundred and fifty numbered copies, of which this is number 113. Unpaginated. Photogravure portrait plates with tissue guards. Full crimson morocco with gilt ruling and elk device to front board. Five raised bands with six gilt-ruled compartments and gilt titles on spine. Marbled endpapers and slipcase. Printed with both English and German texts. Slight rubbing to spine. Bookplate. Otherwise, near fine.

Est.: $800-up
Start Bid: $400

37233   R. Lydekker. *The Great and Small Game of India, Burma & Tibet.* London: Rowland Ward, 1900. **One of five hundred numbered copies signed by the publisher, of which this is number 235.** Quarto. 416 pages. Nine hand-colored plates with numerous reproductions and illustrations. Publisher's green cloth with gilt-stamped titles and ruling to front cover and spine. Some shelf-wear to extremities with minor loss to spine ends. Foot of rear hinge broken, front starting. Some light uniform toning to a few plates. Otherwise, very good.

Est.: $800-up
Start Bid: $400

37234   Arthur H. Neumann. *Elephant-Hunting in East Equatorial Africa.* London: Rowland Ward, 1898. First edition. Octavo. 455 pages. Numerous illustrations by J. G. Millais, E. Caldwell, and G. E. Lodge with a colored plate and folding map in rear pocket. Publisher's full red cloth with black-stamped front and gilt-stamped spine titles. Zebra pattern endpapers. Covers have mild dampstaining and rubbing. Reinforced spine slightly faded. Some shelfwear and bumped corners. Very good.

Est.: $600-up
Start Bid: $300

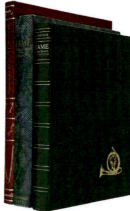

37235   Jack O'Connor. Three Limited Edition Game Books, including: *Game in the Desert.* New York: Derrydale Press, 1939. Limited numbered edition. Fine. [and:] *Game in the Desert Revisited.* Clinton: Amwell Press, 1977. **Signed.** Limited numbered edition. Near fine. [and:] *The Best of Jack O'Connor.* Clinton: Amwell Press, 1977. **Signed.** Limited numbered edition. Slipcase. Fine.

Est.: $600-up
Start Bid: $300

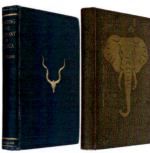

37236   Pair of Books About Elephant Hunting, including: **Captain C. H. Stigand.** *Hunting the Elephant in Africa and Other Recollections of Thirteen Years' Wanderings.* New York: The Macmillan Company, 1913. First edition. Octavo. xv, 379 pages. Illustrated. Original blue cloth with titles in gilt. Top edge gilt. Light restoration to spine ends, else very good condition. [and:] **Commander David Enderby Blunt.** *Elephant.* London: Published by East Africa newspaper, 1933. First edition. Octavo. xi, 260 pages. Illustrated. Original simulated leather with elephant vignette on the front board. Former owner's bookplate on the front endpaper, light scuffing to boards, else very good.

Est.: $600-up
Start Bid: $300

37237   Captain C. H. Stigand. *Hunting the Elephant in Africa and Other Recollections of Thirteen Years' Wanderings.* New York: The Macmillan Company, 1913. First American edition. Octavo. xv, 379 pages. Illustrated. Publisher's burgundy cloth with titles stamped in gilt on the spine. Walter Rutherford Peterson ex-libris mounted to front pastedown. Introduction by Theodore Roosevelt. Modest shelf wear to the extremities of the boards. Otherwise, a fine copy.

Est.: $600-up
Start Bid: $300

37238   The Maharajah of Cooch Behar. *Thirty-Seven Years of Big Game Shooting in Cooch Behar, the Duars, and Assam.* London: Rowland Ward, 1908. First edition. Quarto. 461 pages. Profusely illustrated with reproductions and a folding map at rear. Publisher's blue cloth with gilt-stamped insignia on front, spine titles, blind-stamped publisher's logo on rear. Covers have mild soiling and wear to spine and covers. Interior clean. Generally near fine.

Est.: $600-up
Start Bid: $300

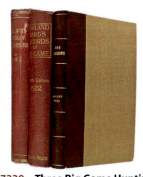

37239   Three Big Game Hunting Books, including: **B. H. Jessen.** *W. N. McMillan's Expeditions and Big Game Hunting in Sudan, Abyssinia, & British East Africa.* London: Merchant Singer & Co., 1906. First edition. Octavo. 415 pages. Illustrated. Map. Publisher's binding. Dampstain to lower portion of boards, else very good. [and:] **J. G. Dollman and J. B. Burlace, editors.** *Rowland Ward's Records of Big Game.* London: Rowland Ward, 1922. Eighth edition. Octavo. 527 pages. Illustrated. Publisher's binding. Fine.[and:] **Roland Ward.** *Horn Measurements and Weights of the Great Game of the World*: London: Privately printed, 1892. First edition. Octavo. 264 pages. Illustrated. Half-leather over tan cloth with gilt-stamped spine titles. Fine.

Est.: $800-up
Start Bid: $400

37240   Rowland Ward. *A Naturalist's Life Study in the Art of Taxidermy.* London: Rowland Ward, Ltd., 1913. First edition "For Private Circulation". Quarto. 227 pages. Illustrated. Publisher's yellow cloth over beveled boards with a title label featuring an elephant mounted to the front board. Titles stamped in gilt on the spine. Trivial shelf wear to boards. Bookplate and gift inscription at front. Else a near fine copy of this scarce book.

Est.: $600-up
Start Bid: $300

37241   Three Books on Southern Africa, including: **William Harvey Brown.** *On the South African Frontier...* New York: Charles Scribner's Sons, 1899. First American edition. [and:] **H. Anderson Bryden.** *Gun and Camera in Southern Africa...* London: Edward Stanford, 1893. First edition. [and:] **W. H. Drummond.** *The Large Game and Natural History of South and South-East Africa.* Edinburgh: Edmonston and Douglas, 1875. First edition. All volumes generally very good.

Est.: $600-up
Start Bid: $300

37242   Three Books on the Alaskan Hunting and Exploration, including: **William N. Beach.** *In the Shadow of Mount McKinley.* New York: Derrydale Press, 1931. One of 750 copies. [and:] **J. W. Eddy.** *Hunting on Kenai Peninsula...* [N.p.]: Lowman & Hanford, 1924. **Inscribed to Beach with his bookplate.** C. R. E. Radclyffe. [and:] *Big Game Shooting in Alaska.* London: Rowland Ward, 1904. All very good or better.

Est.: $600-up
Start Bid: $300

37243   Four Books on Sport in Tibet and the Himalayas, including: **W. N. Fergusson.** *Adventure, Sport and Travel on the Tibetan Steppes.* London: Constable and Company, 1911. First edition. [and:] **H. L. Haughton.** *Sport & Folklore in the Himalaya.* New York: Longmans, Green, and Co., [n.d.]. Later edition. [and:] **R. L. Kennion.** *Sport and Life in the Further Himalaya.* Edinburgh: William Blackwood and Sons, 1910. First edition. [and:] **Alexander A. A. Kinloch.** *Large Game Shooting in Thibet, the Himalayas, Northern and Central India.* Calcutta: Thacker, Spink and Co., 1892. Third edition. Publisher's bindings. All volumes very good.

Est.: $800-up
Start Bid: $400

37244   Six Volumes Elaborately Boxed in African Hunting Reprint Series, including: **Roualeyn Gordon Cumming.** *A Hunter's Life in South Africa, Volumes I and II.* [and:] *The Recollections of William Finaughty, Elephant Hunter 1864-1875.* [and:] **William Charles Baldwin.** *African Hunting.* [and:] **Frederick Courteney Selous.** *A Hunter's Wanderings in Africa* [and:] **Arthur H. Neumann.** *Elephant Hunting in East Equatorial Africa.* Bulawayo: Books of Zimbabwe, 1980-82. Deluxe facsimile editions, limited to 100 copies, though this set is unnumbered. Six octavo volumes. Fully bound in elephant hide with four raised bands and paper labels on spine. Top edges gilt. Housed in a custom wooden shelf display with elephant hide band and back. Spine labels poorly affixed by publisher. Otherwise, near fine.

Est.: $800-up
Start Bid: $400

37245   H. de Brinon. *Recherches sur L'Anesthésie Chirurgicale Obtenue par L'Action Combinée de la Morphine et du Chloroforme.* Paris: Octave Doin, 1878. First edition. **Inscribed by the author.** Light blue printed wrappers. 78 pages. Some rolling to the spine. Some loss to the top edge of the front wrapper. Minor damp-staining to the title page. Very good.

Est.: $600-up
Start Bid: $300

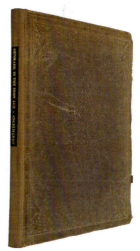

37246   Conrad Engelhardt. *Denmark in the Early Iron Age, Illustrated by Recent Discoveries in the Peat Mosses of Slesvig.* London: Williams and Norgate, 1866. First edition. Quarto. x, 80 pages text, 33 unpaginated plates at rear. Rebacked. Original boards. Inked name of previous owner to front pastedown. Moderate foxing to some of the plates. Corners bumped. Very good.

Est.: $600-up
Start Bid: $300

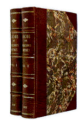

37247 William Jacob. *An Historical Inquiry Into the Production and Consumption of the Precious Metals.* London: John Murray, 1831. First edition. Two octavo volumes. [i]-xvi, [1]-380 pages; [i]-[xii], [1]-415, [1] pages. Modern half leather over marbled boards. Four raised bands on spine with gilt-stamped titles ruling and decoration. New endpapers. Mostly unopened pages. Light foxing to edges and titles. Generally, near fine.

Est.: $600-up
Start Bid: $300

37248 [Haskell Norman]. Diana H. Hook & Jeremy M. Norman. *The Haskell F. Norman Library of Science & Medicine.* San Francisco: Jeremy Norman & Co., Inc., 1991. **Deluxe edition, number 12 of 35 deluxe copies signed by Haskell Norman, Jeremy Norman, Diana Hook, and Steve Renick.** Two folio volumes. lxxviii, [2, Acknowledgements leaf], 511; [xvi, 513-1,005, [1,006, blank], [2, colophon leaf], [4, blank] pages. Specially bound in black over red Nigerian goatskin with gilt titles. All edges gilt. Housed together in the publisher's black cloth dropdown box. Accompanying the deluxe edition is a black cloth chemise containing various artifacts from the construction of the book and assemblage of the text, including manuscript notes, collations, original photographs, typewritten descriptions, first design ideas, page proofs, linotronic pages, a floppy disk containing the cataloger's introduction, and more. Each of these is slipped in a gray paper folder. Also chemise here is a copy of *The Haskell F. Norman Library of Science & Medicine . Selections Exhibited for the International Congress of Bibliophiles* (Jeremy Norman, 1985). A fine copy of this monumental work.

Est.: $600-up
Start Bid: $300

37249 John T. Scopes and James Presley. *Center of the Storm: Memoirs of John T. Scopes.* New York: Holt, Rinehart and Winston, [1967]. First edition, first printing. **Inscribed by Scopes** on the front free endpaper. Octavo. 277 pages. Minor rubbing to extremities. Faint dampstain at base of fore-edge and along a small portion of bottom edge, without intrusion onto pages. A very good copy in a chipped and rubbed dust jacket. Memoirs of John T. Scopes, the school teacher from Dayton, Tennessee who was prosecuted for teaching evolution, resulting in the celebrated, landmark "Monkey Trial."

Est.: $600-up
Start Bid: $300

37250 Ten Various Nineteenth Century Astronomical and Scientific Texts, the majority from *Philosophical Transactions,* including the work of **Peter Barlow, David Brewster, Samuel Hunter Christie, Humphry Davy, James Ivory,** and **John William Lubbock.** Disbound quarto sections in oversized wrappers. Most stapled, some uncut, with a few trimmed. Some illustrated with plates, a few of which are folding. Edges somewhat toned with light rippling to pages. Light offsetting of plates. An interesting collection of writings. All in very good condition. (Detailed list at HA.com).

Est.: $600-up
Start Bid: $300

37251 Carl Barks. *The Fine Art of Walt Disney's Donald Duck.* Scottsdale, Arizona and West Plains, Missouri: Another Rainbow Publishing, [1981]. "McDuck" edition, limited to 1,875 copies **signed by Carl Barks** on limitation page, of which this is number 456. Folio. 311 pages. Profusely illustrated with numerous illustrations in text and 135 full-color plates reproducing Barks' works, many of them folding plates. Publisher's crimson buckram lettered in gilt, with a color illustration inset on front cover. Housed in publisher's matching slipcase. Mild scuffing to edges of slipcase, otherwise fine condition.

Est.: $800-up
Start Bid: $400

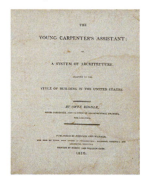

37252 Owen Biddle. *The Young Carpenter's Assistant.* Philadelphia: Johnson and Warner, 1810. Second edition. Quarto. [62] pages. 44 architectural plates. Complete. Contemporary full calf. Front board nearly detached, rear board detached but present, joints split, cords visible, boards worn. Dampstaining to contents. Good. Only the second book on architecture to be written and published in the United States.

Est.: $1,000-up
Start Bid: $500

37253 Eric Clapton. *Eric Clapton: The Autobiography.* London: Century, 2007. Special edition limited to 1,000 copies **signed by Clapton.** Publisher's binding, issued without dust jacket, housed in a slipcase designed to resemble a Fender Twin amplifier. Still in shrinkwrap. As new.

Est.: $600-up
Start Bid: $300

37254 Salvador Dali, [illustrator]. *The Autobiography of Benvenuto Cellini.* Garden City: Doubleday, 1946. Limited to 1000 numbered copies of which this is 791. **Signed by Dali** on limitation page. Octavo. 442 pages. Publisher's full blue cloth with mild abrading to tail of spine. Top edge gilt. **Illustrated with sixteen color plates by Dali.** Lacking slipcase. Near fine.

Est.: $600-up
Start Bid: $300

37255   Anna Gaskell. *Peter Norton Family Christmas Project 2001.* [n. p.]: Intervisual Communications, [ca. 2001]. First edition. Octavo. Unpaginated. Publisher's boards containing accordion "peep show" and laid into cloth chemise with ribbon closure. Mild sunning to extremities of boards. Near fine.

Est.: $600-up
Start Bid: $300

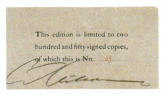

37256   Charles Dana Gibson. *Everyday People.* New York: Charles Scribner's Sons, 1904. **Edition De Luxe, limited to 250 numbered copies signed by the author, of which this is number 59.** Oblong quarto. Unpaginated. Bound in full buckram with gilt-stamped titles on front board. Matching box bound same. Rubbed box has some soiling and areas of dampstaining. Top right corner of box bumped with corresponding bump to textblock. Light wear to boards. Overall, very good. [and:] **Two ALsS of Gibson**: one full page in purple ink on unlined paper, with the other being two pages on his summer home stationery, envelope included.

Est.: $600-up
Start Bid: $300

37257   Thomas Ingoldsby. Hand-Illustrated Manuscript for *The Jackdaw of Rheims.* No place or date of publication. Illustrated with an intricately illustrated title page, frontispiece and detailed illustrations within colorful illuminated capitals at the head of each chapter. Bound in an exquisite Bayntun-Riviere binding of crimson morocco. Custom clamshell case. Fine.

Est.: $600-up
Start Bid: $300

37258   Pablo Picasso. *Le Picador II.* A vibrant multi-colored lithograph from *A Los Toros avec Picasso.* Monte-Carlo: 1961. Trimmed from the book on the left. Wove paper. In very good condition with the exception of light toning to edges and faint bumping to corners of left side. Measures 9.625 x 12.5 inches.

Est.: $600-up
Start Bid: $300

37259   Roger Poulain. *Boutiques 1929.* Paris: Vincent Freal et Cie, [1929]. First edition. Oblong quarto (8 x 11.75 inches). Portfolio of printed paper-covered boards with ribbon ties, containing 72 plates of black and white photographs of interiors and exteriors of Paris shops, boutiques, and other business, all on loose sheets. Wear and loss to cloth spine; some scuffing to boards. Plates are in fine condition. An incredible collection of Paris art deco architecture and design. Scarce.

Est.: $600-up
Start Bid: $300

37260   Edward Ruscha. *Nine Swimming Pools and a Broken Glass.* [N.p.]: Edward Ruscha, 1968. First edition. Twelvemo. Unpaginated. Illustrated with color reproductions. Original printed wrappers with glassine jacket. Rubbed spine and jacket sunned as well as tail edge. Minor chipping to jacket with small stains. Very good.

Est.: $800-up
Start Bid: $400

37261   Edward Ruscha. *Some Los Angeles Apartments.* [Los Angeles]: Edward Ruscha, [1970]. Second edition. Twelvemo. Unpaginated. Illustrated with black and white reproductions. Publisher's printed wrappers with glassine jacket. Titles printed in green on the front panel and spine. Lightly bumped spine. Jacket sunned. Minor chipping to jacket with small tears and a small stain. Some minor shelf wear. Very good.

Est.: $800-up
Start Bid: $400

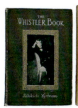

37262   [James McNeill Whistler]. Two Whistler Books, including: E. R. & J. Pennell. *The Whistler Journal.* 1921. Autograph Edition, **signed by Elizabeth and Joseph Pennell.** [and:] **Sadakichi Hartmann.** *The Whistler Book.* 1910. First impression. Both generally very good.

Est.: $600-up
Start Bid: $300

37263   J. M. Barrie. *Peter and Wendy.* New York: Charles Scribner's Sons, [1911]. First American edition. Octavo. 267 pages with thirteen illustrations by F. D. Bedford. Publisher's olive green cloth with gilt titles and decorations to front and spine. Light rubbing to extremities. Owner's bookplate and signature. Custom clamshell case. A bright, attractive copy of this children's classic in near fine condition.

Est.: $600-up
Start Bid: $300

37264   J. M. Barrie. *Quality Street A Comedy in Four Acts.* **Limited Edition Illustrated by Hugh Thompson.** London: Hodder & Stoughton, [1913]. Limited edition of 1,000 hand-numbered copies **signed by the artist Hugh Thompson**, of which this is copy number 298. Octavo. 198 pages. With twenty-two tipped-in color plates under captioned tissue guards. Original vellum lavishly decorated in gilt with purple rules. Ribbon ties intact. Top edge gilt. A beautiful and complete copy, with ever-so-slightly warped boards (typical of these large volumes). Else fine.

Est.: $600-up
Start Bid: $300

37265   [Aubrey Beardsley]. Thomas Malory. *Le Morte Darthur.* [London]: J. M. Dent, 1893-4. One of 1,500 copies. Two quarto volumes. Illustrations by Aubrey Beardsley. Original ivory cloth elaborately decorated in gilt. Cloth darkened a bit. Minor shelfwear. Near fine. 21-year old Beardsley's first illustrated work.

Est.: $600-up
Start Bid: $300

37266   Lewis Carroll. *Through the Looking-Glass and What Alice Found There.* New York: Limited Editions Club, 1935. Special edition limited to 1,500 copies, of which this is number 596, **signed by Alice Hargreaves (nee Alice Liddell, "the original Alice")**. Octavo. xxi, 211 pages. Introduction by Carl Van Doren. Original illustrations by John Tenniel, re-engraved in metal by Frederic Warde. Printed for the members of the Limited Editions Club by the printing house of William Edwin Rudge, Mount Vernon, New York. Publisher's full blue morocco with gilt-stamped fleuron on covers. Titles and portraits of the book's characters stamped in gilt on spine. All edges gilt. Moderate wear to the boards edges. Noticeable rubbing to the spine. Otherwise, a near fine copy.

Est.: $1,000-up
Start Bid: $500

37267   Joseph Crawhall. Three Books Illustrated by Him, including: *Crawhall's Chap-Book Chaplets.* London: Field & Tuer, 1883. [and:] *Olde Ffrendes with Newe Faces.* London: Field & Tuer, 1883. [and:] *"Impress Quaint."* Newcastle: Mawson, Swan, and Morgan, 1889. All quarto. Profusely illustrated; the two with the Field & Tuer imprint are hand-colored. Significant wear to the bindings, with some loss to the spines. The interiors are clean with vibrant illustrations. Overall, very good.

Est.: $600-up
Start Bid: $300

37268   [Walt Disney]. *Walt Disney's Snow White and the Seven Dwarfs.* Chicago/New York: Circle Fine Art Press, [1978]. Limited edition of 9,500 copies, of which this is number 967, with each copy containing four original color serigraphs (created especially for this book) of scenes from Walt Disney's 1937 film. Large oblong quarto. Unpaginated. Lavishly illustrated. Red- and gold-stamped full white leatherette. All edges gilt. Fine in publisher's slipcase.

Est.: $600-up
Start Bid: $300

37269   Franklin W. Dixon. *The Hardy Boys. A Figure in Hiding.* Illustrated by Paul Laune. New York: Grosset & Dunlap Publishers, [1937]. First edition. Octavo. [iv], 212, [6, publisher's advertisements] pages. Publisher's light brown cloth with dark brown titles and decorative stamping. Top edge stained black. Red pictorial endpapers. Original pictorial dust jacket. Noticeable stain to front panel and spine of dust jacket. Very good.

Est.: $600-up
Start Bid: $300

37270   Franklin W. Dixon. Two First Edition Hardy Boys Books, including: *The Secret of the Caves.* [1929]. [and:] *The Mystery of the Cabin Island.* [1929]. New York: Grosset & Dunlap. First editions. Two octavo volumes. Publisher's binding. Both with frontispiece. Abrading to cloth extremities with rounded corners and fraying to spine ends. Two-inch gouge in front free endpaper and frontispiece. Hinges cracked. Occasional soil and wear to pages. Good.

Est.: $600-up
Start Bid: $300

37271 Franklin W. Dixon. *The Hardy Boys. The Hidden Harbor Mystery.* New York: Grosset & Dunlap, [1935]. First edition, first printing. Octavo. 219 pages. Publisher's binding and dust jacket. A few spots of abrading to top edge of front board. Name to recto of frontispiece. Jacket is lightly rubbed with minor wear to extremities and faintly dampstained along bottom edge. Housed in a custom slipcase. Very good.
Est.: $800-up
Start Bid: $400

37272 Franklin W. Dixon. *The Hardy Boys. The Mystery of the Flying Express.* Illustrated by Paul Laune. New York: Grosset & Dunlap Publishers, [1941]. First edition. Octavo. [vi], 217 pages. Publisher's light brown cloth with dark brown titles and decorative stamping. Top edge stained black. Red pictorial endpapers. Original pictorial dust jacket. Spine cocked. Very minor wear to jacket edges, with two tiny closed tears to top edge. An excellent copy.
Est.: $600-up
Start Bid: $300

37273 [Edmund Dulac, illustrator]. *Hans Andersen. Stories from Hans Andersen.* With Illustrations by Edmund Dulac. London: Hodder & Stoughton, [1911]. Edition de Luxe, limited to 750 copies, of which this is number 427, **signed by Edmund Dulac.** Large quarto (12.125 x 9.625 inches). viii, 250, [2] pages. Twenty-eight mounted color plates. Original full vellum, stamped in gilt on front cover and spine. Pictorial endpapers. Top edge gilt, others uncut. Lacking the ties. Binding rubbed and bowing slightly. A little light offsetting from the plates, otherwise near fine.
Est.: $800-up
Start Bid: $400

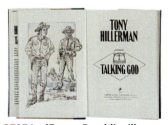

37274 [Ernest Franklin, illustrator]. *Tony Hillerman. Talking God.* New York: Harper & Row, [1989]. First edition, first printing. **With twenty original, signed illustrations by Navajo artist Ernest Franklin.** Publisher's binding and dust jacket. Fine condition. Includes original ink drawings colored with pencil drawn directly on the page and signed by the artist. In a custom slipcase.
Est.: $600-up
Start Bid: $300

37275 **Joel Chandler Harris.** *Uncle Remus. His Songs and Sayings. The Folk-Lore of the Old Plantation.* With Illustrations by Frederick S. Church and James H. Moser. New York: D. Appleton and Company, 1881. First edition, BAL first state, of the author's first book (with "presumptive" in the last line on page 9, and the advertisements on page [233] beginning "New Books. A Treatise on the Practice of Medicine"). Twelvemo. 231, [1, blank], [8, advertisements] pages. Eight wood-engraved plates (including frontispiece) and sixteen wood-engraved text illustrations (including title vignette). Publisher's mustard cloth with front cover pictorially stamped in gilt and black and spine decoratively stamped and lettered in gilt.
Est.: $1,000-up
Start Bid: $500

37276 **Charles Kingsley.** *The Heroes, or Greek Fairy Tales for my Children.* London: Philip Lee Warner, 1912. **One of twelve copies printed on vellum, of which this is number nine.** Quarto. Illustrated with twelve mounted coloured plates by William Russell Flint with captioned tissue guards bound in at the end. Publisher's limp vellum with gilt front and spine titles. Green silk ties and top edge gilt. Covers have light discoloration and one tie missing. Light foxing to page edges and light toning to plates. Bookplate to front pastedown. Printed by The Riccardi Press. Very good copy of a beautifully executed book.
Est.: $1,000-up
Start Bid: $500

37277 **A. A. Milne.** *The Christopher Robin Story Book.* With Decorations by Ernest H. Shepard. New York: E. P. Dutton, [1929]. Large paper edition, limited to 350 copies, this being number 78, **signed by Milne and Shepard.** Square octavo. [xiv], 171 pages. Light green cloth over illustrated paper boards. Green endpapers. Some soiling and light dampstaining to boards; cloth spine a bit faded, some loss to paper spine label. Minor toning to pages; a couple of leaves chipped or torn at fore-edge. Very good.
Est.: $800-up
Start Bid: $400

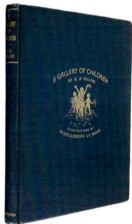

37278 **A. A. Milne.** *A Gallery of Children.* London: Stanley Paul & Company, 1825. **Limited to 500 copies of which this is number 257, signed by Milne.** Large quarto. 105 pages. Twelve illustrated color plates including illustrated title by Saida (H. Willebeek le Mair). Blue cloth over beveled boards, with the David McKay imprint to spine. Top edge gilt. Some light foxing to the plates. Near fine.
Est.: $600-up
Start Bid: $300

37279 **[Kay Nielsen].** *East of the Sun and West of the Moon*. *Old Tales From the North*. New York: George H. Doran, [n.d.]. First American trade edition. Octavo. Illustrated with tipped-in plates throughout. Publisher's full yellow cloth with red-stamped titles on front and spine. Dust jacket. Boards and jacket somewhat rubbed with lightly bumped tips. Generally near fine.

Est.: $800-up
Start Bid: $400

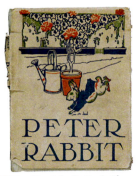

37280 **[Beatrix Potter].** *The Tale of Peter Rabbit*. Philadelphia: Henry Altemus, 1904. First pirated American edition. Sixteenmo. Unpaginated and with 31 color illustrations. Publisher's green cloth binding and dust jacket. Minor rubbing and darkening to cloth extremities with a few small spots of insect damage to board edges. Faint soiling to boards. Plain endpapers. Modest toning to pages and an occasional softly bent corner. Shadow offsetting to a few pages facing illustrations. Scarce jacket is darkened and edge worn with several small chips and tears, and portion of upper rear panel lacking. Very good.

Est.: $600-up
Start Bid: $300

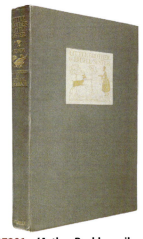

37281 **[Arthur Rackham, illustrator].** *Little Brother & Little Sister and Other Tales*. London: Constable & Co. [1917]. Limited edition, number 433 of 525 numbered copies, **signed by Arthur Rackham**. Large quarto. xi, [1, blank], 250, [1], [1, blank] pages. Thirteen mounted color plates, captioned on mounts, and forty-three drawings in black and white, eight of which are full-page. Page and plate at page 35 supplied, the plate in facsimile. The additional mounted colored plate ("He Hurried Away with Long Strides," facing page 178) not present. Original gray cloth with white cloth panel on front cover pictorially stamped and lettered in gilt.

Est.: $800-up
Start Bid: $400

37282 **[Arthur Rackham, illustrator].** *Ondine*. Paris: Hachette et Cie, 1912. Limited to 390 copies on "papier vélin" of which this is copy number 113. Quarto. viii, 114 pages. Fifteen tipped-in color plates under captioned tissue guards. Original vellum lettered and decorated in gilt on the front board and spine. French text. Top edge gilt, remaining edges untrimmed. Tie closures not present. Bookplate. A beautiful copy in fine condition.

Est.: $800-up
Start Bid: $400

37283 **[Arthur Rackham, illustrator].** *Some British Ballads*. London: Constable and Company, 1919. First edition limited to 575 numbered copies, **signed by Arthur Rackham**. Quarto. 170 pages. Some bumping to the corners. Binding browning and somewhat dull. Some of the signatures a bit loose. Overall, a very good copy, internally fresh and clean.

Est.: $800-up
Start Bid: $400

37284 **Mischa Richter. Artist's Original Mock-ups of** *Geedyup and Friend*, **in Pencil and in Ink,** including: **Mock-up booklet consisting of nine sheets of paper, folded in half to form a booklet, with all text and original drawings by Richter in pencil.** [and:] **Twenty-eight sheets of original drawings in ink.** [and:] **Twenty-nine color separation overlays.** Sheets of varying sizes. All in very good condition or better. Also included is a fine copy of a later printing of the 1968 book, published by Harper & Row.

Est.: $1,000-up
Start Bid: $500

37285 **Dr. Seuss.** *How the Grinch Stole Christmas!* New York: Random House, [1957]. First edition in first issue dust jacket. Publisher's glazed paper boards. Minor wear to edges; light bump to fore-edge of front board and to one corner. Dust jacket with "250/250" price; a couple of small chips, short tears, and some creasing along edges. A very good copy.

Est.: $800-up
Start Bid: $400

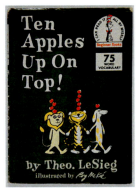

37286 **[Dr. Seuss]. Theo. Le Sieg (pseud.).** *Ten Apples Up on Top!* [New York]: Random House, [1961]. First edition, first issue, with no logo on front board. Illustrations by Roy McKie. Publisher's glazed paper boards and dust jacket with "195/195" price on flap. Minor wear to extremities of binding and jacket. Very good.

Est.: $600-up
Start Bid: $300

37287   Dr. Seuss. Four Seuss First Editions, including: *The Seven Lady Godivas*. New York: Random House, [1939]. Near fine. [and:] *Dr. Seuss's ABC.* 1963. Fine. [and:] *Fox in Sox.* 1965. Near fine. [and:] *The Foot Book.* 1968. Very good. All first editions in first issue dust jackets, except for *ABC*, which is in a later issue jacket.

Est.: $600-up
Start Bid: $300

37288   Jessie Willcox Smith. *The Jessie Willcox Smith Mother Goose.* New York: Dodd, Mead, [1914]. Later issue with plain endpapers. Oblong quarto. 173 pages. Publisher's binding with mild rubbing to cloth extremities and a bit of abrading to lower corner of paper label on front. Name and date to both pastedowns. Foxing to endpapers with fold lines to rear free endpaper. **Illustrated with 12 color plates by Willcox Smith.** Binding cracked and reinforced. Overall about near fine.

Est.: $600-up
Start Bid: $300

37289   [William Steig]. Original Drawing from *Giggle Box*. A delightful original drawing for the Alfred A. Knopf children's anthology, *Giggle Box* (1950), for which Steig provided all of the illustrations. This image is for the excerpt from Glen Rounds' *Pay Dirt*. Executed on a white sheet of sketch paper measuring 7.5 x 10 inches. Beneath the inked image are blue penciled notations for the design department. On the verso is affixed an official Knopf paper shipping label with an inked note to "return to" the publisher's offices. A charming example of the work of a well-known and prolific cartoonist.

Est.: $800-up
Start Bid: $400

37290   Garth Williams. Preliminary drawings and rough sketches for illustrations #1 and #2 appearing in *The Cricket in Times Square*. Pencil on paper (one ink on paper). Thirteen sheets, ranging in size from 8.25 x 6.875 inches to 13 x 8.625 inches. **All initialed by Williams.** All generally fine. *From the Estate of Garth Williams.*

Est.: $400-up
Start Bid: $200

37291   Garth Williams. Preliminary drawings and rough sketches for illustration #3 appearing in *The Cricket in Times Square*. Pencil on paper (two ink on paper). Twenty-one sheets, ranging in size from 8.5 x 5.5 inches to 11 x 8.5 inches. **All initialed by Garth Williams.** All generally fine. *From the Estate of Garth Williams.*

Est.: $400-up
Start Bid: $200

37292   Garth Williams. Preliminary drawings and rough sketches for illustrations #4, #5, and #6 appearing in *The Cricket in Times Square*. Pencil on paper (two ink over pencil). Fifteen sheets, ranging in size from 8.375 x 10.75 inches to 11.5 x 8.625 inches. One with caption in Williams' hand reading "Rough sketch for Tucker Mouse in 'The Cricket in Times Square' / Garth Williams 1960." **One signed in full by Garth Williams, the rest initialed by him.** One with a paper clip stain, else all generally fine. *From the Estate of Garth Williams.*

Est.: $400-up
Start Bid: $200

37293   Garth Williams. Preliminary drawings and rough sketches for illustrations #7, #8, and #9 appearing in *The Cricket in Times Square*. Pencil on paper. Twenty sheets, ranging in size from 10.75 x 8.25 inches to 12.875 x 8.75 inches. Largest sheet has drawings on both sides and has a horizontal crease running along the center of the sheet. **All initialed by Garth Williams.** All generally fine. *From the Estate of Garth Williams.*

Est.: $400-up
Start Bid: $200

37294   Garth Williams. Preliminary drawings and rough sketches for illustrations #10 - #17 and the title page vignette appearing in *The Cricket in Times Square*. Pencil on paper. Nineteen sheets measuring approximately 8.375 x 10.6.25 inches. **All initialed by Garth Williams.** All generally fine. *From the Estate of Garth Williams.*

Est.: $400-up
Start Bid: $200

37295   Garth Williams.
Preliminary drawings and rough sketches for illustrations #18 - #24 appearing in *The Cricket in Times Square*. Pencil on paper. Nineteen sheets measuring approximately 8.25 x 10.75 inches. **All initialed by Garth Williams.** All generally fine. *From the Estate of Garth Williams.*
Est.: $400-up
Start Bid: $200

37296   Garth Williams.
Preliminary drawings and sketches for illustrations appearing in *Little House in the Big Woods* by Laura Ingalls Wilder, 1953. Pencil on tracing paper. Nine sheets, ranging in size from 4.5 x 5.5 inches to 8.875 x 5.875 inches. Two with notes in Williams' hand. **All initialed by Garth Williams.** All generally fine. *From the Estate of Garth Williams.*
Est.: $600-up
Start Bid: $300

37297   Handsome Metal Printing Plate for *Hansel and Gretel*. This wonderful printing relic shows Gretel peeking in a window at the witch's house. The plate is titled at the top "Hansel and Gretel" and includes four lines of text underneath the image. Plate measures 5.25 x 7.75 inches. Framed with a brown-inked impression of the plate to an overall size of 20.75 x 14.5 inches. Not examined outside the frame. Will require third-party shipping. A wonderful example of modern printing arts in fine condition.
Est.: $600-up
Start Bid: $300

37298   Isaac Asimov. *Foundation*. New York: Gnome Press Publishers, [1951]. First edition, first issue (Currey priority A binding). Octavo. 255 pages. Publisher's dark blue cloth with red titles. Original first issue dust jacket with three titles advertised on the rear panel and two on the rear flap. Minor edge wear and light soiling to boards. Bookplate to front pastedown. Some dark soiling to endpapers. Two small tape repairs and some minor spotting to verso. Very good.
Est.: $1,000-up
Start Bid: $500

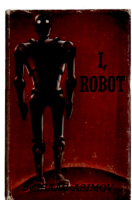

37299   Isaac Asimov. *I, Robot*. New York: Gnome Press, Inc. Publishers, [1950]. First edition. Octavo. 253 pages. Publisher's red cloth with black titles. Original pictorial dust jacket. Light edge wear and minor dustsoiling to boards. Bookplate to front pastedown. Two long closed tears to front free endpaper. Two short tape repairs and some toning to verso of jacket. Very good.
Est.: $800-up
Start Bid: $400

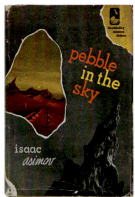

37300   Isaac Asimov. *Pebble in the Sky*. Garden City: Doubleday & Company, 1950. First edition. Octavo. 223 pages. Publisher's tan cloth over boards. Orange lettering to spine. Original pictorial dust jacket. Tiny dark stain to rear board and to the corresponding area of the dust jacket. Bookplate to front pastedown. Text edges and endpapers a touch toned. Very minimal wear to jacket edges. Jacket spine a bit toned on the verso. Very good.
Est.: $600-up
Start Bid: $300

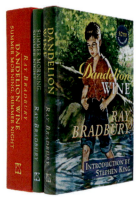

37301   Ray Bradbury. *Dandelion Wine*. [Hornsea]: PS Publishing, 2007. **One of 100 special deluxe sets signed by both Ray Bradbury and Stephen King, of which this is copy number 6.** Octavo. 220 pages. [and:] ***Summer Morning, Summer Night***. [Hornsea]: PS Publishing, 2007. Reprint edition. Octavo. 147 pages. Both volumes in publisher's binding with dust jackets. Ribbon markers. Slipcase with spine titles. Fine.
Est.: $600-up
Start Bid: $300

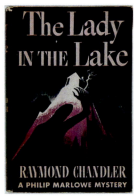

37302   Raymond Chandler. *The Lady in the Lake*. New York: Knopf, 1943. First edition, first printing. Octavo. 216 pages. Publisher's binding and dust jacket. Mild rubbing to cloth extremities. Jacket is lightly toned and edge worn with a few small chips and tears. Very good.
Est.: $800-up
Start Bid: $400

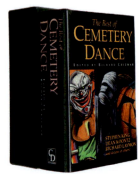

37303   Richard Chizmar, editor. *The Best of Cemetery Dance*. Baltimore: Cemetery Dance Publications, 1998. **One of 400 special signed editions, of which this is number 63. Signed by 64 contributors including the editor, Stephen King, Poppy Z. Brite, and Dean Koontz.** Octavo. 786 pages. Publisher's binding and dust jacket. Slipcase. Ribbon marker. Slight rubbing to bottom of text block. Otherwise, near fine.
Est.: $600-up
Start Bid: $300

37304 [Richard Chizmar and Robert Morriah, editors]. *October Dreams.* Baltimore: Cemetery Dance Publications, 2000. **First deluxe edition limited to 52 letter copies. This being "QQ," signed by over forty contributors to this horror anthology.** Leather-bound. Dust jacket. Publisher's traycase. Fine. [with:] **Halloween Art Portfolio,** with twelve black and white prints as well as a matted color print by Gahan Wilson. Fine.
Est.: $800-up
Start Bid: $400

37305 **Agatha Christie.** *The Secret Adversary.* London: John Lane The Bodley Head, 1922. First edition. Octavo. 312; 4 advertising pages. Publisher's binding with rubbing and abrading to cloth extremities. Some light scuffing and a few small areas of soiling to rear board. Foxing to page edges with staining to top page edges, modestly affecting textblock. Hinges cracking. Name on front pastedown and a crudely crossed-out name on half-title page. Scattered foxing throughout. Overall good.
Est.: $600-up
Start Bid: $300

37306 **Len Deighton. Author's Original Typescript for** *Stranger in Town.* **Signed by Deighton** on title page. Quarto. Four pages, including title page. Stapled along one edge and with two smoothed folds. Hand corrections in pencil. Small chip and staple holes to title page. Also includes a **Typed Note Signed by Deighton** and dated 1967. Laid into a custom clamshell box with lightly abraded leather spine labels. Near fine.
Est.: $600-up
Start Bid: $300

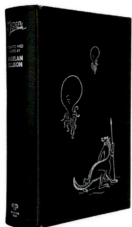

37307 **Harlan Ellison, editor.** *Medea: Harlan's World.* Huntington Woods, Michigan: Phantasia Press, 1985. First edition. **One of 35 specially bound copies signed by the authors and illustrator, of which this is copy G.** Octavo. 532 pages. Nine illustrations (one fold out) by Kelly Freas. Full leather binding with silver illustrations on cover and silver print on spine. Some minor rubbing along lower edges of boards. Near fine.
Est.: $600-up
Start Bid: $300

37308 **Ian Fleming.** *Casino Royale.* New York: Macmillan, 1954. First American edition, first printing. Octavo. 176 pages. Publisher's binding and dust jacket. Mild rubbing to cloth extremities. Light foxing to page edges and endpapers. Jacket is edge worn with several small chips and tears, and darkening to spine. Two-inch tear to front panel. Very good.
Est.: $800-up
Start Bid: $400

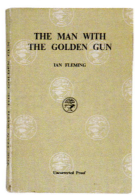

37309 **Ian Fleming.** *The Man With the Golden Gun.* London: Jonathan Cape, [1965]. Uncorrected proof of the first edition. Twelvemo. 221 pages. Publisher's green printed wrappers. Spine cocked. Wrappers somewhat rubbed, lightly soiled, with minor abrading along the joints, and one small, dark abrasion to rear cover. A couple of minor creases to front cover. Text edges just a touch dusty. Internally, the text is very clean. Very good.
Est.: $600-up
Start Bid: $300

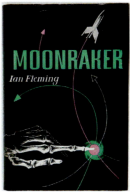

37310 **Ian Fleming.** *Moonraker.* New York: Macmillan, 1955. First American edition, first printing. Octavo. 220 pages. Publisher's binding and dust jacket. Rubbing and abrading to cloth extremities with tape shadows to boards. Ex-library with renewed endpapers. Crude restoration to dust jacket. Good.
Est.: $600-up
Start Bid: $300

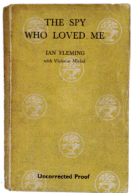

37311 **Ian Fleming with Vivienne Michel.** *The Spy Who Loved Me.* London: Jonathan Cape, [1962]. Uncorrected proof of the first edition. Twelvemo. 221 pages. Publisher's green printed wrappers. Spine cocked. Wrappers somewhat rubbed, soiled and creased. Text edges dusty. Scattered thumb-soiling to text, and some corner creases to leaves. A very good copy of a rare piece of Bondiana.
Est.: $600-up
Start Bid: $300

37312 Ian Fleming. *The Spy Who Loved Me.* London: Jonathan Cape, [1962]. First edition, first printing. Octavo. 221 pages. Publisher's binding and dust jacket. Mild rubbing to cloth extremities. Spine slightly cocked. Minor soiling to page edges. Light wear to jacket extremities with dampstaining to rear panel and faint soiling to inner flaps. Very good.

Est.: $600-up
Start Bid: $300

37313 Ian Fleming. Two James Bond Uncorrected Proofs, including: *You Only Live Twice.* [London]: Jonathan Cape, [1964]. Cocked, as is usual with these ARCs. Minor coffee (tea?) splash to page facing copyright page. [and:] *Octopussy and the Living Daylights*. London: Jonathan Cape, [1966]. A nice square copy with light soiling and sunning to wrappers; a shallow fold affecting last leaf and rear wrapper. Both bound in printed twelvemo wrappers, both very good.

Est.: $600-up
Start Bid: $300

37314 [Ian Fleming]. Two Unique James Bond-Related Books Specially Bound for Kingsley Amis, including: **Kingsley Amis.** *The James Bond Dossier.* [1965]. [and:] **Robert Markham.** *Colonel Sun. A James Bond Adventure.* [1968]. Both very good. Each binding stamped "K. A." and **each accompanied by a separate Typed Note Signed by Kingsley Amis** verifying that each "is an individual production, specially bound by the publishers as my own personal copy. It is unique and no other exists anywhere or has ever existed."

Est.: $600-up
Start Bid: $300

37315 John Grisham. *The Pelican Brief.* New York: Doubleday, [1993]. First edition, limited to 350 numbered copies of which this is 303. **Signed by Grisham.** Octavo. 371 pages. Publisher's binding, glassine dust jacket, and slipcase. Fine.

Est.: $600-up
Start Bid: $300

37316 Tony Hillerman. *The Ghostway.* New York, et al.: Harper & Row, Publishers, [1985]. First trade edition. **With twenty fantastic ink and watercolor drawings signed by Ernest Franklin** within, and illustrating, the text, usually on the blank versos at chapter endings or just under the text closing a chapter. Octavo. [viii], 213 pages. Publisher's blue cloth over brown paper boards with copper foil spine titles. Original pictorial dust jacket. Housed in a brown buckram slipcase. Fine condition.

Est.: $600-up
Start Bid: $300

37317 Robert E. Howard. *Skull-Face and Others.* Sauk City: Arkham House, 1946. First edition. Octavo. 474 pages. Publisher's binding and dust jacket. Light rubbing to cloth with bump to lower corner of rear board and minor fraying at head of spine. Small color-matched area to top edge of front board. Hinges a bit shaken and mild offsetting to endpapers. Jacket is toned and edge worn with several small chips and tears; folds are tender and starting. Very good.

Est.: $600-up
Start Bid: $300

37318 Will James. Four Cowboy Books, including: *Lone Cowboy, My Life Story.* New York: Charles Scribner's, 1930. [and:] *Big-Enough.* 1931. [and:] *Home Ranch.* 1935. [and:] *The American Cowboy.* 1942. All first editions with "A" on copyright page. All in the publisher's binding. All near fine in slightly rubbed dust jackets.

Est.: $600-up
Start Bid: $300

37319 Stuart M. Kaminsky. Author's Typescript for *You Bet Your Life*. Signed by Kaminsky on title page. Quarto. 217 pages. Unbound pages with **author's hand corrections.** Laid into a custom cloth chemise and lightly rubbed slipcase with leather spine labels. Preliminary and a few occasional pages with minor abrading to edges, otherwise near fine.

Est.: $600-up
Start Bid: $300

37320 **Stephen King and Peter Straub.** *Black House.* [Hampton Falls: Donald M. Grant, 2002]. First edition, limited to 1520 copies of which this is 340. **Signed by King and Straub.** Quarto. [640 pages]. Publisher's binding and clamshell box. As new, still sealed in publisher's shrinkwrap.

Est.: $600-up
Start Bid: $300

37321 **Stephen King. Two** *Blockade Billy* **Editions**, including: *Blockade Billy.* Baltimore: Lonely Road Books, 2010. Limited edition of 350 copies **signed by Stephen King (on baseball card) and artists Glen Orbik and Alex McVey.** Original full red leather, in publisher's tray case, with Blockade Billy and Stephen King baseball cards. [and:] *Blockade Billy.* Baltimore: Cemetery Dance, 2010. First edition. Publisher's binding and dust jacket, in slipcase. With Blockade Billy baseball card. Both books in fine condition.

Est.: $600-up
Start Bid: $300

37322 **Stephen King.** *Christine.* West Kingston: Donald M. Grant, [1983]. First edition, limited to 1000 numbered copies of which this is number 121. **Signed by King.** Octavo. 544 pages. Publisher's binding, dust jacket, and slipcase. Fine.

Est.: $600-up
Start Bid: $300

37323 **Stephen King.** *The Colorado Kid.* Hornsea: PS Publishing, 2007. First British and first hardcover edition. **Deluxe edition limited to 33 numbered copies, this being number 5, signed by King, Charles Ardai (who provided the introduction), and artists Edward Miller, Glenn Chadbourne, and J. K. Potter.** Blue leather over boards. In tray-case box. Fine.

Est.: $1,000-up
Start Bid: $500

37324 **Stephen King.** *Stephen King's Creepshow, A George A. Romero Film.* New York: Plume/New American Library, 1982. First edition, first printing. **Signed by Stephen King on the title page.** Large format paperback original. Unpaginated. Art by Berni Wrightson with Michele Wrightson. Cover art by Jack Kamen. Fine. Graphic novel, issued as a companion to the George Romero film of the same name.

Est.: $600-up
Start Bid: $300

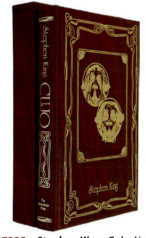

37325 **Stephen King.** *Cujo.* New York: Mysterious Press, [1981]. First edition, limited to 750 numbered copies of which this is 66. **Signed by King.** Octavo. 319 pages. Publisher's binding and slipcase. Fine.

Est.: $600-up
Start Bid: $300

37326 **Stephen King.** *The Eyes of the Dragon.* Bangor: Philtrum Press, 1984. First edition, limited to 1000 numbered copies of which this is 966. **Signed by King on limitation page and additionally inscribed by King on title page.** Quarto. 314 pages. Publisher's binding and slipcase. Modest rubbing to corners. Minor scuffing and soiling to bottom edge of slipcase. Fine.

Est.: $1,000-up
Start Bid: $500

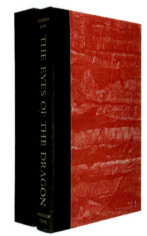

37327 **Stephen King.** *The Eyes of the Dragon.* Bangor: Philtrum Press, 1984. First edition, limited to 1000 numbered copies of which this is 225. **Signed by King.** Quarto. 314 pages. Publisher's binding and slipcase. Modest rubbing to corners and faint sunning to spine. Bookplate. Light scuffing to slipcase. Fine.

Est.: $600-up
Start Bid: $300

37328   Stephen King.
Firestarter. Huntington Woods: Phantasia, 1980. First edition, number 17 of 725 limited edition copies **signed by King** on the limitation page. Octavo. 428 pages. Publisher's binding, dust jacket, and moderately rubbed slipcase. Fine.

Est.: $800-up
Start Bid: $400

37329   Stephen King.
Firestarter. New York: The Viking Press, 1980. First trade edition. **Signed by the author.** Octavo. 428 pages. Publisher's binding and dust jacket. Some age toning and very minor crinkling to jacket at top and bottom. Remainder of bookplate on front pastedown. Light rubbing to edges. Otherwise, very good.

Est.: $800-up
Start Bid: $400

37330   Stephen King. *From a Buick 8.* Baltimore: Cemetery Dance, 2002. First edition, limited to 750 numbered copies of which this is 455. **Signed by King and Bernie Wrightson, illustrator.** Quarto. 408 pages. Publisher's binding, dust jacket, and clamshell box. Fine.

Est.: $600-up
Start Bid: $300

37331   Stephen King. *Full Dark, No Stars.* New York: Scribner, [2010]. First edition, first printing. **Signed by King** on title page. Octavo. 368 pages. Publisher's binding and dust jacket. Fine.

Est.: $600-up
Start Bid: $300

37332   Stephen King. *The Dark Tower: The Gunslinger.* West Kingston: Donald M. Grant Publisher, 1982. First trade edition. Octavo. 224 pages. Illustrated by Michael Whelan. Publisher's binding and dust jacket. Mild rubbing to extremities. Near fine.

Est.: $600-up
Start Bid: $300

37333   Stephen King. Two Copies of *Insomnia,* **Published by Mark V. Ziesing Books,** including: *Insomnia.* Shingletown, 1994. Deluxe leather-bound edition limited to 1,250 numbered copies. **Signed by the author, artist and designer.** Traycase. [and:] *Insomnia.* Shingletown, 1994. Gift edition. Dust jacket. Slipcase. Both fine.

Est.: $600-up
Start Bid: $300

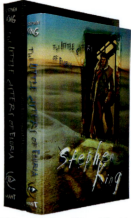

37334   Stephen King. *The Little Sisters of Eluria.* Hampton Falls: Donald M. Grant, [2008]. First edition, limited to 1250 numbered copies of which this is 1246. **Signed by King and Michael Whelan, illustrator.** Quarto. 312 pages. Publisher's binding, dust jacket, and clamshell box. Fine.

Est.: $600-up
Start Bid: $300

37335   Stephen King. *Night Shift.* Garden City, New York: Doubleday & Company, Inc., 1978. First edition, first impression (with code "S52" printed in the gutter of page 336). **Inscribed and signed by King.** Octavo. xxiv, 336 pages. Publisher's binding and dust jacket. Minor shelf wear to boards. Small dampstain to front board, most noticeable on the pastedown. Remnants of a removed bookplate to front free endpaper. Very light thumb-soiling to title page (the author's?). A couple of tiny brown spots to jacket panels and flap edges. An unusually nice copy in near fine condition.

Est.: $800-up
Start Bid: $400

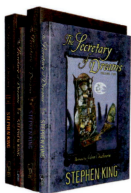

37336   **Stephen King.** *The Secretary of Dreams.* *Volume One and Two.* Baltimore: Cemetery Dance Publications, 2006, 2010. First edition. Each limited to 750 copies, signed by the author and the illustrator, Glenn Chadbourne. Quarto. Publisher's full black leather. Dust jacket. Publisher's brown cloth padded clamshell box. Fine.

Est.: $600-up
Start Bid: $300

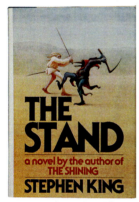

37337   **Stephen King.** *The Stand.* Garden City: Doubleday & Company, 1978. First edition (with code "T39" present in the gutter of page 823). **Inscribed and signed by King on the title page, "To Sally - / With best, / Stephen King / 9/8/79."** Octavo. [xii], 823 pages. Publisher's black cloth over tan paper boards with gilt spine titles. Spine cloth just a touch soiled with rubbing to the gilt titles and a bit of bowing inward of the spine. An excellent copy in near fine condition.

Est.: $800-up
Start Bid: $400

37338   **Stephen King.** *Under the Dome.* New York: Simon & Schuster, 2009. Signed Limited Special Illustrated Collector's edition. **Signed by the author.** Large octavo. 1,074 pages. Includes a shrinkwrapped set of 27 cards by Matthew Diffee. Publisher's binding and dust jacket. Gold silk belly band with jacket. Sewn-in silk bookmark. Still shrinkwrapped. Fine. **[and:]** **Stephen King.** *Under the Dome.* New York: Simon & Schuster, 2009. Special Illustrated Collector's edition. Large octavo. 1,074 pages. Includes a shrink-wrapped set of 27 cards by Diffee. Publisher's binding and dust jacket. Gold silk belly band with jacket. Sewn-in silk bookmark. Still in shrinkwrap, though slightly open. Slight bumping. Near fine.

Est.: $600-up
Start Bid: $300

37339   **Dean Koontz.** *The Book of Counted Sorrows.* New York: Charnel House, 2003. First edition, limited to 1250 numbered copies of which this is 821. **Signed by Koontz.** Octavo. 61; 71 pages. Publisher's binding and slipcase. Fine.

Est.: $600-up
Start Bid: $300

37340   **Johnston McCulley.** *The Mark of Zorro.* New York: Grosset & Dunlap, [1924]. Photoplay edition. Octavo. 300 pages. Publisher's binding and dust jacket. Illustrated with four photographic images from the film. Mild wear to cloth extremities with a few small indentations to front board. A touch of foxing to page edges and endpapers. Jacket is toned and edge worn with several small chips and tears; tape at head of spine. Very good.

Est.: $600-up
Start Bid: $300

37341   **Abraham Merritt.** *Creep, Shadow!* Garden City: The Crime Club, Inc. by Doubleday, Doran & Company, [1934]. First edition. 301 pages. Publisher's black cloth over boards with green spine stamping. Original pictorial dust jacket. Minor edge wear to boards. Bookplate to front pastedown. Five small chips to jacket edges (including two at the spine ends affecting a few letters in the title and imprint, and a couple of closed edge tears. Light rubbing to dust jacket. Overall, a very good, internally sound copy. Currey, page 364.

Est.: $600-up
Start Bid: $300

37342   **Abraham Merritt:** *Dwellers in the Mirage.* New York: Liveright, Inc., [1932]. First edition. Octavo. 295 pages. Publisher's black cloth with gilt titles. Original pictorial dust jacket. Light rubbing to spine cloth. Bookplate to front pastedown. Minor edge wear to jacket. Vertical crease running the length of the jacket spine. Very good condition.

Est.: $600-up
Start Bid: $300

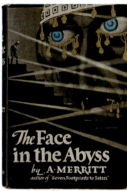

37343   **Abraham Merritt.** *The Face in the Abyss.* New York: Horace Liveright, [1931]. First edition. Octavo. 343 pages. Publisher's yellow cloth with black titles. Original pictorial dust jacket. Minimal shelf wear. Very minor dustsoiling to boards. Bookplate to front pastedown. Minor edge wear and rubbing to jacket, with a tiny closed tear to the bottom edge of the rear panel. Very good.

Est.: $600-up
Start Bid: $300

37344 **Mickey Spillane.** *I, the Jury.* E. P. Dutton & Company, 1947. First edition. Laid in is a bookplate **signed by Mickey Spillane.** Mild cocking to binding. Some chipping to a slightly rubbed and browned dust jacket. In custom slipcase. Overall, a very good copy of Spillane's first and most well-known book.
Est.: $1,000-up
Start Bid: $500

37345 **H. G. Wells.** *The Outline of History, Being a Plain History of Life and Mankind.* London: George Newnes Limited, [1919-1920]. First edition, in magazine format. Twenty-four quarto issues (complete series). 780 continuous pages, including the Index in volume 24. Forty-seven color and miscellaneous black and white illustrations throughout. Original wrappers with full color covers. Housed in a handsome, but slightly worn half leather slipcase. Tape repairs to covers of part 1. A few covers lightly creased. Cover to part 17 with a small abrasion and minor clip to corner. Most spines unusually fresh. All in all, a near fine copy. This first printing of the classic original magazine series was published fortnightly, from November 1919 to November 1920.
Est.: $600-up
Start Bid: $300

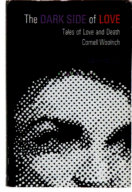

37346 **Cornell Woolrich.** *The Dark Side of Love.* New York: Walker, [1965]. First edition, first printing. Octavo. 181 pages. Publisher's binding and dust jacket. Minor wear to extremities of binding with some soft bumping and occasional insect nibbling. Light rubbing to jacket. Very good.
Est.: $600-up
Start Bid: $300

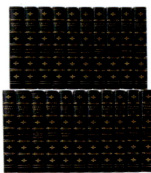

37347 **Thomas Hardy.** *The Writings of Thomas Hardy in Prose and Verse, with Prefaces and Notes.* New York and London: Harper & Brothers, 1920. Anniversary edition, one of 1,250 sets; this one unnumbered. Twenty-one octavo volumes. Bound by Brentano's in half royal blue leather over blue cloth with gilt ruling. Five raised bands on spine with gilt ornaments, ruling, and titles. Top edges gilt. Uncut page edges. Marbled endpapers. Extremities very lightly rubbed. Some shelf wear. Otherwise, near fine copies in this handsome set.
Est.: $1,000-up
Start Bid: $500

37348 **Elbert Hubbard.** *Contemplations.* East Aurora: Roycrofters, 1902. First edition. **Limited to 100 copies, this being number 35, signed by Hubbard.** Quarto. 120 double-columned pages. Frontispiece signed in pencil by the photographer. Engraved title. Half morocco over marbled boards. Marbled endpapers. Very minor rubbing to the joints. Some scuffing to the publisher's wood veneer box which has some loss to the rear panel. Very good.
Est.: $600-up
Start Bid: $300

37349 **Histories of England by Hume and Smollett. David Hume.** *The History of England, from the Invasion of Julius Caesar to the Revolution in 1688.* [and:] **Tobias Smollett.** *The History of England, from the Revolution in 1688, to the Death of George II. Designed as a continuation of Hume.* Both books published by R. Scholey and B. Crosby in London, 1808-1811. Sixteen large octavo volumes. Embellished with numerous engravings. Bound in polished calf with blind-tooled and gilt-stamped borders on covers, gilt-tooled board edges and inside boards. Five raised gilt-tooled bands on spine with gilt-stamped devices and titles. Marbled page edges. Light offsetting to engravings throughout. Some shelfwear to extremities. A very good set.
Est.: $600-up
Start Bid: $300

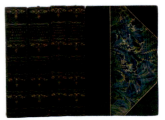

37350 **John Keats.** *The Complete Works.* Edited by Nathan Haskell Dole. London and Boston: Virtue & Company Publishers, [1904-1906]. Laurel edition, number 281 of 1,000 copies. Four octavo volumes. Sumptuous three-quarter green morocco over marbled boards with gilt titles and rules and five raised spine bands. Top edges gilt, others uncut. Marbled endpapers. Some shelf wear, with rubbed corners. Spines a touch darkened. Volumes one, two and four each have varying degrees of splitting to the joints. Front hinge of volume one just starting. Short tear to front cover spine leather of volume two; front board halfway detached; light ink staining to rear flyleaves. Front hinge of volume four cracked at the limitation page. Very good.
Est.: $600-up
Start Bid: $300

37351 **Samuel Richardson.** *The Works of Samuel Richardson.* London: James Carpenter and William Miller, 1811. First collected edition. Complete in nineteen twelvemo volumes. Bound in dark blue half calf over marbled boards. Four gilt-stamped bands on spine with gilt-stamped titles on morocco labels. Rubbing to extremities. Volume One has loss at spine foot. Generally, a very good set.
Est.: $600-up
Start Bid: $300

37352 **[Sangorski & Sutcliffe].** **Omar Khayyam.** *Rubaiyat of Omar Khayyam.* London: Siegle, Hill & Co., [n.d., ca. 1910]. Edition limited to 550 copies, of which this is number 54, **signed by Sangorski and Sutcliffe.** Large quarto. Unpaginated. 12 striking illustrations, many initials, and several decorations throughout highlighted in gold. Bound in vellum, front cover with elaborate gilt peacock. A few scuff marks and a couple of bumps to slightly bowing boards. Endpapers toned. Else, a stunningly beautiful work in near fine condition.

Est.: $600-up
Start Bid: $300

37353 **Percy Bysshe Shelley.** *The Complete Works.* Edited by Nathan Haskell Dole. London and Boston: Virtue & Company Publishers, [1904-1906]. Laurel edition, number 281 of 1,000 copies. Eight octavo volumes. Sumptuous three-quarter green morocco over marbled boards with gilt titles and rules and five raised spine bands. Top edges gilt, others uncut. Marbled endpapers. Some shelf wear, with very mild abrading to some spine leather, and rubbed corners. Spines a touch darkened. Short splits to the joints of two volumes. Rear fore-edge of board of volume one bumped, and rear hinge cracked. Overall, a very attractive, well-maintained set in very good condition.

Est.: $800-up
Start Bid: $400

37354 **George Newnes, editor.** *The Strand Magazine.* *An Illustrated Monthly.* London: Burleigh Street and George Newnes, 1891-1900. Twenty consecutive octavo volumes. Illustrated throughout. Publisher's blue cloth over beveled boards with black titles and illustration on front and gilt-stamped and black titles on spine. General shelfwear, mostly to spine and corners. Some spines with small tears or sunned. Very good.

Est.: $1,000-up
Start Bid: $500

37355 **Robert Arnot, Managing Editor.** *The Immortals: Masterpieces of Fiction Crowned by the French Academy.* With a Preface to each Volume by an Immortal and a General Introduction Conveying Official Sanction by Gaston Boissier Secrétaire Perpétual de L'Académie Française. Paris: Maison Mazarin, [1905]. Richelieu Edition. **One of fifty numbered sets signed by both Arnot and Boissier on the limitation page, of which this is number four.** Twenty octavo volumes. Frontispiece portraits after various artists, with printed tissue guards. Bound in full black crushed levant morocco with gilt-tooled decorations, each with metal medallion portrait of Cardinal Richelieu set into front cover.

Est.: $1,000-up
Start Bid: $500

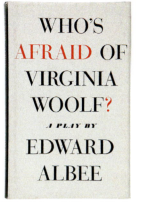

37356 **Edward Albee.** *Who's Afraid of Virginia Woolf?* New York: Atheneum, 1962. First edition, first printing. **Inscribed by Albee** on half-title page. Octavo. 242 pages. Publisher's binding and dust jacket. Minor rubbing to cloth and spine titles with a bit of abrading to extremities. Slight lean to spine and modest thumbing to pages. Jacket shows mild rubbing with light wear to head of spine. Small area of soiling to front panel. Very good.

Est.: $600-up
Start Bid: $300

37357 **Horatio Alger, Jr.** *Ragged Dick; or, Street Life in New York with the Boot-Blacks.* Boston: Loring, [1868]. First edition, later impression. Octavo. 296 pages. Publisher's binding with wear and abrading to extremities. Spine leaning with a few sprung gatherings. Rear joint split and glued. Name on front free endpaper. Bookplate to verso of front free endpaper. Illustrated half-title with Dick and three friends. Mild toning to pages with an occasional spot soiling. Overall good condition.

Est.: $600-up
Start Bid: $300

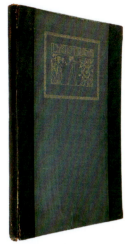

37358 **Aristophanes.** *Lysistrata.* London: Fanfrolico Press, [1926]. **Limited to 725 copies, signed by the translator, Jack Lindsay.** Folio. 51 pages. Illustrated by Norman Lindsay. Original half morocco. Gilt lettering to spine. Gilt title to top board. Top edge gilt. Some scuffing and bumping to the binding. Very good.

Est.: $600-up
Start Bid: $300

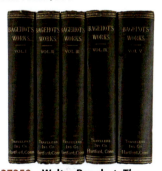

37359 **Walter Bagehot.** *The Works of Walter Bagehot.* Hartford: Travelers Insurance Company, 1889. Five octavo volumes. Index in volume V. Frontispiece. Olive cloth over boards. Gilt lettering to spines. Cracked hinge to final volume. Very good.

Est.: $600-up
Start Bid: $300

37360 [Bruce Francis, editor]. *Literature, Art and Artifacts That Will Forever Remain Among The Undead: The Book Sail 16th Anniversary Catalogue.* Orange: McLaughlin Press, 1984. First edition, limited to 50 copies lettered with a character from Venusian alphabet. **Signed by Elvira, Rowena Morrill, Ray Bradbury, Robert Bloch, and William F. Nolan** (in Nolan's *The Dandelion Chronicles* pamphlet inserted in pocket at rear). Also with an **original Hannes Bok drawing** inserted in pocket at front. Octavo. Unpaginated. Publisher's quarter leather over cloth boards with lenticular image of Elvira mounted to front board. Includes Dracula edition color, lenticular, 8 x 10 inch, **signed photograph of Elvira,** housed in publisher's enclosure and slipcase. Seldom seen set in fine condition.
Est.: $600-up
Start Bid: $300

37361 [Charlotte Brontë]. *Jane Eyre. An Autobiography.* Edited by Currer Bell. Boston: Wilkins, Carter & Co., 1848. First American hardcover edition. Twelvemo. (1-3), 4-483 pages. Bound in contemporary half leather over mottled paper boards. Spine has four raised bands with blindstamped floral decoration and gilt titles and ruling. Well worn boards with splitting to top of joints and loose spine head. Several signatures sprung at front and two at rear standing proud. Hinges broken with front hanging by a cord. Page edges toned with some staining throughout text. Otherwise, a good copy for rebinding.
Est.: $600-up
Start Bid: $300

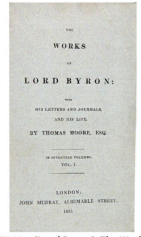

37362 [Lord Byron]. *The Works of Lord Byron with his Letters and Journals and his Life*, by *Thomas Moore, Esq.* London: John Murray, 1835. Later edition. Seventeen twelvemo volumes. Bound in full leather with double-fillet borders on diced covers. Blind-tooled design on covers and edges of boards. Four raised bands on spine with gilt and blind-stamped ruling. Morocco labels on spine with gilt titles. Marbled edges and endpapers. Engraved frontispieces and half-titles. Shelfwear to extremities. Some minor chipping to spine ends. Light foxing throughout. Gift inscription. Very good.
Est.: $600-up
Start Bid: $300

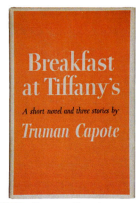

37363 Truman Capote. *Breakfast at Tiffany's.* New York: Random House, [1958]. First edition, first printing. Octavo. [viii], [1]-179 pages. Publisher's yellow cloth with gilt spine titles. Original dust jacket, price-clipped. Minor edge wear to boards. Spine cloth and dust jacket spine slightly sunned. Small bit of toning to fore-edge margin of page 179. Near fine condition.
Est.: $600-up
Start Bid: $300

37364 Miguel Cervantes de Saavedra. *The Life and Exploits of the ingenious gentleman Don Quixote de la Mancha. Translated from the original Spanish by Charles Jarvis.* London: J. and R. Tonson, S. Draper, R. Dodsley, 1749. Stated Second Edition. Two octavo volumes. xxii, [26], 406 pages; [16], 422 pages. With 24 copper-engraved plates by George Vander Gucht. Tastefully rebacked with diced full polished calf covers with gilt borders. Blind-stamped modern spines with black and red morocco labels, gilt decoration, ruling and titles. Speckled edges. New preliminaries and terminals. Minor foxing to endpapers and pages. Generally near fine.
Est.: $800-up
Start Bid: $400

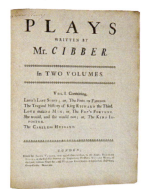

37365 [Colley Cibber]. *Plays Written by Mr. Cibber.* London: Jacob Tonson, et al., 1721. First edition. Two large quarto volumes. 406; 463 pages. Custom uniform full cloth with leather spine labels. Minor rubbing and toning to cloth extremities. Pages show darkened edges and toning with scattered foxing and occasional abrading to edges. Volume I with one leaf detached. Rear hinge of Volume II cracking. Neat name on title page of both volumes. Very good.
Est.: $800-up
Start Bid: $400

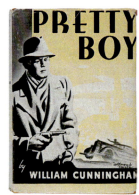

37366 William Cunningham. *Pretty Boy.* First edition. New York: The Vanguard Press, 1936. The rare second novel by the author of The *Green Corn Rebellion*, which, like this novel, was also a story championing the depression-era Oklahoma proletariat. Cunningham was the first director of the Oklahoma Federal Writers' Project. Some moderate chipping to the dust jacket. Very good.
Est.: $600-up
Start Bid: $300

37367 [Charles Dickens]. *Sketches by Boz Illustrative of Every-Day Life and Every-Day People.* London: Chapman and Hall, 1839. First one-volume book edition. Octavo. viii, 248, 241-526 pages.
Est.: $600-up
Start Bid: $300

37368 [Charles Dickens].
Memoirs of Joseph Grimaldi.
London: Richard Bentley, 1838.
First edition, first issue.
Est.: $600-up
Start Bid: $300

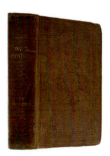

37369   Charles Dickens.
The Personal History of David
Copperfield. With Illustrations by
H. K. Browne. London: Bradbury
& Evans, 1850. First edition in
book form. Octavo. [8], [vii]-xiv,
624 pages. Errata leaf (pp. xv/xvi)
bound following the half-title (pp.
[i/ii]). Forty etched plates, including
frontispiece and added vignette
title, by H. K. Browne ("Phiz"). Later
state of the vignette title, without
the 1850 date and with the imprint
"Chapman & Hall, 193, Piccadilly."
Est.: $800-up
Start Bid: $400

37370   [Charles Dickens, edi-
tor]. *The Pic Nic Papers.* London:
Henry Colburn, 1841. First edition,
second issue, with the G. J. Palmer
imprint on the verso of the title
page of Volume I and the error
"publisher young" corrected to
"young publisher" on p. [iii] of the
Introduction. Three twelvemo
volumes.
Est.: $600-up
Start Bid: $300

37371   [Thomas D'Urfey]. *The*
Comical History of Don Quixote,
as it is Acted at the Queens
Theatre in Dorset-Garden, by
Their Majesties Servants. Part
I and Part the Second. London:
Samuel Briscoe, 1694. Small quarto.
[8], 63, [1]; [8], 64 pages. Two parts
bound as single volume. Spine
rebacked with linen and rear cover
appears renewed. Front cover with
lettering over "London." Chipping
and abrading to preliminary pages,
affecting some text. Occasional
minor soiling and abrading
throughout with infrequent notations. Pages generally toned, but
still soft. Fragile, but overall good
condition.
Est.: $600-up
Start Bid: $300

37372   Lee Fairchild. *Don Juan's*
Bouquet. New York: Edwin C. Hill,
1903. Limited to 500 copies of
which this is number 1. Inscribed
by the author. Almost 100 original
watercolors throughout this slim
book of poetry. Lavishly bound
by Curtis Walters in full morocco.
Gilt tooling and floral onlays. Full
morocco doublures and watered
silk endpapers. Moderate scuffing.
Terminal blanks detached. Overall,
a stunningly designed and embellished book in very good condition.
Est.: $600-up
Start Bid: $300

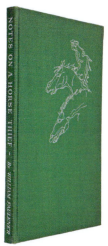

37373   William Faulkner. *Notes*
on a Horse Thief. Greenville: Levee
Press, 1950. First edition, limited
to 975 numbered copies of which
this is 840. **Signed by Faulkner.**
Small quarto. 71 pages. Publisher's
binding with light rubbing to cloth
extremities. Mild foxing to page
edges and offsetting to endpapers.
Name on front free endpaper. Near
fine.
Est.: $800-up
Start Bid: $400

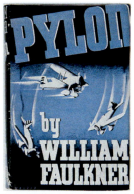

37374   William Faulkner. *Pylon.*
New York: Harrison Smith and
Robert Haas, 1935. First edition,
first printing. Octavo. 315 pages.
Publisher's binding and dust jacket.
Rubbing to cloth extremities and
gilt titles. Scattered soiling with
sunning to spine. Light foxing to
page edges and endpapers. Price
clipped jacket is mildly rubbed
with a one-inch tear and abrasion
to tail of spine. Modest abrading
to bottom edge of inner flaps. Very
good.
Est.: $600-up
Start Bid: $300

37375   William Faulkner.
Requiem for a Nun. New York:
Random House, [1951]. First edition. Limited to 750 copies of
which this is number 694, and
signed by Faulkner. Octavo.
286 pages. Publisher's half black
cloth with gilt stamping on spine,
marbled paper boards and acetate
wrapper. Housed in a custom clamshell box. A fine copy.
Est.: $1,000-up
Start Bid: $500

37376   Ian Fleming. *Dr. No.*
London: Jonathan Cape, [1958].
First edition, first printing. Octavo.
256 pages. Publisher's binding
and dust jacket. Modest rubbing
to cloth with a touch of abrading
to head of spine. General foxing to
jacket with tape shadows on inner
flaps. Smoothed fold line along
length of bottom edge. Very good.
Est.: $600-up
Start Bid: $300

37377 Ian Fleming. *For Your Eyes Only.* London: Jonathan Cape, [1960]. First edition, first printing. Octavo. 252 pages. Publisher's binding and dust jacket. Slight lean to spine with a few spots of soiling to page edges. Jacket is rubbed and edge worn with several small chips and tears. Very good.

Est.: $600-up
Start Bid: $300

37378 Ian Fleming. *The Man with the Golden Gun.* London: Jonathan Cape, [1965]. First edition, first printing. Octavo. 221 pages. Publisher's binding and dust jacket. Faint foxing to page edges. Jacket shows insect nibbling to extremities with areas of dampstaining to spine and rear panel. Front fold reinforced. Very good.

Est.: $600-up
Start Bid: $300

37379 Ian Fleming. *On Her Majesty's Secret Service.* London: Jonathan Cape, [1963]. First edition, first printing. Octavo. 288 pages. Publisher's binding and dust jacket. General rubbing and light abrading to cloth extremities with a slight spine lean. Mild foxing and soiling to page edges with a touch of foxing to endpapers. A few tiny spots of abrading to foreedge. Minor rubbing and toning to jacket edges with some faint foxing to front panel and internal tape to spine ends. Overall very good.

Est.: $600-up
Start Bid: $300

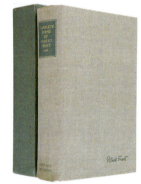

37380 Robert Frost. *Complete Poems of Robert Frost 1949.* New York: Henry Holt, [1949]. First edition, limited to 500 numbered copies of which this is number 357. **Signed by Frost.** Octavo. 642 pages. Publisher's binding and slipcase. Modest toning to spine ends. Light rubbing and wear to slipcase. Letter from publisher, dated 1949, responding to an inquiry about purchasing a copy of this title. Includes envelope. A fine copy.

Est.: $600-up
Start Bid: $300

37381 Graham Greene. *The Confidential Agent.* London: William Heinemann, [1939]. First edition. Octavo. [vi], 286 pages. Modern three-quarter green morocco over green cloth boards with gilt spine titles and five raised spine bands by Period Bookbinders of Bath, England. Scattered foxing throughout. Very good.

Est.: $600-up
Start Bid: $300

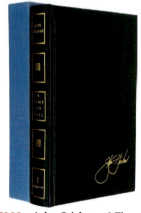

37382 John Grisham. *A Time to Kill.* New York: Doubleday, [1993]. Leatherbound slipcased edition. **Limited to 350 numbered copies signed by the author, of which this is number 66.** Octavo. 487 pages. Publisher's binding. Blue spray to edges. Slipcase rubbed. Otherwise, near fine.

Est.: $600-up
Start Bid: $300

37383 Nathaniel Hawthorne. *The Complete Works of Nathaniel Hawthorne,* with *Introductory Notes by George Parsons Lathrop and Illustrated with Etchings by Blum, Church, Dielman, Gifford, Shirlaw, and Turner, in Twelve Volumes.* Cambridge: The Riverside Press, 1883. Riverside Edition. Twelve octavo volumes. Limited to 250 sets, this being number 232. Frontispieces. Illustrations. Recased in tan cloth over boards. Original paper title labels mounted to spines. Foxing to frontispieces and title pages. Hinge of Volume I cracked. Overall, a near fine set. BAL 7643.

Est.: $600-up
Start Bid: $300

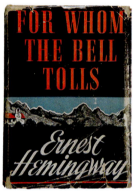

37384 Ernest Hemingway. *For Whom the Bell Tolls.* New York: Charles Scribner's Sons, 1940. First edition, first printing. Octavo. [x], 471, [1, blank] pages. Publisher's oatmeal cloth and first issue dust jacket, lacking photographer's credit on rear panel. Boards slightly sunned along the edges, especially the spine panel. Contents slightly toned with occasional minor foxing. Jacket chipped and worn along the edges with some small areas of loss. Generally very good.

Est.: $600-up
Start Bid: $300

37385   Ernest Hemingway. *God Rest You Merry Gentlemen.* New York: House of Books, 1933. First edition. Limited to 300 numbered copies, of which this is number 20. Twelvemo. 10 unnumbered pages. Red cloth over boards. Fine in the original publisher's glassine, which is chipped, torn, and creased.

Est.: $1,200-up
Start Bid: $600

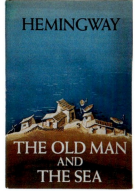

37386   Ernest Hemingway. *The Old Man and the Sea.* New York: Charles Scribner's Sons, 1952. First edition, in the first state dust jacket with image on rear panel tinted in blue. Octavo. 140 pages. Publisher's binding and dust jacket with $3.00 price. Mild fading to spine and board edges. Minor expert restoration and a couple of tiny holes to jacket spine. A near fine copy in a remarkably bright and crisp dust jacket, housed in a custom blue cloth slipcase with gilt-stamped black morocco label.

Est.: $1,000-up
Start Bid: $500

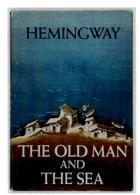

37387   Ernest Hemingway. *The Old Man and the Sea.* New York: Scribner's, 1952. First edition, first state dust jacket. Octavo. 140 pages. Publisher's binding and dust jacket. Moderate toning to cloth with light abrading to extremities. Minor wear to jacket edges with chipping at spine head and a one-half-inch folded tear to top edge of rear panel. Very good.

Est.: $600-up
Start Bid: $300

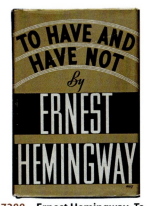

37388   Ernest Hemingway. *To Have and Have Not.* New York: Charles Scriber's Sons, 1937. First edition, with "A" and Scribner's seal on copyright page. Octavo. 262 pages. Bottom edge of boards slightly rubbed. Top edge dusty. A very nice dust jacket (with $2.50 price) with light chipping to edges, and a four-inch straight scratch to the front panel. Bookplate to front pastedown. A bright, clean copy in very good condition.

Est.: $600-up
Start Bid: $300

37389   Two A. E. Housman related items, including: **Robert Bridges.** *New Verse, written in 1921.* Oxford: Clarendon Press, 1925. First edition. **Presentation copy to the scholar and poet A. E. Housman.** Octavo. 88 pages. Publisher's white paper boards with blind-stamped borders and gilt-stamped titles on front and spine. Housman's bookplate. Covers lightly soiled with sunned spine. Shelfwear to extremities. Front joints starting. Very good. [and:] **Richard Perceval Graves.** *A. E. Housman. The Scholar Poet.* New York: Charles Scribner's Sons, [1980]. First U.S. edition. **Signed dedication bookplate.** Octavo. 304 pages. Publisher's binding and price-clipped dust jacket. Shelfwear to foot of boards. Spine of jacket faded. Custom clamshell case with modern reprint photo of Bridges included. Very good.

Est.: $600-up
Start Bid: $300

37390   Henrik Ibsen. *The Works of Henrik Ibsen.* The Viking Edition. New York: Charles Scribner's Sons, 1911, 1912. **Limited to 256 sets, signed by the publisher.** Sixteen octavo volumes. Bound by Stikeman in half morocco. Gilt designs and lettering to spines. Top edges gilt. Some rubbing to the extremities, joints showing moderate cracking. Very good.

Est.: $600-up
Start Bid: $300

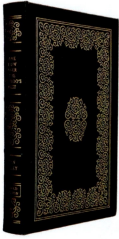

37391   Ken Kesey. *One Flew Over the Cuckoo's Nest.* Norwalk: The Easton Press, [1999]. Leather-bound edition. **Signed by the author.** Octavo. 311 pages. Publisher's full leather with gilt-stamped decoration and ruling to front and rear cover and gilt-stamped titles and decoration to spine. All edges gilt. Silk moire end-papers. Ribbon marker. Near fine.

Est.: $600-up
Start Bid: $300

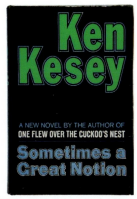

37392   Ken Kesey. *Sometimes a Great Notion.* New York: The Viking Press, [1964]. First edition. **Signed by the author** on a special autograph plate affixed to the front free endpaper. Octavo. [viii], 628 pages. Publisher's gray and blue weaved cloth with green and blue titles. Top edge stained green. Viking ship present on the half title page. In the original first issue dust jacket with the Hank Krangler photo credit and two lines of biographical information on the author on the rear flap. Minor dust-soiling to text edges. Minimal edge wear to jacket. Very minor foxing and a small dark stain at the spine tail on the verso of jacket. Near fine.

Est.: $600-up
Start Bid: $300

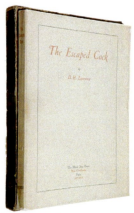

37393   D. H. Lawrence. *The Escaped Cock.* Paris: The Black Sun Press, 1929. First edition, limited to 450 numbered copies, of which this is number 35. Octavo. 96 pages. Frontispiece. Publisher's wrappers and glassine. Marbled paper-covered slipcase. Very good condition. [and:] *The Man Who Died.* New York: Alfred A. Knopf, 1931. First American edition, advance reader's copy. Octavo. 103 pages. Publisher's binding. Review slip tipped in. Fine.

Est.: $800-up
Start Bid: $400

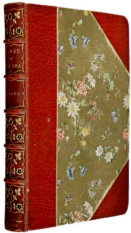

37394   Charles Godfrey Leland. *Songs of the Sea and Lays of the Land.* London: Adam and Charles Black, 1895. First edition. Octavo. 278 pages. Custom half morocco by Charles E. Lauriat. **With 12 original signed water color illustrations by Leland's wife, Bella.** Modest rubbing and scuffing to binding with a touch of darkening to spine. A near fine copy with wonderful, one-of-a-kind illustrations.

Est.: $600-up
Start Bid: $300

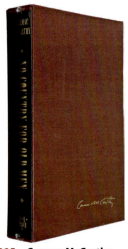

37395   Cormac McCarthy. *No Country For Old Men.* [New Orleans: Trice, 2005]. First edition, limited to 325 numbered copies of which this is 83. **Signed by McCarthy.** Octavo. Publisher's binding and slipcase. Fine and still sealed in publisher's shrinkwrap.

Est.: $800-up
Start Bid: $400

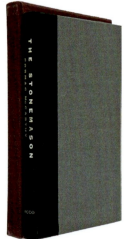

37396   Cormac McCarthy. *The Stonemason.* [Hopewell]: Ecco Press, [1994]. First edition, limited to 350 numbered copies of which this is 109. **Signed by McCarthy.** Octavo. 133 pages. Publisher's binding and slipcase. Fine.

Est.: $600-up
Start Bid: $300

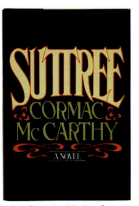

37397   Cormac McCarthy. *Suttree.* New York: Random House, 1979. First edition. Octavo. 471 pages. Square stain on front free endpaper from removed resale sticker. Faint red remainder stamp of the Random House logo on bottom edge. Overall, a near fine copy in a nearly flawless dust jacket.

Est.: $1,000-up
Start Bid: $500

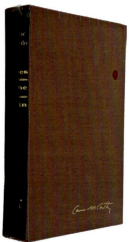

37398   Cormac McCarthy. *Cities of the Plains.* [New Orleans: Trice, 1998]. First edition, limited to 300 numbered copies of which this is 61. **Signed by McCarthy.** Octavo. Publisher's binding and slipcase. Fine and still sealed in publisher's shrinkwrap.

Est.: $800-up
Start Bid: $400

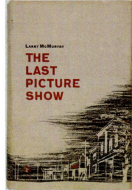

37399   Larry McMurtry. *The Last Picture Show.* New York: Dial, 1966. First edition, first printing. Octavo. 280 pages. Publisher's binding and dust jacket. Slight lean to spine. Mild rubbing and darkening to jacket. Repriced in ink on front inner flap. Near fine.

Est.: $600-up
Start Bid: $300

37400   Herman Melville. *Moby Dick or, The Whale.* [Mount Vernon]: The Artist's Limited Edition, 1975. **One of 1,500 copies with a signed serigraph frontispiece by the artist LeRoy Neiman and the preface signed by Jacques Yves-Cousteau, of which this is number 265.** Folio. 272 pages. Illustrated with twelve double-page spreads and a serigraph frontispiece by LeRoy Neiman. Bound in full leather with gilt-stamped illustration to front and spine titles. Five raised bands. Slip-on case with leather ends and cloth sides. Near fine.

Est.: $600-up
Start Bid: $300

37401   Margaret Mitchell.
Gone with the Wind. New York:
Macmillan, 1936. First edition, first
printing with "Published May, 1936"
on copyright page and no note
of other printings. Octavo. 1037
Pages. Publisher's binding and dust
jacket. Minor rubbing and darkening to cloth with abrading to
extremities. Splits to head and tail
with light chipping. Foxing to endpapers and preliminary pages with
lightly scattered foxing throughout. Later issue jacket with no price
and reviews on rear panel. Jacket is
edge worn with several small chips
and tears. Overall very good.
Est.: $600-up
Start Bid: $300

**37402   [John Henry Nash,
printer]. Three Books Printed
by John Henry Nash,** including:
Elizabeth Barrett Browning.
Sonnets from the Portuguese.
1927. [and:] **John Dryden.** *All
For Love.* 1929. [and:] **Alexander
Pope.** *An Essay on Criticism.* 1928.
All books printed in San Francisco
for William Andrews Clark, Jr. by
John Henry Nash. Each title limited
to 250 numbered copies, and each
in a slipcase with companion facsimile volume. Quarto. Half vellum
over paper boards. Some moderate
shelf wear and minor chipping to
the slipcase. Overall, near fine, in
clean, crisp condition.
Est.: $600-up
Start Bid: $300

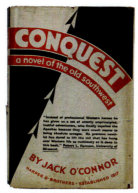

37403   Frank O'Connor.
*Conquest: A Novel of the Old
Southwest.* New York: Harper
& Brothers, 1930. First edition.
Octavo. 293 pages. Publisher's rus-
set cloth with orange stamped titles on front panel and spine. Dust
jacket. Extremities and corners
lightly rubbed. Rear hinge starting.
Dust jacket shows toning and light
staining with small chips. Overall,
a very good copy of the author's
scarce first book.
Est.: $600-up
Start Bid: $300

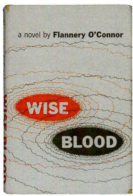

37404   Flannery O'Connor. *Wise
Blood.* New York: Harcourt, Brace,
[1952]. First edition. Octavo. 232
pages. Publisher's binding and dust
jacket. Spine ends and extremities
rubbed with shelfwear. Jacket is
price-clipped with new price in
marker. Chipping to spine of jacket
and edges worn. Small closed
tears. Otherwise, very good.
Est.: $1,000-up
Start Bid: $500

**37405   [Fore-Edge Painting].
Thomas Park [editor].** *The British
Poets: with the Most Approved
Translations of the Greek and
Roman Poets. Vols. LXI and LXII.*
London: J. Sharpe, 1810-1824. First
edition. Twelvemo. [2], vii, [1], 184,
[2], 171, [5] pages. **With a fore-
edge painting depicting a religious structure.** Contemporary
full morocco with gilt titles
and decoration. All edges gilt.
Bookplate. Engraved frontispiece
and one additional plate. Mild rubbing and scuffing to binding. Faint
toning to some pages. Housed in a
custom clamshell box. Near fine.
Est.: $600-up
Start Bid: $300

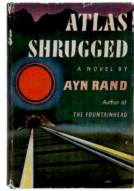

37406   Ayn Rand. *Atlas
Shrugged.* New York: Random
House, [1957]. First edition, first
printing. Octavo. 1,168 pages.
Publisher's binding and dust jacket.
Cloth is rubbed and dampstained
with abraded extremities. Titles
and gilt rubbed. Areas of dampstaining and discoloration along
bottom rear edge of textblock.
Hinges reinforced. Bookplate.
Small label on rear free endpaper.
Jacket is edge rubbed and edge
worn with several small chips and
tears, and staining to bottom edge
of rear panel and front fold. Overall
very good.
Est.: $600-up
Start Bid: $300

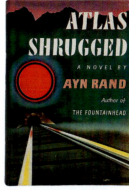

37407   Ayn Rand. *Atlas
Shrugged.* New York: Random
House, [1957]. First edition. Octavo.
1,168 pages. Publisher's green
cloth, front cover stamped in gilt,
spine stamped in gilt and black,
dust jacket. Jacket spine slightly
browned, some rubbing to edges,
some restoration to headcap,
some rubbing and soiling to cloth.
Overopened at title page. Very
good.
Est.: $1,000-up
Start Bid: $850

37408   J. D. Salinger. *The
Complete Uncollected Short
Stories. Volume 1 and 2.* [n. p.: n.
d., 1974]. Second issue of pirated
edition. Two octavo volumes. 88;
107 pages. Publisher's wrappers.
Mild rubbing to covers with a few
spots of foxing. Small area of soiling to fore-edge of Volume 1. A
near fine set.
Est.: $600-up
Start Bid: $300

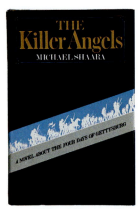

37409   Michael Shaara. *The Killer Angels.* New York: David McKay Company, Inc., [1974]. First edition, review copy with slip laid in. Publisher's binding and dust jacket with $8.95 price. Foxing to top page edges; short closed tear to rear panel of jacket. Else fine. Civil War novel, winner of the Pulitzer Prize for Fiction in 1975.
Est.: $1,000-up
Start Bid: $500

37410   [William] Shakespeare. *Hamlet, Prince of Denmark.* London: Selwyn & Blount, n.d. 175 pages. Decorated by John Avsten. Publisher's black paper over boards with gilt-stamped and green titles and decoration on front cover. White cloth backstrip with gilt-stamped titles and decoration. Fore-edge and bottom edge uncut. Covers rubbed with slight damp-staining. Extremities rubbed with loss at corners. Spine has light soiling. Foxing and toning to preliminaries and terminals. Pages lightly toned. Generally very good.
Est.: $600-up
Start Bid: $300

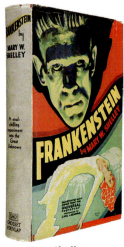

37411   Mary Shelley. *Frankenstein*. New York: Grosset & Dunlap, [1931]. "Illustrated with scenes from the Universal Photoplay." White stain to the front pastedown. Inked name of previous owner to rear pastedown. Minor chipping to the dust jacket. The jacket illustration of Karloff as the monster and Mae Clarke in a deep swoon is bright and vibrant. In a custom box. A superior copy in very good condition of one of the most sought-after photoplay editions.
Est.: $1,000-up
Start Bid: $500

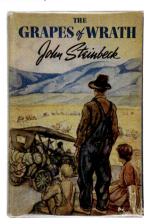

37412   John Steinbeck. *The Grapes of Wrath.* New York: Viking, [1939]. First edition. Octavo. 619 pages. Publisher's binding and dust jacket (with "First Edition" tag on the lower front flap, as issued). Front hinge cracking. Jacket is lightly toned and rubbed with some chipping to extremities and moderate insect damage to lower corner of front panel. Very good.
Est.: $600-up
Start Bid: $300

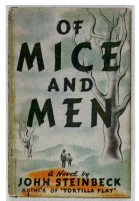

37413   John Steinbeck. *Of Mice and Men.* New York: Covici Friede, [1937]. First edition, first issue, with a bullet between the "8"s on page 88 and "pendula" on page 9, line 21. Octavo. 186 pages. Publisher's tan cloth with orange and black stamping. Original pictorial dust jacket. Minimal soiling and one tiny bubble to cloth. Text edges mildly dustsoiled. Internally, the text is very clean. Minor chipping and a few closed tears to jacket edges. One small hole on the jacket spine near the "E" in "MEN." Overall, a very good copy of a scarce first printing.
Est.: $800-up
Start Bid: $400

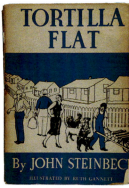

37414   John Steinbeck. *Tortilla Flat.* New York: Covici Friede, [1935].First edition, issued in wrappers, one of approximately only 500 copies. Publisher's square binding with blank stiff cream covers, sewed and wrapped in the illustrated dust jacket. Both the front blank cover and the illustrated wrapper have cleanly separated from the binding at the front joint but are still present. Jacket panels toned, spine darkened. One corner chipped. A fragile item in good to very good condition. Goldstone A4a.
Est.: $800-up
Start Bid: $400

37415   Alfred Lord Tennyson. *The Death of Oenone, Akbar's Dream, and Other Poems.* London: Macmillan, 1892. One of five hundred numbered copies, of which this is number 125. Quarto, Large Paper Edition. 111 pages. Contains five steel engravings of Lord Tennyson, complete with tissue guards. White cloth over boards with front gilt border and gilt spine titles. Two small indentations to spine. Slight soiling to top edge. Foxing and toning throughout, particularly to edges of engravings. Many pages unopened. Binding still tight. Bookplate on front pastedown. Original dust jacket included, though missing spine and in pieces. Generally very good.
Est.: $600-up
Start Bid: $300

37416   Alfred Tennyson. *Idylls of the King.* London: Edward Moxon & Co., 1859. First edition, later state, 8 pages of unopened "December, 1859" advertisements at front. Octavo. 261 pages. Publisher's green cloth over boards with blindstamping and gilt spine titles. Boards somewhat faded with rubbing and bumped corners. Spine sunned with small tears and loss at ends. Binding loose with some pages separating but held by binding threads. Slightly cocked. Minimal foxing. Bookplate on front pastedown. Handwritten two and a quarter page "Dedication" from "The Poet Laureate to the late Prince Consort" as well as an inscription from Queen Victoria's obstetrician Charles B. Locock, bart. Generally very good.
Est.: $600-up
Start Bid: $300

37417   Alfred Tennyson. *Poems, Chiefly Lyrical.* London: Effingham Wilson Royal Exchange, Cornhill, 1830. First edition, first issue with rare leaf of errata but lacking advertisements at rear, and page 91 misnumbered as 19. Twelvemo. 154 pages. Full leather with extensive gilt decoration and borders. Five raised bands on spine with gilt decoration and titles. Top edge gilt. Marbled endpapers with rich inner dentelles. Bookplate on verso of last free endpaper. Front board detached with rear hinge rubbed. Lightly bumped corners and head of spine rubbed with minor loss. Scattered foxing throughout. Otherwise, very good.
Est.: $800-up
Start Bid: $400

37418   Hunter S. Thompson. *Fear and Loathing in America.* *The Brutal Odyssey of an Outlaw Journalist, 1968-1976.* New York: Simon & Schuster, [2000]. First edition. **Signed by the author.** Octavo. 756 pages. Publisher's full red leather with gilt-stamped Gonzo device on front cover and gilt-stamped titles and decoration on spine. All edges gilt. Silk moire endpapers. Ribbon marker. Slightly overopened at tipped-in signature page. Otherwise, near fine.
Est.: $600-up
Start Bid: $300

37419   Hunter S. Thompson. *Fear and Loathing in Las Vegas.* *A Savage Journey to the Heart of the American Dream.* New York: Random House, [1971]. First edition. **Signed by the author.** Octavo. 206 pages. Illustrations by Ralph Steadman. Publisher's binding and dust jacket. Boards slightly faded at both head and tail. Light foxing to top corners of endpapers. Some staining and light foxing to all edges. Rubbed jacket has light toning to edges. Very good.
Est.: $600-up
Start Bid: $300

37420   Mark Twain [Samuel L. Clemens]. *The Adventures of Tom Sawyer.* Hartford: The American Publishing Company, 1876. First edition, third printing. Printed on laid paper. Four page publisher's catalog in back dated December 1, 1876. Octavo. 275 pages. Profusely illustrated in text. Original full sheepskin (only 1,500 in this binding) Boards detached, along with preliminary and terminal blanks. Much of the leather has been worn from the spine. Boards bumped and scuffed. Previous owner's name in pencil to two of the blank preliminary pages. An early state in this rare form, internally very good.
Est.: $600-up
Start Bid: $300

37421   Jules Verne. *Michael Strogoff.* New York: Scribner, Armstrong & Co., 1877. First American edition. Octavo. 377 pages. Illustrated. Publisher's reddish brown cloth. Rubbing to extremities. Slightly cocked and a bit shaken. Very good.
Est.: $600-up
Start Bid: $300

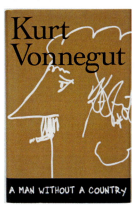

37422   Kurt Vonnegut, Jr. *A Man Without a Country.* New York: Seven Stories, [2005]. First edition, first printing. **Signed by Vonnegut on half-title page and with drawing.** Octavo. 146 pages. Publisher's binding and dust jacket. Fine.
Est.: $600-up
Start Bid: $300

 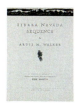

37423   Ardis M. Walker. *Sierra Nevada Sequence.* [n. p.]: Sierra Trails Press, [1968]. First edition, limited to 107 numbered copies of which this is 38. Quarto. Unpaginated. Publisher's unbound sheets laid into a cloth folding box with gilt titles. Illustrated with 32 tipped-in wood-engraved plates, **signed by Kirk Martin.** A fine set.
Est.: $600-up
Start Bid: $300

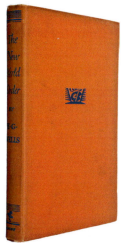

37424   H. G. Wells. *The New World Order.* New York: Alfred A. Knopf, 1940. Second printing of the first American edition. **Signed by Wells** on the half-title page. Octavo. 145 pages. Orange cloth over boards. Spine slightly darkened and frayed at the head. Mild soiling to boards. Overall, a very good, tight copy.
Est.: $1,000-up
Start Bid: $500

37425 **Walt Whitman.** *The Complete Writings of Walt Whitman.* New York: G. Putnam's Sons / Knickerbocker Press, 1902. The Paumanok Edition, limited to 300 numbered sets, of which this is number 12, printed on Ruisdael hand-made paper. Nine quarto volumes only, of the ten-volume set. Frontispieces. Illustrations. Original full polished morocco. Gilt floral designs to boards. Raised bands, gilt lettering and designs to spines. Top edges gilt. Interior doublures with green suede endpapers. Some browning to the edges of suede free endpapers. Missing Volume X. Near fine. BAL 21454C.

Est.: $600-up
Start Bid: $300

37426 **[Oscar Wilde]. Robert Ernest Cowan and William Andrews Clark, Jr. [editors].** *Wilde and Wildeiana: The Library of William Andrews Clark, Jr.* San Francisco: Printed by John Henry Nash, 1922-1923. First edition, limited to 100 sets. Six octavo volumes. Uniform publisher's quarter green cloth with paper boards. Sunning to backstrips. All volumes in publisher's slipcases with minor soiling. A near fine set.

Est.: $800-up
Start Bid: $400

37427 **Tennessee Williams.** *Cat on a Hot Tin Roof.* [New York]: New Directions, [1955]. First edition, first printing. Octavo. 197 pages. Publisher's binding and dust jacket. Modest wear to cloth extremities with a tiny spot of abrading to fore-edge. Jacket shows mild rubbing to extremities. Near fine.

Est.: $600-up
Start Bid: $300

37428 **Thomas J. Wise.** *A Bibliography of the Writings in Prose and Verse of William Wordsworth.* London: Richard Clay, 1916. First edition, limited to 100 copies. **Inscribed by Wise to Harold B. Wrenn, son of noted collector John Henry Wrenn.** Octavo. 268 pages. Publisher's binding with general rubbing and abrading to extremities. Offsetting and occasional foxing to endpapers. Title page and frontispiece show offsetting from tissue guard. Overall very good.

Est.: $600-up
Start Bid: $300

END OF AUCTION

Terms and Conditions of Auction

Auctioneer and Auction:

1. This Auction is presented by Heritage Auction Galleries, a d/b/a/ of Heritage Auctions, Inc., or its affiliates Heritage Numismatic Auctions, Inc., or Heritage Vintage Sports Auctions, Inc., or Currency Auctions of America, Inc., as identified with the applicable licensing information on the title page of the catalog or on the HA.com Internet site (the "Auctioneer"). The Auction is conducted under these Terms and Conditions of Auction and applicable state and local law. Announcements and corrections from the podium and those made through the Terms and Conditions of Auctions appearing on the Internet at HA.com supersede those in the printed catalog.

Buyer's Premium:

2. On bids placed through Auctioneer, a Buyer's Premium of fifteen percent (15%) will be added to the successful hammer price bid on lots in Coin, Currency, and Firearms Auctions or nineteen and one-half percent (19.5%) on lots in all other Auctions. There is a minimum Buyer's Premium of $14.00 per lot. In Gallery Auctions (sealed bid auctions of mostly bulk numismatic material), the Buyer's Premium is 19.5%.

Auction Venues:

3. The following Auctions are conducted solely on the Internet: Heritage Weekly Internet Auctions (Coin, Currency, Comics, Rare Books, Jewelry & Watches, Guitars & Musical Instruments, and Vintage Movie Posters); Heritage Monthly Internet Auctions (Sports, World Coins and Rare Wine). Signature® Auctions and Grand Format Auctions accept bids from the Internet, telephone, fax, or mail first, followed by a floor bidding session; HeritageLive! and real- time telephone bidding are available to registered clients during these auctions.

Bidders:

4. Any person participating or registering for the Auction agrees to be bound by and accepts these Terms and Conditions of Auction ("Bidder(s)").
5. All Bidders must meet Auctioneer's qualifications to bid. Any Bidder who is not a client in good standing of the Auctioneer may be disqualified at Auctioneer's sole option and will not be awarded lots. Such determination may be made by Auctioneer in its sole and unlimited discretion, at any time prior to, during, or even after the close of the Auction. Auctioneer reserves the right to exclude any person from the auction.
6. If an entity places a bid, then the person executing the bid on behalf of the entity agrees to personally guarantee payment for any successful bid.

Credit:

7. Bidders who have not established credit with the Auctioneer must either furnish satisfactory credit information (including two collectibles-related business references) well in advance of the Auction or supply valid credit card information. Bids placed through our Interactive Internet program will only be accepted from pre-registered Bidders; Bidders who are not members of HA.com or affiliates should pre-register at least 48 hours before the start of the first session (exclusive of holidays or weekends) to allow adequate time to contact references. Credit may be granted at the discretion of Auctioneer. Additionally Bidders who have not previously established credit or who wish to bid in excess of their established credit history may be required to provide their social security number or the last four digits thereof to us so a credit check may be performed prior to Auctioneer's acceptance of a bid.

Bidding Options:

8. Bids in Signature. Auctions or Grand Format Auctions may be placed as set forth in the printed catalog section entitled "Choose your bidding method." For auctions held solely on the Internet, see the alternatives on HA.com. Review at HA.com/common/howtobid.php.
9. Presentment of Bids: Non-Internet bids (including but not limited to podium, fax, phone and mail bids) are treated similar to floor bids in that they must be on-increment or at a half increment (called a cut bid). Any podium, fax, phone, or mail bids that do not conform to a full or half increment will be rounded up or down to the nearest full or half increment and this revised amount will be considered your high bid.
10. Auctioneer's Execution of Certain Bids. Auctioneer cannot be responsible for your errors in bidding, so carefully check that every bid is entered correctly. When identical mail or FAX bids are submitted, preference is given to the first received. To ensure the greatest accuracy, your written bids should be entered on the standard printed bid sheet and be received at Auctioneer's place of business at least two business days before the Auction start. Auctioneer is not responsible for executing mail bids or FAX bids received on or after the day the first lot is sold, nor Internet bids submitted after the published closing time; nor is Auctioneer responsible for proper execution of bids submitted by telephone, mail, FAX, e-mail, Internet, or in person once the Auction begins. Bids placed electronically via the internet may not be withdrawn until your written request is received and acknowledged by Auctioneer (FAX: 214-443-8425); such requests must state the reason, and may constitute grounds for withdrawal of bidding privileges. Lots won by mail Bidders will not be delivered at the Auction unless prearranged.
11. Caveat as to Bid Increments. Bid increments (over the current bid level) determine the lowest amount you may bid on a particular lot. Bids greater than one increment over the current bid can be any whole dollar amount. It is possible under several circumstances for winning bids to be between increments, sometimes only $1 above the previous increment. Please see: "How can I lose by less than an increment?" on our website. Bids will be accepted in whole dollar amounts only. No "buy" or "unlimited" bids will be accepted.

The following chart governs current bidding increments.

Current Bid	Bid Increment	Current Bid	Bid Increment
<$10	$1	$20,000 - $29,999	$2,000
$10 - $29	$2	$30,000 - $49,999	$2,500
$30 - $49	$3	$50,000 - $99,999	$5,000
$50 - $99	$5	$100,000 - $199,999	$10,000
$100 - $199	$10	$200,000 - $299,999	$20,000
$200 - $299	$20	$300,000 - $499,999	$25,000
$300 - $499	$25	$500,000 - $999,999	$50,000
$500 - $999	$50	$1,000,000 - $1,999,999	$100,000
$1,000 - $1,999	$100	$2,000,000 - $2,999,999	$200,000
$2,000 - $2,999	$200	$3,000,000 - $4,999,999	$250,000
$3,000 - $4,999	$250	$5,000,000 - $9,999,999	$500,000
$5,000 - $9,999	$500	>$10,000,000	$1,000,000
$10,000 - $19,999	$1,000		

12. If Auctioneer calls for a full increment, a bidder may request Auctioneer to accept a bid at half of the increment ("Cut Bid") only once per lot. After offering a Cut Bid, bidders may continue to participate only at full increments. Off-increment bids may be accepted by the Auctioneer at Signature® Auctions and Grand Format Auctions. If the Auctioneer solicits bids other than the expected increment, these bids will not be considered Cut Bids.

Conducting the Auction:

13. Notice of the consignor's liberty to place bids on his lots in the Auction is hereby made in accordance with Article 2 of the Texas Business and Commercial Code. A "Minimum Bid" is an amount below which the lot will not sell. THE CONSIGNOR OF PROPERTY MAY PLACE WRITTEN "Minimum Bids" ON HIS LOTS IN ADVANCE OF THE AUCTION; ON SUCH LOTS, IF THE HAMMER PRICE DOES NOT MEET THE "Minimum Bid", THE CONSIGNOR MAY PAY A REDUCED COMMISSION ON THOSE LOTS. "Minimum Bids" are generally posted online several days prior to the Auction closing. For any successful bid placed by a consignor on his Property on the Auction floor, or by any means during the live session, or after the "Minimum Bid" for an Auction have been posted, we will require the consignor to pay full Buyer's Premium and Seller's Commissions on such lot.
14. The highest qualified Bidder recognized by the Auctioneer shall be the Buyer. In the event of a tie bid, the earliest bid received or recognized wins. In the event of any dispute between any Bidders at an Auction, Auctioneer may at his sole discretion reoffer the lot. Auctioneer's decision and declaration of the winning Bidder shall be final and binding upon all Bidders. Bids properly offered, whether by floor Bidder or other means of bidding, may on occasion be missed or go unrecognized; in such cases, the Auctioneer may declare the recognized bid accepted as the winning bid, regardless of whether a competing bid may have been higher.
15. Auctioneer reserves the right to refuse to honor any bid or to limit the amount of any bid, in its sole discretion. A bid is considered not made in "Good Faith" when made by an insolvent or irresponsible person, a person under the age of eighteen, or is not supported by satisfactory credit, collectibles references, or otherwise. Regardless of the disclosure of his identity, any bid by a consignor or his agent on a lot consigned by him is deemed to be made in "Good Faith." Any person apparently appearing on the OFAC list is not eligible to bid.
16. Nominal Bids. The Auctioneer in its sole discretion may reject nominal bids, small opening bids, or very nominal advances. If a lot bearing estimates fails to open for 40–60% of the low estimate, the Auctioneer may pass the item or may place a protective bid on behalf of the consignor.
17. Lots bearing bidding estimates shall open at Auctioneer's discretion (approximately 50%-60% of the low estimate). In the event that no bid meets or exceeds that opening amount, the lot shall pass as unsold.
18. All items are to be purchased per lot as numerically indicated and no lots will be broken. Auctioneer reserves the right to withdraw, prior to the close, any lots from the Auction.
19. Auctioneer reserves the right to rescind the sale in the event of nonpayment, breach of a warranty, disputed ownership, auctioneer's clerical error or omission in exercising bids and reserves, or for any other reason and in Auctioneer's sole discretion. In cases of nonpayment, Auctioneer's election to void a sale does not relieve the Bidder from their obligation to pay Auctioneer its fees (seller's and buyer's premium) and any other damages or expenses pertaining to the lot.
20. Auctioneer occasionally experiences Internet and/or Server service outages, and Auctioneer periodically schedules system downtime for maintenance and other purposes, during which Bidders cannot participate or place bids. If such outages occur, we may at our discretion extend bidding for the Auction. Bidders unable to place their Bids through the Internet are directed to contact Client Services at 1-800-872-6467.
21. The Auctioneer, its affiliates, or their employees consign items to be sold in the Auction, and may bid on those lots or any other lots. Auctioneer or affiliates expressly reserve the right to modify any such bids at any time prior to the hammer based upon data made known to the Auctioneer or its affiliates. The Auctioneer may extend advances, guarantees, or loans to certain consignors.
22. The Auctioneer has the right to sell certain unsold items after the close of the Auction. Such lots shall be considered sold during the Auction and all these Terms and Conditions shall apply to such sales including but not limited to the Buyer's Premium, return rights, and disclaimers.

Payment:

23. All sales are strictly for cash in United States dollars (including U.S. currency, bank wire, cashier checks, travelers checks, eChecks, and bank money orders, all subject to reporting requirements). All are subject to clearing and funds being received in Auctioneer's account before delivery of the purchases. Auctioneer reserves the right to determine if a check constitutes "good funds" when drawn on a U.S. bank for ten days, and thirty days when drawn on an international bank. Credit Card (Visa or Master Card only) and PayPal payments may be accepted up to $10,000 from non-dealers at the sole discretion of the Auctioneer, subject to the following limitations: a) sales are only to the cardholder, b) purchases are shipped to the cardholder's registered and verified address, c) Auctioneer may pre-approve the cardholder's credit line, d) a credit card transaction may not be used in conjunction with any other financing or extended terms offered by the Auctioneer, and must transact immediately upon invoice presentation, e) rights of return are governed by these Terms and Conditions, which supersede those conditions promulgated by the card issuer, f) floor Bidders must present their card.
24. Payment is due upon closing of the Auction session, or upon presentment of an invoice. Auctioneer reserves the right to void an invoice if payment in full is not received within 7 days after the close of the Auction. In cases of nonpayment, Auctioneer's election to void a sale does not relieve the Bidder from their obligation to pay Auctioneer its fees (seller's and buyer's premium) on the lot and any other damages pertaining to the lot.
25. Lots delivered to you, or your representative in the States of Texas, California, New York, or other states where the Auction may be held, are subject to all applicable state and local taxes, unless appropriate permits are on file with Auctioneer. (Note: Coins are only subject to sales tax in California on invoices under $1500 and in Texas on invoices under $1000. Check the Web site at: http://coins.ha.com/c/ref/sales-tax.zx for more details.) Bidder agrees to pay Auctioneer the actual amount of tax due in the event that sales tax is not properly collected due to: 1) an expired, inaccurate, inappropriate tax certificate or declaration, 2) an incorrect interpretation of the applicable statute, 3) or any other reason. The appropriate form or certificate must be on file at and verified by Auctioneer five days prior to Auction or tax must be paid; only if such form or certificate is received by Auctioneer within 4 days after the Auction can a refund of tax paid be made. Lots from different Auctions may not be aggregated for sales tax purposes.
26. In the event that a Bidder's payment is dishonored upon presentment(s), Bidder shall pay the maximum statutory processing fee set by applicable state law. If you attempt to pay via eCheck and your financial institution denies this transfer from your bank account, or the payment cannot be completed using the selected funding source, you agree to complete payment using your credit card on file.
27. If any Auction invoice submitted by Auctioneer is not paid in full when due, the unpaid balance will bear interest at the highest rate permitted by law from the date of invoice until paid. Any invoice not paid when due will bear a three percent (3%) late fee on the invoice amount or three percent (3%) of any installment that is past due. If the Auctioneer refers any invoice to an attorney for collection, the buyer agrees to pay attorney's fees, court costs, and other collection costs incurred by Auctioneer. If Auctioneer assigns collection to its in-house legal staff, such attorney's time expended on the matter shall be compensated at a rate comparable to the hourly rate of independent attorneys.
28. In the event a successful Bidder fails to pay any amounts due, Auctioneer reserves the right to sell the lot(s) securing the invoice to any underbidders in the Auction that the lot(s) appeared, or at subsequent private or public sale, or relist the lot(s) in a future auction conducted by Auctioneer. A defaulting Bidder agrees to pay for the reasonable costs of resale (including a 10% seller's commission, if consigned to an auction conducted by Auctioneer). The defaulting Bidder is liable to pay any difference between his total original invoice for the lot(s), plus any applicable interest, and the net proceeds for the lot(s) if sold at private sale or the subsequent hammer price of the lot(s) less the 10% seller's commissions, if sold at an Auctioneer's auction.
29. Auctioneer reserves the right to require payment in full in good funds before delivery of the merchandise.

Terms and Conditions of Auction

30. Auctioneer shall have a lien against the merchandise purchased by the buyer to secure payment of the Auction invoice. Auctioneer is further granted a lien and the right to retain possession of any other property of the buyer then held by the Auctioneer or its affiliates to secure payment of any Auction invoice or any other amounts due the Auctioneer or affiliates from the buyer. With respect to these lien rights, Auctioneer shall have all the rights of a secured creditor under Article 9 of the Texas Uniform Commercial Code, including but not limited to the right of sale. In addition, with respect to payment of the Auction invoice(s), the buyer waives any and all rights of offset he might otherwise have against the Auctioneer and the consignor of the merchandise included on the invoice. If a Bidder owes Auctioneer or its affiliates on any account, Auctioneer and its affiliates shall have the right to offset such unpaid account by any credit balance due Bidder, and it may secure by possessory lien any unpaid amount by any of the Bidder's property in their possession.
31. Title shall not pass to the successful Bidder until all invoices are paid in full. It is the responsibility of the buyer to provide adequate insurance coverage for the items once they have been delivered to a common carrier or third-party shipper.

Delivery; Shipping; and Handling Charges:

32. Buyer is liable for shipping and handling. Please refer to Auctioneer's website www.HA.com/common/shipping.php for the latest charges or call Auctioneer. Auctioneer is unable to combine purchases from other auctions or affiliates into one package for shipping purposes. Lots won will be shipped in a commercially reasonable time after payment in good funds for the merchandise and the shipping fees is received or credit extended, except when third-party shipment occurs.
33. Successful international Bidders shall provide written shipping instructions, including specified customs declarations, to the Auctioneer for any lots to be delivered outside of the United States. NOTE: Declaration value shall be the item'(s) hammer price together with its buyer's premium and Auctioneer shall use the correct harmonized code for the lot. Domestic Buyers on lots designated for third-party shipment must designate the common carrier, accept risk of loss, and prepay shipping costs.
34. All shipping charges will be borne by the successful Bidder. On all domestic shipments, any risk of loss during shipment will be borne by Heritage until the shipping carrier's confirmation of delivery to the address of record in Auctioneer's file (carrier's confirmation is conclusive to prove delivery to Bidder; if the client has a Signature release on file with the carrier, the package is considered delivered without Signature) or delivery by Heritage to Bidder's selected third-party shipper. On all foreign shipments, any risk of loss during shipment will be borne by the Bidder following Auctioneer's delivery to the Bidder's designated common carrier or third-party shipper.
35. Due to the nature of some items sold, it shall be the responsibility for the successful Bidder to arrange pick-up and shipping through third-parties; as to such items Auctioneer shall have no liability. Failure to pick-up or arrange shipping in a timely fashion (within ten days) shall subject Lots to storage and moving charges, including a $100 administration fee plus $10 daily storage for larger items and $5.00 daily for smaller items (storage fee per item) after 35 days. In the event the Lot is not removed within ninety days, the Lot may be offered for sale to recover any past due storage or moving fees, including a 10% Seller's Commission.
36. The laws of various countries regulate the import or export of certain plant and animal properties, including (but not limited to) items made of (or including) ivory, whalebone, turtleshell, coral, crocodile, or other wildlife. Transport of such lots may require special licenses for export, import, or both. Bidder is responsible for: 1) obtaining all information on such restricted items for both export and import; 2) obtaining all such licenses and/or permits. Delay or failure to obtain any such license or permit does not relieve the buyer of timely compliance with standard payment terms. For further information, please contact Ron Brackemyre at 800-872-6467 ext. 1312.
37. Any request for shipping verification for undelivered packages must be made within 30 days of shipment by Auctioneer.

Cataloging, Warranties and Disclaimers:

38. NO WARRANTY, WHETHER EXPRESSED OR IMPLIED, IS MADE WITH RESPECT TO ANY DESCRIPTION CONTAINED IN THIS AUCTION OR ANY SECOND OPINE. Any description of the items or second opine contained in this Auction is for the sole purpose of identifying the items for those Bidders who do not have the opportunity to view the lots prior to bidding, and no description of items has been made part of the basis of the bargain or has created any express warranty that the goods would conform to any description made by Auctioneer. Color variations can be expected in any electronic or printed imaging, and are not grounds for the return of any lot. NOTE: Auctioneer, in specified auction venues, for example, Fine Art, may have express written warranties and you are referred to those specific terms and conditions. .
39. Auctioneer is selling only such right or title to the items being sold as Auctioneer may have by virtue of consignment agreements on the date of auction and disclaims any warranty of title to the Property. Auctioneer disclaims any warranty of merchantability or fitness for any particular purposes. All images, descriptions, sales data, and archival records are the exclusive property of Auctioneer, and may be used by Auctioneer for advertising, promotion, archival records, and any other uses deemed appropriate.
40. Translations of foreign language documents may be provided as a convenience to interested parties. Auctioneer makes no representation as to the accuracy of those translations and will not be held responsible for errors in bidding arising from inaccuracies in translation.
41. Auctioneer disclaims all liability for damages, consequential or otherwise, arising out of or in connection with the sale of any Property by Auctioneer to Bidder. No third party may rely on any benefit of these Terms and Conditions and any rights, if any, established hereunder are personal to the Bidder and may not be assigned. Any statement made by the Auctioneer is an opinion and does not constitute a warranty or representation. No employee of Auctioneer may alter these Terms and Conditions, and, unless signed by a principal of Auctioneer, any such alteration is null and void.
42. Auctioneer shall not be liable for breakage of glass or damage to frames (patent or latent); such defects, in any event, shall not be a basis for any claim for return or reduction in purchase price.

Release:

43. In consideration of participation in the Auction and the placing of a bid, Bidder expressly releases Auctioneer, its officers, directors and employees, its affiliates, and its outside experts that provide second opines, from any and all claims, cause of action, chose of action, whether at law or equity or any arbitration or mediation rights existing under the rules of any professional society or affiliation based upon the assigned description, or a derivative theory, breach of warranty express or implied, representation or other matter set forth within these Terms and Conditions of Auction or otherwise. In the event of a claim, Bidder agrees that such rights and privileges conferred therein are strictly construed as specifically declared herein; e.g., authenticity, typographical error, etc. and are the exclusive remedy. Bidder, by non-compliance to these express terms of a granted remedy, shall waive any claim against Auctioneer.
44. Notice: Some Property sold by Auctioneer are inherently dangerous e.g. firearms, cannons, and small items that may be swallowed or ingested or may have latent defects all of which may cause harm to a person. Purchaser accepts all risk of loss or damage from its purchase of these items and Auctioneer disclaims any liability whether under contract or tort for damages and losses, direct or inconsequential, and expressly disclaims any warranty as to safety or usage of any lot sold.

Dispute Resolution and Arbitration Provision:

45. By placing a bid or otherwise participating in the auction, Bidder accepts these Terms and Conditions of Auction, and specifically agrees to the dispute resolution provided herein. Consumer disputes shall be resolved through court litigation which has an exclusive Dallas, Texas venue clause and jury waiver. Non-consumer dispute shall be determined in binding arbitration which arbitration replaces the right to go to court, including the right to a jury trial.
46. Auctioneer in no event shall be responsible for consequential damages, incidental damages, compensatory damages, or any other damages arising or claimed to be arising from the auction of any lot. In the event that Auctioneer cannot deliver the lot or subsequently it is established that the lot lacks title, or other transfer or condition issue is claimed, in such cases the sole remedy shall be limited to rescission of sale and refund of the amount paid by Bidder; in no case shall Auctioneer's maximum liability exceed the high bid on that lot, which bid shall be deemed for all purposes the value of the lot. After one year has elapsed, Auctioneer's maximum liability shall be limited to any commissions and fees Auctioneer earned on that lot.
47. In the event of an attribution error, Auctioneer may at its sole discretion, correct the error on the Internet, or, if discovered at a later date, to refund the buyer's purchase price without further obligation.
48. Dispute Resolution for Consumers and Non-Consumers: Any claim, dispute, or controversy in connection with, relating to and /or arising out of the Auction, participation in the Auction, award of lots, damages of claims to lots, descriptions, condition reports, provenance, estimates, return and warranty rights, any interpretation of these Terms and Conditions, any alleged verbal modification of these Terms and Conditions and/or any purported settlement whether asserted in contract, tort, under Federal or State statute or regulation shall or any other matter: a) if presented by a consumer, be exclusively heard by, and the parties consent to, exclusive in personam jurisdiction in the State District Courts of Dallas County, Texas. THE PARTIES EXPRESSLY WAIVE ANY RIGHT TO TRIAL BY JURY. Any appeals shall be solely pursued in the appellate courts of the State of Texas; or b) for any claimant other than a consumer, the claim shall be presented in confidential binding arbitration before a single arbitrator, that the parties may agree upon, selected from the JAMS list of Texas arbitrators. The case is not to be administrated by JAMS; however, if the parties cannot agree on an arbitrator, then JAMS shall appoint the arbitrator and it shall be conducted under JAMS rules. The locale shall be Dallas Texas. The arbitrator's award may be enforced in any court of competent jurisdiction. Any party on any claim involving the purchase or sale of numismatic or related items may elect arbitration through binding PNG arbitration. Any claim must be brought within one (1) year of the alleged breach, default or misrepresentation or the claim is waived. This agreement and any claims shall be determined and construed under Texas law. The prevailing party (party that is awarded substantial and material relief on its claim or defense) may be awarded its reasonable attorneys' fees and costs.
49. No claims of any kind can be considered after the settlements have been made with the consignors. Any dispute after the settlement date is strictly between the Bidder and consignor without involvement or responsibility of the Auctioneer.
50. In consideration of their participation in or application for the Auction, a person or entity (whether the successful Bidder, a Bidder, a purchaser and/or other Auction participant or registrant) agrees that all disputes in any way relating to, arising under, connected with, or incidental to these Terms and Conditions and purchases, or default in payment thereof, shall be arbitrated pursuant to the arbitration provision. In the event that any matter including actions to compel arbitration, construe the agreement, actions in aid or arbitration or otherwise needs to be litigated, such litigation shall be exclusively in the Courts of the State of Texas, in Dallas County, Texas, and if necessary the corresponding appellate courts. For such actions, the successful Bidder, purchaser, or Auction participant also expressly submits himself to the personal jurisdiction of the State of Texas.
51. These Terms & Conditions provide specific remedies for occurrences in the auction and delivery process. Where such remedies are afforded, they shall be interpreted strictly. Bidder agrees that any claim shall utilize such remedies; Bidder making a claim in excess of those remedies provided in these Terms and Conditions agrees that in no case whatsoever shall Auctioneer's maximum liability exceed the high bid on that lot, which bid shall be deemed for all purposes the value of the lot.

Miscellaneous:

52. Agreements between Bidders and consignors to effectuate a non-sale of an item at Auction, inhibit bidding on a consigned item to enter into a private sale agreement for said item, or to utilize the Auctioneer's Auction to obtain sales for non-selling consigned items subsequent to the Auction, are strictly prohibited. If a subsequent sale of a previously consigned item occurs in violation of this provision, Auctioneer reserves the right to charge Bidder the applicable Buyer's Premium and consignor a Seller's Commission as determined for each auction venue and by the terms of the seller's agreement.
53. Acceptance of these Terms and Conditions qualifies Bidder as a client who has consented to be contacted by Heritage in the future. In conformity with "do-not-call" regulations promulgated by the Federal or State regulatory agencies, participation by the Bidder is affirmative consent to being contacted at the phone number shown in his application and this consent shall remain in effect until it is revoked in writing. Heritage may from time to time contact Bidder concerning sale, purchase, and auction opportunities available through Heritage and its affiliates and subsidiaries.
54. Rules of Construction: Auctioneer presents properties in a number of collectible fields, and as such, specific venues have promulgated supplemental Terms and Conditions. Nothing herein shall be construed to waive the general Terms and Conditions of Auction by these additional rules and shall be construed to give force and effect to the rules in their entirety.

State Notices:

Notice as to an Auction in California. Auctioneer has in compliance with Title 2.95 of the California Civil Code as amended October 11, 1993 Sec. 1812.600, posted with the California Secretary of State its bonds for it and its employees, and the auction is being conducted in compliance with Sec. 2338 of the Commercial Code and Sec. 535 of the Penal Code.

Notice as to an Auction in New York City. These Terms and Conditions of Sale are designed to conform to the applicable sections of the New York City Department of Consumer Affairs Rules and Regulations as Amended. This sale is a Public Auction Sale conducted by Heritage Auction Galleries, Inc. #41513036. The New York City licensed auctioneers are: Sam Foose, #095260; Kathleen Guzman, #0762165; Nicholas Dawes, #1304724; Ed Beardsley, #1183220; Scott Peterson, #1306933; Andrea Voss, #1320558, who will conduct the Sale on behalf of Heritage Numismatic Auctions, Inc. (for Coins and Currency) and Heritage Auction Galleries Inc. (for other items). All lots are subject to: the consignor's rights to bid thereon in accord with these Terms and Conditions of Sale, consignor's option to receive advances on their consignments, and Auctioneer, in its sole discretion, may offer limited extended financing to registered bidders, in accord with Auctioneer's internal credit standards. A registered bidder may inquire whether a lot is subject to an advance or a reserve. Auctioneer has made advances to various consignors in this sale. On lots bearing an estimate, the term refers to a value range placed on an item by the Auctioneer in its sole opinion but the final price is determined by the bidders.

Notice as to an Auction in Texas. In compliance with TDLR rule 67.100(c)(1), notice is hereby provided that this auction is covered by a Recovery Fund administered by the Texas Department of Licensing and Regulation, P.O. Box 12157, Austin, Texas 78711 (512) 463-6599. Any complaints may be directed to the same address.

Notice as to an Auction in Ohio: Auction firm and Auctioneer are licensed by the Dept. of Agriculture, and either the licensee is bonded in favor of the state or an aggrieved person may initiate a claim against the auction recovery fund created in Section 4707.25 of the Revised Code as a result of the licensee's actions, whichever is applicable.

Rev. 7-25-11

Terms and Conditions of Auction

How to Ship Your Purchases

Agent Shipping Release
Authorization form

Heritage Auction Galleries requires "Third Party Shipping" for certain items in this auction not picked up in person by the buyer. It shall be the responsibility of the successful bidder to arrange pick up and shipping through a third party; as to such items auctioneer shall have no liability.

Steps to follow:

1. Select a shipping company from the list below or a company of your choosing.

2. Complete, sign, and return an Agent Shipping Release Authorization form to Heritage (this form will automatically be emailed to you along with your winning bid(s) notice or may be obtained by calling Client Services at 866-835-3243). The completed form may be faxed to 214-409-1425.

3. Heritage Auctions' shipping department will coordinate with the shipping company you have selected to pick up your purchases.

Shippers that Heritage has used are listed below. However, you are not obligated to choose from the following and may provide Heritage with information of your preferred shipper.

Navis Pack & Ship	The Packing & Moving Center	Craters & Freighters
161 Pittsburgh St	2040 E. Arkansas Lane, Ste #222	2220 Merritt Drive, Suite 200
Dallas, TX 75207	Arlington, TX 76011	Garland, TX 75041
Ph: 972-870-1212	Ph: 817-795-1999	Ph: 972-840-8147
Fax: 214-409-9001	Fax: 214-409-9000	Fax: 214-780-5674
Navis.Dallas@GoNavis.com	thepackman@sbcglobal.net	dallas@cratersandfreighters.com

- It is the Third Party Shipper's responsibility to pack (or crate) and ship (or freight) your purchase to you. Please make all payment arrangements for shipping with your Shipper of choice.

- Any questions concerning Third Party Shipping can be addressed through our Client Services Department at 1-866-835-3243.

- Successful bidders are advised that pick-up or shipping arrangements should be made within ten (10) days of the auction or they may be subject to storage fees as stated in Heritage's Terms & Conditions of Auction, item 35.

HERITAGE

JANUARY 2012 | ORLANDO

SMITHSONIAN
BENEFIT AUCTION

SUPPORT THE SMITHSONIAN'S
NATIONAL NUMISMATIC COLLECTION

HOW YOU CAN HELP

In January 2012, Heritage will host an auction of coins and notes donated by collectors to create an endowment for the National Numismatic Collection. This special auction will feature no seller's commissions and no buyer's premiums. Heritage is donating all of our commissions and services, *so 100% of your numismatic or cash donation will go directly to the Smithsonian.*

Here's how it will work:

1. Call 800-872-6467 to speak with a Consignment Director.

2. Consign a coin/currency valued over $500 or a group of coins/currency valued over $1,000. Or, designate the proceeds of an existing consignment toward the NNC Endowment Fund.

3. After the auction, receive a gift receipt from the Smithsonian for the sale price of your consignment.

4. All proceeds raised benefitting the NNC Endowment will be transferred to the National Museum of American History after each auction.

Visit HA.com/Smithsonian for more information.

No coins from the Smithsonian or the NNC will be auctioned and the consigned coins are not intended for acquisition by the Smithsonian or the NNC. Neither the NNC nor the Smithsonian makes any representation or warranty as to the provenance, condition, grading, or value of any coin for auction.

Annual Sales Exceed $700 Million | 600,000+ Online Bidder-Members

HERITAGE
AUCTIONS   HA.com

3500 MAPLE AVE • DALLAS, TEXAS 75219 • 800-872-6467 • HA.com

DALLAS | NEW YORK | BEVERLY HILLS | SAN FRANCISCO | PARIS | GENEVA

FL licenses: Heritage Numismatic Auctions, Inc.: AB665; Currency Auctions of America: AB2218;
FL Auctioneer licenses: Samuel Foose AU3244; Mike Sadler AU3795; Andrea Voss AU4034.
This auction subject to a 15% buyer's premium.

Steve Ivy
Jim Halperin
Greg Rohan
Leo Frese
Warren Tucker
Todd Imhof
Michael Moline

 P·N·G
Knowledge. Integrity. Responsibility.

21509OTH

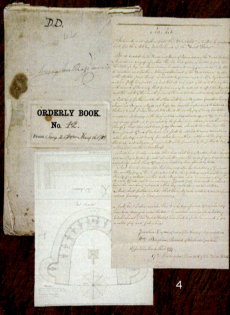

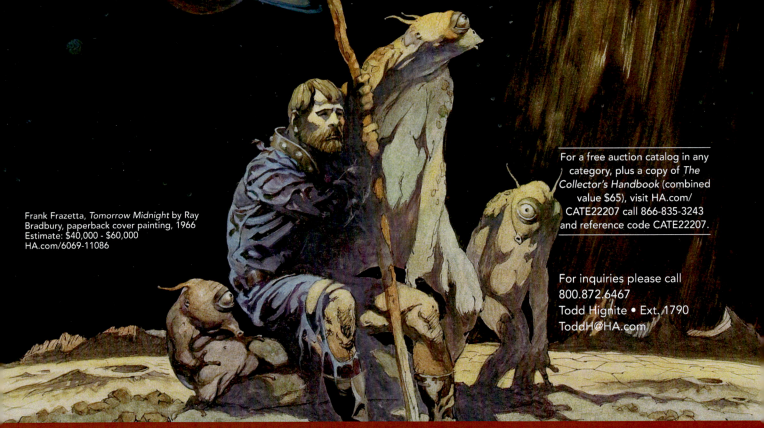

HERITAGE
ARMS & ARMOR

GREG MARTIN AUCTIONS

Visit HA.com/Arms to View and Bid Online

SEPTEMBER 18, 2011 | DALLAS | LIVE & ONLINE

The Alfred Cali Collection of Important Colt Firearms

For a free auction catalog in any category, plus a copy of *The Collector's Handbook* (combined value $65), visit HA.com/CATM22207 or call 866-835-3243 and reference code CATM22207.

Fine and Exceptional Colt Walker Model Civilian Series Revolver, with Period Flap Leather Holster, Known as "The Thumbprint Walker"
Estimate: $600,000-$800,000
HA.com/6073-11006

Exceptional, Rare and Fine Cased and Shell Carved Ivory-Gripped Texas or Holster Model No. 5 Paterson Revolver, with 9-inch Barrel and Attached Loading Lever
Estimate: $700,000-$900,000
HA.com/6073-11005

Historic Cased, Gustave Young-Engraved and Ivory-Gripped Colt Third Model Dragoon Revolver, Inscribed "Colonel P.M. Milliken."
Estimate: $500,000-$750,000
HA.com/6073-11009

Exceptional Historic, Cased, Engraved and Presentation Inscribed Colt Model 1861 New Model Navy Revolver, from the Colt Company to E.W. Parsons, of Adams Express Co., Hartford
Estimate: $400,000-$600,000
HA.com/6073-11029

Session 2:
Fine and Collectible Arms, Armor and Sporting Guns
featuring over 300 lots of quality offerings

Department Specialists

For the extensions below, please dial 800.872.6467

Comics & Comic Art

HA.com/Comics

Ed Jaster, Ext. 1288 • EdJ@HA.com

Lon Allen, Ext. 1261 • LonA@HA.com

Barry Sandoval, Ext. 1377 • BarryS@HA.com

Todd Hignite, Ext. 1790 • ToddH@HA.com

Fine Art

American, Western & European Art

HA.com/FineArt

Ed Jaster, Ext. 1288 • EdJ@HA.com

Marianne Berardi, Ph.D., Ext. 1506 • MarianneB@HA.com

Ariana Hartsock, Ext. 1283 • ArianaH@HA.com

Kirsty Buchanan, Ext. 1741 • KirstyB@HA.com

Mary Adair Dockery, Ext. 1799 • MaryD@HA.com

Decorative Arts & Design

HA.com/Decorative

Tim Rigdon, Ext. 1119 • TimR@HA.com

Karen Rigdon, Ext. 1723 • KarenR@HA.com

Nicholas Dawes, Ext. 1605 • NickD@HA.com

Carolyn Mani, Ext. 1677 • CarolynM@HA.com

Illustration Art

HA.com/Illustration

Ed Jaster, Ext. 1288 • EdJ@HA.com

Todd Hignite, Ext. 1790 • ToddH@HA.com

Lalique & Art Glass

HA.com/Design

Nicholas Dawes, Ext. 1605 • NickD@HA.com

Modern & Contemporary Art

HA.com/Modern

Frank Hettig, Ext. 1157 • FrankH@HA.com

Silver & Vertu

HA.com/Silver

Tim Rigdon, Ext. 1119 • TimR@HA.com

Karen Rigdon, Ext. 1723 • KarenR@HA.com

Texas Art

HA.com/TexasArt

Atlee Phillips, Ext. 1786 • AtleeP@HA.com

Vintage & Contemporary Photography

HA.com/ArtPhotography

Ed Jaster, Ext. 1288 • EdJ@HA.com

Rachel Peart, Ext. 1625 • RPeart@HA.com

Handbags & Luxury Accessories

HA.com/Luxury

Matt Rubinger, Ext. 1419 • MRubinger@HA.com

Historical

American Indian Art

HA.com/AmericanIndian

Delia Sullivan, Ext. 1343 • DeliaS@HA.com

Americana & Political

HA.com/Historical

Tom Slater, Ext. 1441 • TomS@HA.com

John Hickey, Ext. 1264 • JohnH@HA.com

Michael Riley, Ext. 1467 • MichaelR@HA.com

Don Ackerman, Ext. 1736 • DonA@HA.com

Arms & Armor

HA.com/Arms

Greg Martin, Ext. 1883 • GregM@HA.com

Jemison Beshears, Ext. 1886 • JemisonB@HA.com

Cliff Chappell, Ext. 1887 • CliffordC@HA.com

Roger Lake, Ext. 1884 • RogerL@HA.com

David Carde, Ext. 1881 • DavidC@HA.com

Civil War & Militaria

HA.com/CivilWar

Dennis Lowe, Ext. 1182 • DennisL@HA.com

Historical Manuscripts

HA.com/Manuscripts

Sandra Palomino, Ext. 1107 • SandraP@HA.com

Rare Books

HA.com/Books

James Gannon, Ext. 1609 • JamesG@HA.com

Joe Fay, Ext. 1544 • JoeF@HA.com

Space Exploration

HA.com/Space

John Hickey, Ext. 1264 • JohnH@HA.com

Michael Riley, Ext. 1467 • MichaelR@HA.com

Texana

HA.com/Historical

Sandra Palomino, Ext. 1107 • SandraP@HA.com

Jewelry

HA.com/Jewelry

Jill Burgum, Ext. 1697 • JillB@HA.com

Movie Posters

HA.com/MoviePosters

Grey Smith, Ext. 1367 • GreySm@HA.com

Bruce Carteron, Ext. 1551 • BruceC@HA.com

Music & Entertainment Memorabilia
HA.com/Entertainment

Margaret Barrett, Ext. 1912 • MargaretB@HA.com
Kristen Painter, Ext. 1149 • KristenP@HA.com
John Hickey, Ext. 1264 • JohnH@HA.com
Garry Shrum, Ext. 1585 • GarryS@HA.com

Vintage Guitars & Musical Instruments
HA.com/Guitar

Mike Gutierrez, Ext. 1183 • MikeG@HA.com
Isaiah Evans, Ext. 1201 • IsaiahE@HA.com

Natural History
HA.com/NaturalHistory

David Herskowitz, Ext. 1610 • DavidH@HA.com

Numismatics

Coins – United States
HA.com/Coins

Leo Frese, Ext. 1294 • Leo@HA.com
David Mayfield, Ext. 1277 • DavidM@HA.com
Jessica Aylmer, Ext. 1706 • JessicaA@HA.com
Win Callender, Ext. 1415 • WinC@HA.com
Chris Dykstra, Ext. 1380 • ChrisD@HA.com
Sam Foose, Ext. 1227 • SamF@HA.com
Jim Jelinski, Ext. 1257 • JimJ@HA.com
Bob Marino, Ext. 1374 • BobMarino@HA.com
Mike Sadler, Ext. 1332 • MikeS@HA.com
Beau Streicher, Ext. 1645 • BeauS@HA.com

Rare Currency
HA.com/Currency

Len Glazer, Ext. 1390 • Len@HA.com
Allen Mincho, Ext. 1327 • Allen@HA.com
Dustin Johnston, Ext. 1302 • Dustin@HA.com
Michael Moczalla, Ext. 1481 • MichaelM@HA.com
Jason Friedman, Ext. 1582 • JasonF@HA.com
Brad Ciociola, Ext. 1752 • BradC@HA.com

World & Ancient Coins
HA.com/WorldCoins

Cristiano Bierrenbach, Ext. 1661 • CrisB@HA.com
Warren Tucker, Ext. 1287 • WTucker@HA.com
David Michaels, Ext. 1606 • DMichaels@HA.com
Scott Cordry, Ext. 1369 • ScottC@HA

Sports Collectibles
HA.com/Sports

Chris Ivy, Ext. 1319 • CIvy@HA.com
Peter Calderon, Ext. 1789 • PeterC@HA.com
Derek Grady, Ext. 1975 • DerekG@HA.com
Mike Gutierrez, Ext. 1183 • MikeG@HA.com
Lee Iskowitz, Ext. 1601 • LeeI@HA.com
Mark Jordan, Ext. 1187 • MarkJ@HA.com
Chris Nerat, Ext. 1615 • ChrisN@HA.com
Jonathan Scheier, Ext. 1314 • JonathanS@HA.com

Timepieces
HA.com/Timepieces

Jim Wolf, Ext. 1659 • JWolf@HA.com

Wine
HA.com/Wine

Frank Martell, Ext. 1753 • FrankM@HA.com
Poppy Davis, Ext. 1559 • PoppyD@HA.com

Services

Appraisal Services
HA.com/Appraisals

Meredith Meuwly, Ext. 1631• MeredithM@HA.com

Corporate & Institutional Collections/Ventures
Karl Chiao, Ext. 1958 • KarlC@HA.com

Credit Department
Marti Korver, Ext. 1248 • Marti@HA.com
Eric Thomas, Ext. 1241 • EricT@HA.com

Media & Public Relations
Noah Fleisher, Ext. 1143 • NoahF@HA.com

Trusts & Estates
HA.com/Estates

Mark Prendergast, Ext. 1632 • MPrendergast@HA.com
Karl Chiao, Ext. 1958 • KarlC@HA.com
Shaunda Fry, Ext. 1159 • ShaundaF@HA.com

Locations

Dallas (World Headquarters)
214.528.3500 • 800.872.6467
3500 Maple Ave.
Dallas, TX 75219

Beverly Hills
310.492.8600
9478 W. Olympic Blvd.
Beverly Hills, CA 90212

New York
212.486.3500
445 Park Avenue
New York, NY 10022

DALLAS | NEW YORK | SAN FRANCISCO
BEVERLY HILLS | PARIS | GENEVA

Corporate Officers

R. Steven Ivy, Co-Chairman
James L. Halperin, Co-Chairman
Gregory J. Rohan, President
Paul Minshull, Chief Operating Officer
Todd Imhof, Executive Vice President
Leo Frese, Managing Director-Beverly Hills
Kathleen Guzman, Managing Director-New York

U.S. Rare Coin Auctions	Location	Auction Dates	Consignment Deadline
U.S. Rare Coins	Long Beach	September 7-11, 2011	Closed
U.S. Coin ANA	Pittsburgh	October 13-16, 2011	Closed
U.S. Rare Coins	Baltimore	November 15-16, 2011	October 2, 2011
U.S. Rare Coins	New York	December 7-11, 2011	October 28, 2011
World & Ancient Coin Auctions	Location	Auction Dates	Consignment Deadline
World Coin	Long Beach	Sept. 7-10 & 12, 2011	Closed
World Coin	New York	January 1-2, 2012	November 5, 2011
World Coin Online	Dallas	January 10, 2012	November 5, 2011
Rare Currency Auctions	Location	Auction Dates	Consignment Deadline
Currency	Long Beach	Sept. 7-10 & 12, 2011	Closed
Currency	Orlando	January 4-9, 2012	November 19, 2011
Fine & Decorative Arts Auctions	Location	Auction Dates	Consignment Deadline
Fine Silver & Vertu	Dallas	September 26, 2011	Closed
The Estate Auction	Dallas	September 27, 2011	Closed
Illustration Art	New York	October 22, 2011	Closed
Modern & Contemporary Art	Dallas	October 26, 2011	Closed
Texas Art	Dallas	November 5, 2011	Closed
Art of the American West	Dallas	November 5, 2011	Closed
American, Western & European Art	Dallas	November 8, 2011	September 6, 2011
Lalique and Art Glass	New York	November 19, 2011	September 17, 2011
Vintage & Contemporary Photography	New York	November 19, 2011	September 17, 2011
Fine Silver & Vertu	Dallas	December 7, 2011	October 5, 2011
Decorative Art	Dallas	December 7, 2011	October 5, 2011
The Estate Auction	Dallas	February 7, 2012	December 6, 2011
Illustration Art	Beverly Hills	February 23-24, 2012	December 22, 2011
Texas Art	Dallas	May 5, 2012	March 3, 2012
Art of the American West	Dallas	May 5, 2012	March 3, 2012
Modern & Contemporary Art	Dallas	May 29, 2012	March 27, 2012
Jewelry, Timepieces & Luxury Accessory Auctions	Location	Auction Dates	Consignment Deadline
Watches & Fine Timepieces	New York	November 18, 2011	September 17, 2011
Fine Jewelry	Dallas	December 5, 2011	September 26, 2011
Handbags & Luxury Accessories	Dallas	December 6, 2011	October 3, 2011
Vintage Movie Posters Auctions	Location	Auction Dates	Consignment Deadline
Vintage Movie Posters	Dallas	November 18-19, 2011	September 27, 2011
Comics Auctions	Location	Auction Dates	Consignment Deadline
Comics & Original Comic Art	Beverly Hills	November 10-12, 2011	September 27, 2011
Music & Entertainment Memorabilia Auctions	Location	Auction Dates	Consignment Deadline
The John Wayne Collection	Los Angeles	October 3-6, 2011	Closed
Vintage Guitars & Musical Instruments	Dallas	October 21-22, 2011	Closed
Music, Celebrity & Hollywood Memorabilia	Dallas	December 13-14, 2011	October 22, 2011
Vintage Guitars & Musical Instruments	Dallas	December 16-17, 2011	October 25, 2011
Historical Grand Format Auctions	Location	Auction Dates	Consignment Deadline
Jerry Weist Collection (Books)	Beverly Hills	September 12, 2011	Closed
Rare Books	Beverly Hills	September 12-14, 2011	Closed
Historical Manuscripts	Beverly Hills	September 12-14, 2011	Closed
Art of the Americas	Dallas	September 16-17, 2011	Closed
Arms & Armor	Dallas	September 18, 2011	Closed
Americana & Political	Dallas	November 12, 2011	September 21, 2011
Militaria	Dallas	November 12, 2011	September 21, 2011
Space Exploration	Dallas	November 30, 2011	October 9, 2011
Rare Books	New York City	December 8-9, 2011	October 17, 2011
Historical Manuscripts	New York City	December 8-9, 2011	October 17, 2011
Arms & Armor	Las Vegas	January 22-23, 2012	December 1, 2011
Texana	Dallas	March 10, 2012	January 18, 2012
Art of the Americas	Dallas	Spring 2012	January 12, 2012
Vintage Sports Collectibles Auctions	Location	Auction Dates	Consignment Deadline
Vintage Sports Collectibles	Dallas	November 10-11, 2011	September 19, 2011
Vintage Sports Collectibles	Dallas	April 26-27, 2012	March 5, 2012
Natural History Auctions	Location	Auction Dates	Consignment Deadline
Natural History	Beverly Hills	January 8, 2012	October 1, 2011
Fine & Rare Wine Auctions	Location	Auction Dates	Consignment Deadline
Fine & Rare Wine	Beverly Hills	September 23-24, 2011	Closed

HA.com/Consign • Consignment Hotline 800-872-6467 • All dates and auctions subject to change after press time. Go to HA.com for updates.

HERITAGE WEEKLY INTERNET COIN AUCTIONS • Begin and end every Sunday & Tuesday of each week at 10 PM CT.
HERITAGE MONTHLY INTERNET WORLD COIN AUCTIONS • Begin and end the second Tuesday of each month at 10 PM CT.
HERITAGE TUESDAY INTERNET CURRENCY AUCTIONS • Begin and end every Tuesday at 10 PM CT.
HERITAGE WEEKLY INTERNET COMICS AUCTIONS • Begin and end every Sunday at 10 PM CT.
HERITAGE WEEKLY INTERNET MOVIE POSTER AUCTIONS • Begin and end every Sunday at 10 PM CT.
HERITAGE WEEKLY INTERNET SPORTS AUCTIONS • Begin and end every Sunday at 10 PM CT, with extended bidding available.
HERITAGE WEEKLY INTERNET WATCH & JEWELRY AUCTIONS • Begin and end every Tuesday at 10 PM CT.
HERITAGE WEEKLY INTERNET VINTAGE GUITAR & MUSICAL INSTRUMENT AUCTIONS • Begin and end every Thursday at 10 PM CT.
HERITAGE WEEKLY INTERNET RARE BOOKS AUCTIONS • Begin and end every Thursday at 10 PM CT.
HERITAGE MONTHLY INTERNET WINE AUCTIONS • Begin and end the second Thursday of each month at 10 PM CT

8-12-5011

Auctioneers: Samuel Foose: TX 11727; CA Bond #RSB2004178; FL AU3244; GA AUNR3029; IL 441001482; NC 8373; OH 2006000048; MA 03015; PA AU005443; TN 6093; WI 2230-052; NYC 0952360; Denver 1021450; Phoenix 07006332. Robert Korver: TX 13754; CA Bond #RSB2004179; FL AU2916; GA AUNR003023; IL 441001421; MA 03014; NC 8363; OH 2006000049; TN 6439; WI 2412-52; Phoenix 07102049; NYC 1096338; Denver 1021446. Teia Baber: TX 16624; CA Bond #RSB2005525. Ed Beardsley: TX Associate 16632; NYC 1183220. Nicholas Dawes: NYC 1304724. Marsha Dixey: TX 16493. Chris Dykstra: TX 16601; FL AU4069; WI 2566-052; TN 6463; IL 441001788; CA #RSB2005738. Jeff Engelken: CA Bond #RSB2004180. Alissa Ford: CA Bond #RSB2005920. Leo Frese: CA Bond #RSB2004176; NYC 1094963. Shaunda Fry: TX 16448; FL AU3915; WI 2577-52; CA Bond #RSB2005396. Kathleen Guzman: NYC 0762165. Stewart Huckaby: TX 16590. Cindy Isennock, participating auctioneer: Baltimore Auctioneer license #AU10. Carolyn Mani: CA Bond #RSB2005661; Bob Merrill: TX 13408; MA 03022; WI 2557-052; FL AU4043; IL 441001683, CA Bond #RSB2004177. Cori Mikeals: TX 16582; CA #RSB2005645. Scott Peterson: TX 13256; NYC 1306933; IL 441001659; WI 2431-052; CA Bond #RSB2005395. Tim Rigdon: TX 16519. Michael J. Sadler: TX 16129; FL AU3795; IL 441001478; MA 03021; TN 6487; WI 2581-052; NYC 1304630; CA Bond #RSB2005412. Eric Thomas: TX 16421; PA AU005574; NYC 6515. Andrea Voss: TX 16406; FL AU4043; MA 03019; WI 2576-052; CA Bond #RSB2004676; NYC #1320558. Jacob Walker: TX 16413; FL AU4031; WI 2567-052; IL 441001677; CA Bond #RSB2005394. Peter Wiggins: TX 16635. (Rev. 5-15-11)